19

# Praise for *Behin*

*Told in the authentic voices of parents who have lived the experience of seeking help for their children and confronting mental illness, [this] collection promises to offer guidance and hope to parents who are just starting down the same path . . . One of my responsibilities within NAMI (National Alliance on Mental Illness) is monitoring and reviewing books in our field . . .* Behind the Wall *is unique and will help fill an important niche in meeting the ever-increasing demand for information about parenting children and adolescents with emotional disorders.*

—Bob Carolla, J.D.
Director of Media Relations, NAMI

*It is one thing to learn about mental illness in the classroom. It is another to learn about it through the eyes of those who love someone suffering with it. Every doctor, lawyer, psychologist, therapist, every person in a "helping" profession including paramedics and police during their career will encounter someone suffering with a serious mental illness. As with substance addiction, mental illness is misunderstood and misdiagnosed. It is shrouded in shame, isolation, and fear.* Behind the Wall *lifts the veil of secrecy to look at this devastating illness from those who know it best.* Behind the Wall *should be required reading for everyone entering or currently in the helping professions and recommended reading for those who simply want to understand an illness that touches us all.*

—Alice Tanner, Addiction Consultant/Intervention Specialist
Owner, Addiction Recovery Consulting Services

*This important book is a must-read for parents who are struggling with the vicissitudes of a beloved child's mental illness. It also provides a view on the family struggle that is essential for helping professionals who are trying to see the whole picture. It describes the experiences of five individual parents and two pairs of parents as they ride the roller coaster of feelings, chaotic experiences, and systemic disorganization that becomes the substance of their lives with a mentally ill child. Words like "the new normal," stigma, grief, denial, guilt, coping, revised expectations, and hope describe a process that can best be shared one parent to another. As one mother said, "I wanted to reach out (to another parent coping with learning of her child's mental illness) and tell her 'I've been there, it's okay.'" In reading these powerful, sometimes raw, stories, one senses that it is never really okay, but there is support, knowledge, and understanding available as one learns to deal with illnesses often compounded by substance abuse and societal judgments. Applause for the parents who have broken down the wall of silence and shared their stories and for the authors who deftly wove them together with great skill and the empathy forged by their own life experiences.*

—Rev. Dr. Judith A. B. Lee, DMin, DSW, MSW, LCSW
Professor Emerita University of Connecticut School of Social Work, Pastoral Counselor and Clinical Social Worker

*In this collection of starkly rendered accounts by parents of adult children living with mental illness, the reader is taken on a private journey through personal, often dark and difficult territory. For these parents, the simplest things in their adult child's life are often the most difficult; basic milestones that others take for granted are major achievements. These children do not navigate the path to adulthood in a straight and narrow line. And despite the obvious challenges, mothers and fathers show how to love and support their child while grief, frustration, and disappointment are sometimes the dominant emotional experiences. Parents make mistakes, have regrets, offer advice, and show there is hope. Most of all, they never give up on their children.* Behind the Wall: The True Story of Mental Illness as Told by Parents *is an important book to read for both mental health professionals and struggling families alike.*

—Deborah Rich, MSW, LCSW

*This is an important work—not just for families, extended families, friends, teachers, neighbors, and skeptics, but for the professional community as well. As a child psychiatrist with over thirty years of experience, I listen to my patients' stories as they unfold, but too often find it difficult to know what really goes on behind the wall. I vividly remember sitting with a mother who held her eleven-year-old son, who lives with bipolar, in her arms like a small child as he sucked on her arm and whimpered; she cried with helpless grief. I was dumbstruck. Neither my prescription pad nor my psychotherapeutic expertise was a match for this depth of despair.*

*Years later, an experience in my own family prompted me to join an online support group sponsored by TheBalancedMind.org. There I heard the human stories behind the wall of mental illness. Behind the Wall, by Widdifield and Widdifield provides us with the same privileged access. Their sensitive handling of the interviewing and writing process and the bravery and candor of the families they interviewed allow us to understand the impact of mental illness as the families themselves do. What a gift.*

—Ruth Noel, M.D. Child, Adolescent and Adult Psychiatry Assistant Clinical Professor, University of California, San Francisco

# BEHIND THE WALL

GRIEF HOPE RECOVERY

# BEHIND
# THE WALL

## THE TRUE STORY OF MENTAL
## ILLNESS AS TOLD BY PARENTS

MARY WIDDIFIELD AND ELIN WIDDIFIELD, MA
FOREWORD BY JOHN G. LOONEY, MD, MBA

LANGDON STREET PRESS | MINNEAPOLIS

**IMPORTANT NOTE TO READERS**

This publication should not be used as a substitute for professional medical advice or care. The reader should consult a physician in matters relating to the topics discussed in this book. In particular, the reader should consult with a competent medical professional before undertaking any form of treatment or acting on any of the information or advice contained in this book. Also, the reader should not stop existing treatments based on the information in this book until they have consulted with a competent medical professional. Modifying a medical regimen can be very dangerous. Any side effects should be reported promptly to a physician. A reader concerned about the adverse effects of any medical evaluation or treatment should discuss with a competent medical doctor the benefits as well as the risks of receiving the medical evaluation or treatment.

The information contained in this book regarding health and medical treatments is the result of extensive personal interviews with parents of children living with serious mental illness. Although this book is nonfiction, some of the names and distinguishing traits of patients, family, doctors, and staff have been changed.

The literature on this topic at times reflects conflicting conclusions and opinions. The authors have expressed their views on many issues; the reader should understand that experts may disagree. The author and publisher specifically disclaim any and all liability arising directly or indirectly from the use or application of any information contained in this book.

Visit the *Behind the Wall* blog: http://behindthewallstories.wordpress.com
Like us at *Behind the Wall*: www.facebook.com/StoriesBehindTheWall

Copyright © 2015 by Mary Widdifield and Elin Widdifield, MA

Langdon Street Press
322 First Avenue N, 5th floor
Minneapolis, MN 55401
612.455.2293
www.langdonstreetpress.com

ISBN-13: 978-1-63413-204-6
LCCN: 2014921048

Distributed by Itasca Books

Cover Design by James Arneson
Typeset by Mary Kristin Ross

*Printed in the United States of America*

*Dedicated to all those living with serious mental illness and to those who care and advocate for them.*

*Simply hearing the story of someone's experience with mental illness has been shown to increase acceptance.*

—National Alliance On Mental Illness

*I'd like to learn what to anticipate from parents whose children are older, who've been through similar experiences.*

—Esme, Parent/Contributor

# CONTENTS

# Foreword

Gird your loins, strap on your armor, and prepare to do battle—
battle with the demons of serious mental illness. Be warned,
the book you are about to read can be difficult. What follows
are the raw accounts by parents dealing with severe brain
disorders in their offspring. Although you will find much of
the material painful, read it you should. Read it in order to be
more appreciative if your family has been spared the pain so
dramatically described in this book. Read it to become more
giving, sympathetic, and understanding toward families who
have endured such pain. Read this book if you have had such
pain in your family because reading it will help you feel less
alone. Read it and vow to insist on more and better treatment
options for people experiencing such pain.

*Behind the Wall* also proves there is hope. With a
combination of parental patience and strictness, plus good
treatment, a recovering state can be achieved. This book by Mary
Widdifield and Elin Widdifield is the most recent of a small
genre of works explaining mental illness from the perspective
of those who experience it—this time with a revealing focus
based on the perspective and insight of parents.

Prior contributions are relevant.

The first substantive subjective description of mental
illness by a person experiencing it was the book *A Mind
That Found Itself* by Clifford Whittington Beers. Beers was a
graduate of Yale in 1897. Within a few years after graduation
he was confined to a private mental institution. He had tried
to kill himself by throwing himself from a bedroom window.
He experienced hallucinations and paranoia. He would be
confined to several institutions and, in total, spent many years

hospitalized. He died in a mental institution. The effect of genetics was particularly cruel in the Beers family. His mother and his aunt both had brain disorders, probably, like Clifford, bipolar disorder. Clifford had four siblings, one of whom died early with seizures. The three remaining siblings all died in mental health institutions, two by suicide.

Beers's book documented the conditions in mental institutions—bleak, lonely, and vulnerable to abuse by staff. Yet, the time away from the stresses of the outside world allowed some degree of healing. Beers regained lucidity and wrote his powerful book. Out of this abject misery came some good things. One was a movement to improve mental hospitals. This movement was also fostered by Dorothea Dix, who facilitated the opening of humane institutions around the country. The book also stimulated the idea that better outpatient treatment might prevent hospitalization. The Clifford Beers Clinic was opened in New Haven.

Another major advance resulting from Beers's work was the mental hygiene movement. It was thought that practices of mental hygiene, like physical hygiene, could help ward off psychiatric illness. Another very powerful part of the mental hygiene movement was the concept that problems could be spotted early in children, and professional assistance could help prevent mental illness later. The child guidance movement in America emerged.

Another selected contribution to this genre is *Families in Pain* by Phyllis Vine. A member of Vine's family lived with mental illness. Her book is comprised of selected stories from seventeen families that were willing to share their experiences. The book's impact is poignantly described by the publisher: "From the shock of the first emergency hospitalization to the final acceptance of chronic mental illness, seventeen families share their own experiences and their own solutions to the overwhelming emotional, financial and practical demands of caring for a mentally ill relative."

With time, subjective descriptions of mental illness have increased. Poets and novelists such as Sylvia Plath and William Styron have written poignantly about their own experiences. Plath's, of course, are all the more poignant because she did ultimately die by suicide. Descriptions of mental illness by mental health professionals have begun to appear in the recent past as well. Kay Redfield Jamison's description of bipolar disorder in her family and herself is powerful.

Are we making any progress? Compare the current state with the picture painted by Clifford Beers a century ago. What hasn't changed is the lack of doctors who know how to treat severe and persistent mental illness, particularly such illness in the young. In 1983, the American Academy of Child and Adolescent Psychiatry put together a think tank of leaders in the field to assess the future. One finding was very pessimistic. The subspecialty of child and adolescent psychiatry would be the one group of physicians in the shortest supply for the rest of the century and beyond. That prediction has come true. Even though we have tried to increase the size of our training programs, child and adolescent psychiatry is still the smallest specialty in medicine. The situation is similar for child psychologists.

Something else that has not changed is the stigmatization of mental illness. Some say it has improved, and perhaps it has. However, if you talk to families who have a very ill child or adolescent, you will realize how lonely and isolated they are. They were emotionally isolated at the turn of the century, and they are now. We are still much too slow to diagnose emerging illnesses in children and adolescents. Authors of the current book point out that they were even told that it was not proper to diagnose a personality disorder before adulthood. That incorrect convention has been widely accepted in the diagnostic system.

Patients and their doctors continue to dance to different music. Neither listens to the other long enough to try to get in tune. For whatever reason, smooth communication is often lacking. In the past it may have been because doctors insisted on fitting patients into theoretical conceptions about mental illness—from different "schools" of thought—rather than really listening to them. In the present, doctors complain that skimpy reimbursement by managed care does not give time for adequate dialogue. At times parents have preconceived notions of what is wrong with their children and do not want to hear professional points of view that differ.

No money, no treatment. Even though we are supposed to have a better insurance system in America and even though we are supposed to have parity in payment between traditional medical disorders and mental disorders, there is still inequity. Being of means can secure treatment unavailable to most—children especially, and also adults. Being of means in this instance means being wealthy. In the past, the great private psychiatric hospitals in America (Menninger Clinic, The Institute for Living, McLean Hospital, Sheppard and Enoch Pratt Hospitals, Timberlawn Hospital, and others) evolved for the care of those who could pay. Those who could not went to state facilities with little treatment other than the tincture of time.

What things might be different? One is that hospital treatment of adequate length is no longer available to anyone. Hospitalization of three years, as experienced by Clifford Beers, now appears nowhere. Even in private hospitals, hospital treatment does little other than stabilize a horrible acute situation, provide medication, and send the patient out into the world. In the 1970s and '80s, I was at one of the private hospitals mentioned above. Our hospital treated children and adolescents who had been treatment failures in shorter forms of treatment or in other hospitals. Our average length of stay was about nine months. However, the daily cost to receive this treatment was less than $100. Now it is thousands of dollars. We need to reduce the cost. Yet, whatever the cost, we need hospitalization of adequate length, and we do not have it.

Something else that has certainly changed is the increasing use of medication. In years past, hospital insulation from the stresses of the greater world, time, and benevolent attitude by professionals were the primary ingredients for positive change. Over time, talking therapies of various types evolved. Then, in the 1950s, psychotropic medications were discovered, and there has been a relentless march over time to develop more of them and to use more of them. Now there are those who say that all of these medicines are actually making us worse. Thus, Robert Whitaker and his recent provocative book, *Anatomy of an Epidemic*, shows that keeping up with all of these developments in pharmacology and prescribing the drugs has consumed the time of psychiatrists. Now they rarely do talking therapy.

One good thing that has been different in recent years has been the emergence of specific types of psychotherapies, such as cognitive behavioral therapy and dialectical behavioral therapy, that are aimed at specific types of disorders such as depression, borderline personality disorder, and other serious brain disorders. These therapies have been standardized so that one practitioner is using them similarly to other practitioners. That standardization has allowed for research to document the effectiveness of these therapies.

I warned the reader at the beginning that this book is tough to read. I also realize that I have given the reader some pessimistic facts which might make the reading that much harder. Yet we must foster optimism. We can. We now have a law in the land that should help pay for treatment for a wider economic group in our population. We are working hard to train more doctors who can help children with these terrible disorders. We have strong advocacy groups such as NAMI to lobby for better government support. We have brave people like Widdifield and Widdifield who share stories in an attempt to destigmatize these illnesses and help people not feel so terribly alone.

For over a century we have been saying each decade that

we will do better in providing good mental health care for our children and adolescents. It is time now to fulfill that pledge.

John G. Looney, MD, MBA
Durham, NC
August 2014

*Dr. Looney is Professor of Psychiatry and Behavioral Science at Duke University Medical Center. He is the prior director of both the Division of Child and Adolescent Psychiatry and the Substance Abuse Treatment Program for Youth.*

# PREFACE

When we began talking about our project, we received two distinct responses and rarely anything between. The first response was an expression of visible discomfort. Once, an acquaintance unconsciously backed away before politely changing the subject. But another response was one of interest, even relief, as we were then told about a sister, brother, parent, spouse, or friend living with mental illness. We didn't speak knowingly about living with a person struggling with mental illness, either, until Elin's son was diagnosed and our family was confronted. Mental illness is a family illness; it runs in families and profoundly impacts all its members. It was natural, therefore, that as sisters we, along with the ongoing support from our third (middle) sister, Joan, and the rest of our clan, pursued information about our new reality together. We learned through this process from other families that supporting *all* immediate family members of a person diagnosed with mental illness (parents and siblings) is vitally important.

Those of us with a loved one living with persistent mental illness have learned of its prevalence. According to the National Institute of Mental Health, 6 percent—about eighteen million Americans, live with a *serious* mental illness, and nearly 50 percent will meet the criteria for a mental illness at some point in their lifetime. Among those diagnosed with mental illness, 60 percent are dually diagnosed with substance abuse. There are tens of millions more whose lives are profoundly changed by the onset of mental illness in a loved one. Mental illness statistics are the same across the globe, afflicting those of all religions, ethnicities, and socioeconomic backgrounds. And yet, in a society where the popular culture encourages personal confessions and seemingly no subject is taboo, it is hard to find honest discussion about mental illness.

The stigma drives many parents of children living with mental illness to guard privacy. Parents don't trust how the community will judge their child or their parenting; parents know that others couldn't possibly understand. And frankly, the emotional extremes and practical requirements are often incomprehensible. No parent, for example, ever wants to admit there are times when one secretly wishes her child to precede her in death. No one ever thinks that. But this is not an uncommon or unjustified thought for a parent to have while her child is suffering from a particularly devastating episode related to mental illness. That's how painful the journey can become when one's child lives with severe mental illness such as bipolar disorder, borderline personality disorder, schizophrenia, schizoaffective disorder, or severe anxiety and/or depression.

The stigma, misunderstandings about mental illness, and manifestations of the illness, such as disordered thinking and psychotic behavior, are some factors that often drive parents to withdraw. Brick by brick, parents construct a wall that isolates them from community, friends, and acquaintances.

Ironically, there is another mother, father, sister, or spouse living just down the way who shares a similar experience and who could provide solace with his own story. And a mental illness diagnosis doesn't eliminate the possibility of a fulfilling life. There is treatment. There is hope. There are parents who attest this truth. As our family grappled with the reality of mental illness for one of our own, we began a search for answers from parents because we knew parents often provide some of the best advice and support.

While scientific studies inform best practices, researchers and clinicians don't always live with the person who has a mental illness. We are not experts in the science of parenting a child living with mental illness and can't claim to possess all the answers. But we do know there is value in learning the stories of those who've traveled a similar path. Our experience hearing these stories has helped us to be better parents to our children—to those living with mental illness and not—and to be more empathic to others in our family and community who live with brain disorders.

But talking about it isn't easy, and the interviews didn't always come easily, either. A common reality for our contributors is that life is experienced day by day; recovery is day by day, and a crisis may arise without warning. Flexibility was essential for scheduling (and rescheduling) initial and follow-up interviews. Sometimes, well-intentioned contributors had to cancel altogether. Finding contributors posed unique challenges, as well. Even if we knew where to find parents—treatment centers, for example—direct solicitation breaches confidentiality. We talked about our project and waited to be approached. Luckily we were, even by a father who had never talked about his daughter's illness to anyone outside immediate family. He thought maybe others could benefit from a viewpoint of someone just like him. He was right.

Our contributors and their children, who are from across the United States, remain anonymous. We will always be grateful for their generosity and bravery. What goes on behind the wall—the learning, advocating, grieving, coping, and even triumph—is contained in these stories told by parents.

Mary Widdifield and Elin Widdifield
August 2014

# Introduction

We interviewed parents individually, in two cases both parents together, to hear stories of seven children in uninterrupted entirety and devoid of outside influences. We conducted follow-up interviews and in most cases have ongoing communication. Our contributors often answered our prepared questions and provided much more without our prompting. We cannot account for why mothers were more willing to share their experience and perspective, although Dan, a father who did come forward, provides some thought on this matter in a later chapter about his daughter's recovery.

Our contributors want to show there is hope, offer advice on how to cope, and assure parents they are not alone in the difficult journey of caring and advocating for a child who lives with a mental illness. As one of our contributors says of another mother whose child was recently diagnosed, she "wanted to reach out and tell her, 'I've been there; it's okay.'"

In real life, it is hard to reach out to others affected by mental illness. Through this collection of stories, contributors endeavor to reach out to those burdened by stigma, grief, and isolation. We present these stories as they might be heard in a group meeting, a safe, private environment, perhaps a comfortable living room where everyone understands and hears.

Stories in Part I begin with a group discussion such as in a support group, with each mother, including author Elin Widdifield, introducing her child through recollections from the early years. This chapter is followed by single-narrative stories from Esme, Kerri, Bianca, and Tessa that contain experiences common to many parents in the beginning of their journey parenting a child with mental illness. Esme struggles to get proper diagnosis and treatment, Kerri faces tremendous obstacles to obtain treatment and support, Bianca balances everyday logistics while keeping her son in recovery, and Tessa fights to keep her son on medication and safe.

In Part II, parents address their worst fears. But they also offer hope, recovery, and coping. Though Catherine's story in chapter six is heartbreaking and tragic, we can learn from her story. In chapter seven, Nathalie and Delia's family is saved when they find proper treatment. Dan and Rebecca tell an inspiring story in chapter eight of parenting a daughter who lives with schizophrenia.

In Part III, chapter nine, author Elin Widdifield rejoins four mothers—Esme, Kerri, Bianca, and Tessa—to discuss experiences with grief and guilt. They offer invaluable advice for helping one's child and coping. In chapter ten, discussion turns to revising expectations for one's child, defining "recovery," and finding a "new normal." All our contributors throughout these pages express thoughts about what scares them and what gets them through each day.

The stories and lessons contained herein are not only for those who have children diagnosed with mental illness. These parents offer valuable perspectives beneficial to all parents. These are insights about advocating for one's child, having realistic expectations, meeting them where they are, never giving up on them, and guiding with patience, understanding, and unconditional love.

# PART I

*The journey begins with chaos, diagnosis, and seeking treatment.*

Parents introduce their children, describe how mental illness first presented, and how their own lives began to change. A person with persistent mental illness creates chaos in the home and impacts all family members. There are challenges in getting a proper diagnosis and treatment, and scant support when trying to commit an adult child into treatment. Most frightening for parents is that people experiencing psychosis put themselves in real danger.

Meet the parents.

**Esme** exudes warmth and confidence. She is very fit and dresses in crisp business attire that matches her proven work ethic. She speaks honestly from her heart, a place of deep compassion and experience. She has excellent posture and sits relaxed with her hands folded. Her daughter is Jennifer.

**Kerri** is petite, competent, highly industrious, and organized. She is welcoming, energetic, and her unlined face belies her age. It is no surprise she teaches preschool. She and her husband are active in their community and maintain busy social lives. Her son is Thomas.

**Bianca** is the kind of nurse a patient would be grateful to have. She has a wicked sense of humor and a joy for life that enables her to put any situation in perspective. Her relationship with both of her sons is honest and loving. Miguel is her younger son.

**Tessa** is passionate, fun loving, and has a natural outdoorsy tan from the many hours she spends hiking trails with her own dogs and those of her clients. She is petite and laughs easily, and one can see when talking to her, she has fight in her. She is in her fifties and fit, but at times seems exhausted. Her son, Riley, is the oldest among the group's children.

# CHAPTER ONE: MEET MY CHILD

*The way we were.*

*Miguel could always land on his feet instantly.
He oozed charm!*

*Of course, hindsight is twenty-twenty. At the
time you just think,
"Well, she's a sensitive child."*

*Riley had Olympic athlete potential.*

*Joseph, born in 1988, is the younger of our two boys and was the
easiest baby. He ate well, slept well, and rarely cried. He grew well
and was always healthy. Later, as he grew into toddlerhood, he
began to entertain us with funny songs and dances he created on his
own. He was always very clever, creative, imaginative, and bright,
which carried on into his school years. Joseph was academic, and
his teachers always gave positive feedback, telling us in conferences
that there were "no issues." Joseph was very active and athletic.
He broke his arm three times and his finger once, and excelled
in sports. He's always loved music. During high school concerts,
he performed drum solos, and there was a time when he was a
member of several bands simultaneously. His drum teacher came
to us and said, "There's not much more I can teach him." But from
an early age he was very sensitive and we often had to talk him
out of feeling others' comments too personally. At that early age,
though, we were unconcerned about his sensitive qualities because
it was also what drove him to ask a disabled girl to the school dance
and express genuine empathy for the homeless. That was the way
Joseph was—our creative, sometimes dreamy, often funny child.*

3

*And then, when he was sixteen, he began to change. At first manifesting as substance use, we realized much later it was much more serious.*

*The onset of mental illness occurs for most during the late teens after what many parents describe as "normal" childhoods with family trips, birthday parties, and team sports. Many contributors note that during their child's younger years, they possessed remarkable talent or were gifted in music, art, athletics, or academics. There are often few, if any, definitive indicators of a serious mental illness that may bloom later. Behaviors such as being "overly sensitive" or having "too much anger" become indicators in hindsight. Some parents were even reassured by mental health professionals that their child's excessive emotional outbursts or anger fell within a normal range of "teenage angst."*

*But some parents know something is different about their child right away, well before the teen years. Many parents marvel at the striking and distinct differences between versions of their child before illness took hold, and after.*

*Meet the children.*

**ESME:** Jennifer was a great child. Colicky as a baby, but once she got past that she was very playful, smart, and active. Developmentally she was on par. She has always been bright, able to pick up things. She started reading when she was four.

Jennifer was always a good student, interested in a lot of things, eager to learn. She was in Girl Scouts and was good at gymnastics. She had good friendships, and nothing about these relationships seemed problematic or indicative of what was to come. When she was young, we went to India, which she loved, and we traveled to other places and attended big family reunions.

Jennifer was never good with transitions. I'd always have to tell her in advance if I was going to stop to pick up milk after day care. If I didn't warn her, she would be very unsettled. Looking back, I recognize there were signs of her sensitivity while in day care, as she would often complain that someone

4

wasn't nice to her. But I really started noticing her sensitivity when she was in kindergarten, though I didn't think it any different than what a typical child might experience. She's my first, so I had yet to have a comparison. Later, Jennifer's sensitivity affected her interactions with teachers and coaches. Of course, hindsight is twenty-twenty. At the time you just think, "Well, she's a sensitive child."

At ten or eleven years old, her moods started growing progressively more volatile. I chalked it up to her female cycle, which began early, at barely eleven years old. During her middle school years, Jennifer excelled in academics, sports, and other activities. But she also continued to grow more sensitive. She complained about feeling alienated from friends and then experienced a bullying incident. I didn't typically get involved in these incidents unless it became extreme. I wasn't one of those helicopter parents who would be on top of every single thing that was happening.

In seventh grade, Jennifer wrote me a note that said she tried to overdose. I think it was aspirin. We took her to counseling right away. She explained she was feeling very sad and lonely. The counselor didn't give us *any* indication there were serious issues going on with Jennifer. After six sessions the counselor didn't think there was a need to continue counseling and Jennifer wanted to stop. Because this kind of behavior was new, I followed Jennifer's lead but more vigilantly monitored how she was doing.

I had noted incidents of increased sensitivity during second grade but didn't worry because that was a transitional time for her, having just started at a new school, which was a kindergarten-through-eighth-grade Catholic school. I thought it normal that a child required time to adjust. But she was still at that same school in eighth grade, with many of the same kids she'd known for several years, and she continued to be overly sensitive with friends—often feeling alienated—and frequently thought others did not like her. Jennifer *perceived* she wasn't liked. *She was extremely sensitive.*

**KERRI:** We knew something was wrong from the beginning. Thomas was born with low birth weight, and at five weeks old, he contracted meningitis. He was colicky and cried a lot.

As a boy, he was bright and always asked a lot of questions but seemed overly sensitive. He made friends in kindergarten, but with the exception of one loyal friend, all of them left him when he got "weird." He began having trouble in school around sixth grade and showed signs of OCD.[1] He could hardly pay attention. For example, when the teacher talked, he counted the syllables and even as he read, he had some kind of counting system.

Thomas was still wetting the bed at age nine. Also at that age, his grandfather died and he became very depressed. He believed he caused his grandfather's death. He told me he jumped off the coffee table a certain number of times but it wasn't the *right* number of times so his grandfather died.

He can become extremely angry and was often aggressive toward his younger sister. We were afraid to leave him alone with her. By seventh grade we had to limit TV and video games because once he started to watch or play, he couldn't stop, and asking him to quit caused fights. We tried introducing him to other activities and interests such as sports, music, and art but were unsuccessful. He wasn't interested in any of these things.

**BIANCA:** Miguel was a joyous kid who was happy-go-lucky and made friends easily.

We were a very tight-knit family; there are four of us, and Miguel is younger than his brother, Arturo. Miguel was born overseas because his dad, Carlo, had a job there at the time. Carlo changed jobs frequently, at least every two years. Though we moved around a lot, Miguel could always land on his feet instantly. He oozed charm!

Miguel was a teeny, tiny kid. I thought being five feet tall would be a handicap. I hauled him to endocrinologists to determine whether we should give him growth hormones. We didn't, and now, at five-foot-eleven, he's the tallest member of the family.

He loved lacrosse, but he was so small that the high school coach said, "I cannot safely let him on the team because he'll get creamed." He became the manager instead. He always had friends, was invited places, and had fun, social things to do. He liked to roller-skate and swim. At the time of our last move to this town, he was involved in diving and also enjoyed baseball. Miguel's dad and older brother were deep into martial arts, which Miguel did for a short time. But Miguel is a pacifist and doesn't like to fight, so he didn't stay with that.

Miguel has always had severe learning disabilities and a central auditory processing disability that affects the way he speaks. What he hears takes him longer to process and get speech back out again. He also has dyslexia. He's very bright, but he's had to overcome disabilities all his life. We didn't push him since he had to spend so much time with schoolwork.

He loved music and is a very talented, brilliant cellist. In fourth grade he wasn't tall enough to play cello, so he took piano. Later he studied both. In sixth grade, he could choose instruments. Both teachers wanted him because he was a natural musician. Now he plays guitar, which he taught himself.

Miguel didn't have serious girlfriends in high school or junior high. I made it clear from the beginning it was not the best thing. But he was always such a charmer! When Miguel was a kindergartener, our boys earned fake money for good behavior. They'd save it to go to the movies. Miguel saved his all year long and then took five little girls to the movies with him. They were thrilled to have been asked to go to the movies with Miguel, and all came to school dressed up. He looked like a rock star walking down the hall with his groupies! They arranged themselves around him like little flowers. Here was this little, teeny-tiny thing, shorter than everybody, sitting there surrounded by girls, grinning.

We were talking at dinner one time when the boys were

young, and his brother, Arturo, said, "I hope to have at least ten girlfriends." Miguel replied, "I hope to have a hundred. At the same time." Arturo looked at him and said, "Miguel, that's not safe."

I thought he could pull it off!

**TESSA:** When Riley was three, his father and I divorced. His father moved away and was not around for the everyday things. Riley was a bright, sweet boy. I homeschooled him for kindergarten, then he went to school in first grade. He was a popular, normal, happy-go-lucky child and was always well behaved. He would spend the night at a friend's home and the parent would say, "He's such a delight!"

Riley's childhood was similar to any normal kid's. He loved school and was involved in extracurricular activities. He was active! He mountain-biked, Rollerbladed, played basketball, and swam. He was in bilingual classes and was an honors student. Riley had started swimming as a "Tadpole" at three, and by twelve years old an Olympic swimming coach approached me to ask if he could take my son to Colorado Springs to train. Riley had Olympic athlete potential. But he didn't want to go.

At thirteen, Riley stole baseball cards, and luckily the police just tried to scare him. He told the police he liked baseball cards and wanted to see if he could get away with it. That was the only time he stole, but the incident made me think he needed his dad around, a good role model. His father and I had earlier made an agreement that when Riley hit puberty, he would live near his father. It was time. We moved to California. His dad was in graduate school at that time, though he already had another graduate degree from Harvard. He was working on a master's in psychotherapy for young people. That now seems ironic.

At first Riley was excited to be in California, but the move ended up being difficult for him. In Colorado, Riley had always been well rounded and had many close friends. He had always been involved in sports and, other than the baseball card incident, had never gotten into trouble. Once he was adventurous on a mountain bike and got stuck in a pond. But that was the extent of it.

Once we were in California, things seemed to become harder for Riley. Riley and I shared an apartment with Ted, his father, because money was tight. Unfortunately, Ted and I were butting heads, so I got my own apartment, and Riley and his dad lived together without me. But Riley and Ted had a tumultuous relationship, partly because his dad had been out of his life for a long time. Riley would say, "Who do you think you are, coming back into my life now, telling me what to do?" After about a month, Riley, who was thirteen, tried to run away a few times. Once he was found walking across a freeway bridge. You're not supposed to walk across that bridge.

---

*Parents brighten when talking about their child's early years, before signs of mental illness became manifest. Even when a child expressed atypical behaviors, memories from a child's early years represent more joyful times. Characteristics parents come to know in childhood, such as cognitive abilities, talents, interests, and even one's style of humor, may provide the benchmark for which to define recovery. There is so much behavioral volatility later and grief for the parent, these memories from babyhood and childhood can also offer a sense of grounding, something to which a parent can hold fast. For these stated reasons, we always asked contributors to describe their child before the illness progressed. We wanted to know our contributors' children from their lenses to better understand the profound challenges that came later. Most adults who live with mental illness experience a relatively typical childhood, which is why the changes that often begin during adolescence can feel so devastating.*

## CHAPTER TWO: ESME AND JENNIFER

*The journey begins, chaos erupts,
and diagnosis seems elusive.*

*This was like having a different child.
It was as if one day we opened the door to find
someone else had moved in.*

*Esme agreed to meet after the lunch rush in the cafeteria of the prominent hospital where her daughter, Jennifer, had received outpatient treatment. A public place with fluorescent lights and practical linoleum floors seems an odd location to find privacy for an interview, but it's an environment with which parents with children who live with persistent brain disorders are well acquainted. And Esme, having identified her desire to make a concerted effort to help other parents, was unguarded, her attitude reflected in the phrase, "It is what it is." At the time of our meeting, Jennifer, who was born in 1992, was a month shy of her nineteenth birthday. From the beginning of Jennifer's symptoms to the present, Esme has worked diligently on an intellectual, spiritual, and practical level to address the particular needs of a family that must thrive with mental illness woven into its daily dynamic. Esme was in the process of resigning from some commitments to become more involved with helping other parents, but with a demanding full-time job and two daughters who needed her, she still had limited availability. It was "serendipity," she said, when she learned about the* Behind the Wall *project because it allowed her to begin contributing and helping others.*

*Symptoms of mental illness seem to emerge in a series of increasingly concerning episodes and odd behaviors that may include extreme moodiness, anger, or decreasing competence at school or in social situations. In some cases, a child's substance use in adolescence exacerbates and complicates behaviors. Parents struggle to make sense of these new and extreme behaviors. One or both parents may suspect a child's behaviors are more severe than what falls within a normal range of adolescent angst. A parent's intuition is usually correct, even though it is sometimes in conflict with a spouse who interacts less with the child, other family members, or professionals.*

*A child's confusing behaviors cause chaos in the house and alter familial relationships. Household members feel as if they are "walking on eggshells" around the ill person and feel relief when their family member goes to a hospital or inpatient treatment. Attention becomes focused on the ill child, whether diagnosed and in treatment or not, which stresses a marriage and diverts attention from other children. Friction between spouses is exacerbated by the unpredictability of the illness, the different paces at which parents come to understand mental illness, differing parenting styles, grief experienced by parents for the loss of the child they once knew, and the intensity of advocating for a child in crisis. A family may also be significantly impacted by increased financial and time demands required to provide treatment for their loved one.*

*The path toward a mental health diagnosis can be fraught with emotional conflict. Extreme behaviors a parent witnesses may not be exhibited for a medical professional during an office visit. Sometimes symptoms change and shift in severity. Alcohol and substance use can impede proper diagnosis. Parents also express frustration over a common policy in the mental health profession to abstain from diagnosing minors, which puts effective treatment further out of reach. Even while seeking a diagnosis and knowing in one's heart a son or daughter is unwell, a parent never wants to learn their child has a mental illness; stigma makes acceptance difficult.*

*This is Esme's story.*

**ESME:** I always feared in the back of my mind that mental illness would hit me, my family, my *kids*. It's prevalent. It hit two nephews who now have life-impacting mental illnesses and another who has depression. My mother had mental illness but never acknowledged it and would never go on medication. I never had the tools to address mental illness, nor did my siblings. She ignored it, or "dealt with it." Not in a good way because there was dysfunction in our family. I've lived through other really bad scenarios with my brother's schizophrenia. Because of things that he experienced, I knew the situation could be worse than whatever we were dealing with. But until we got the diagnosis, I didn't know what to do for Jennifer, and that was frustrating. For a long time, I didn't know what *it* was in terms of a specific diagnosis. I recognized that she had depression and anxiety. But I thought her behavior was hormonal. I really did.

By her adolescent years, parenting Jennifer became difficult. Coping with the chaos in the house was hard because she didn't follow rules. I came to intuitively understand that grounding her by taking her phone or computer away wasn't the right punishment. In fact it was the reverse of helping her because she would isolate herself and then go into a depression. Removing social ties, even if they were electronic, was not the right solution for Jennifer. What worked for other children wouldn't work for her and wasn't an appropriate way to change her behavior.

During her early adolescence, we moved to a new town. Jennifer had chosen to continue at the same school, which had progressed into an all-girls Catholic school. I thought it was a good idea to stay at the same school and be stable since change had been hard for her in the past. She had a great year in eighth grade, but the moods were always tough. Getting her to school every morning was a battle. In the fall of ninth grade, she was dressed in a ball gown for a dance she was going to with her boyfriend. Her arms were bare in this gown, and we noticed she had been cutting. We were devastated. We got her into counseling right away. Interestingly, before that night, she had let on about a friend from school who'd been cutting.

In hindsight, I think she had wanted to see what my reaction might be.

But still, her moods and sensitivity created chaos and affected her relationships. Finally, her boyfriend's family said, "That's enough; it's too much." It was too much for him to absorb and take her rages. I remember this incident when I took her to see him play soccer in a town an hour away. Apparently, she was trying to get his attention during the game but he ignored her. His parents had requested that he not have contact with her and he was trying to distance himself. The whole ride home she raged like nobody I'd ever seen before. I was terrified she was going to open the door in mid-flight.

Jennifer transitioned to public school for tenth grade. She still had a few close friends though she started alienating herself from another group of friends. I started to see that kind of pattern. During the high school years she continued to be moody, volatile, and had behavior that continued to be concerning. When she's in a state, she's irrational. You can't reason with her. You could say the wrong thing at any time that would set her off. That phrase—"walking on eggshells"—used to describe her illness is spot-on because you never know what is going to happen. But during freshman year she had learned good coping skills in counseling that helped somewhat. Because she is creative, we gave her art supplies to help her vent.

Over the next few years her moods became increasingly more difficult. The second time she cut, my husband witnessed it. That was traumatic. Who can watch their child cut themselves? We made a few trips to the hospital around that time. After an incident where she was in the ER, a counseling center was recommended. By her junior year, again, after a breakup, she cut herself in school. Had the damage been any more severe, she wouldn't have survived.

We got her into an outpatient program again right away. She participated better in the program than she had with previous counseling. We kept her out of school, and she finished the program in a few days. We thought a cooling-off period away from school could help and wanted to keep her home the next few days that led up to April vacation. But she insisted on going back before vacation. She wanted to talk to her guidance counselor and to the girl who had found her in the bathroom. Jennifer was concerned about what information had been disseminated to kids at school. The girl, luckily, had been spoken to by the administration, but whether she abided by it . . . you know, kids are kids. It was tough.

She finished junior year. The summers were okay because she had friends and free time. She had jobs dealing with children. She's a child magnet—very good and patient with them, which is interesting because otherwise she's critical and thinks in black and white terms. One job she had was at a place where there's a jumpy blow-up thing and pizza parties for little kids. She did that for a while until she perceived her boss was being mean to her and she quit. In that incident, I talked to her boss because it was confirmed by one of Jennifer's friends that the woman had been inappropriate. I intervened because Jennifer was not showing up or calling because she couldn't confront her boss. I felt the need to explain for her. But I didn't usually intervene for her. The following year, Jennifer got a job at a similar place coaching gymnastics for kids. She was happy until the manager asked her to work on her day off. Jennifer said, "I think I can," but she was returning from a college visit with my husband and they hit traffic. She called her boss to say she was running late, but the woman went off on her, which my husband confirmed because he could hear her yelling through the phone. Of course that ended that job and she never got her last check.

Throughout those high school years, she had extreme moods, volatility, and rages, and we were unable to put restrictions on her. She couldn't follow rules. It was difficult trying to impose rules and expect a child to abide and obey, and she simply would not. It was *not* going to be in her plan

15

to follow! I don't know if she deliberately disobeyed or was incapable of follow through. It seemed as though she couldn't absorb what we said, nor could she carry out our instructions into action. Getting her to do anything was difficult.

And there was drama. In one incident that happened between Jennifer's junior and senior years, while we were on vacation, the police called us from her boyfriend's house. She had been drinking, and was raging and throwing things. Then a different time, during her senior year, Jennifer had threatened over the phone to her boyfriend that she would kill herself. He called the police who then came to our door at two in the morning and woke us. "Does Jennifer live here? She's threatening to kill herself." I let the police in. Of course they had to force her to go to the hospital. I didn't believe she was suicidal but that her threats were more about her expressing how she felt.

Then she had a boyfriend who was a college freshman. We discovered sometime in December that she'd been sneaking off to visit him and staying over the weekend. When we found out, we grounded her. I drew a very clear boundary. Then she stole money from me and left in the middle of the night. She got a ride to the train station and went to see him. The following morning he called us to say he was bringing her home, to the hospital actually, and that she was in bad shape. Of course, Jennifer was grounded for that, and she and her boyfriend split. Luckily he gave advance warning and she handled it well, which was surprising, given her past history of handling breakups.

To celebrate our twenty-fifth wedding anniversary, we went with both girls to the Dominican Republic during a break in Jennifer's senior year. I had convinced my husband to go on a family vacation, expecting that Jennifer would soon be going to college. Of course we'd started the whole college process in the fall and had been talking about it since the year before.

It was the second or third vacation that was ruined . . . that's not fair . . . *impacted*, is a better way to say it, by her behavior. This

16

time it started with her tantrum over a room. Jennifer wanted a particular room her sister, Laura, who is three years younger, also wanted, and there became a dispute and accusations, "You like Laura better," which was a constant thread throughout this entire period.

Jennifer was exhibiting very impulsive behavior. We had met people on the trip, and she was staying at the disco a little bit late with them. I stayed with her for a while, and then I said, "I'm going now, but you need to be back in an hour." Then she didn't show up at all. We hunted all over the resort for her and feared the worst, not knowing where she was. That turned into a raging incident in the hotel room because she had been drinking and, of course, lying.

After we got back from that vacation she started skipping school and didn't go back. Things escalated from there. She was depressed and not participating in things. She left home, and we didn't know where she was and couldn't find her. She wouldn't return calls for days. We had no idea what was going on with her. We finally reconnected and tried to get her back in school. She had to make up schoolwork, a silly senior project, and earn a credit and a half in English, which had always been her best subject. Before that, she'd always taken mostly honors and AP college classes. But she just couldn't do it. She couldn't function, couldn't read. She'd get to school and immediately have anxiety. Eventually there was no repair to be done.

We tried a tutor, but she didn't commit to it; then there was either miscommunication or she wasn't paying attention and the school cancelled tutoring. We had to meet with the school administration. We said, "Look, this is the situation: she can't be here; it's too difficult for her." The counselor agreed, "Yes, she's definitely experiencing anxiety." We were able to get a section 504[2] so she could be on leave and receive different kinds of treatment and continue her schooling. We decided to let it rest as it was, let it go over the summer, and try to engage her in school again in the fall and see how she felt. She had the opportunity to take classes at a college over the summer to make up her English course. She could have handled the work and had flexibility to do that. She chose not to. It was really hard at that point. She was babysitting part time. She'd had that job for three summers. But once we got past the summer and school started, she wasn't able to go back to school.

She wasn't always like that. When she was younger, she would get up early on a Saturday and get her homework done. I would think, "Gosh, she's sleeping late!" I'd open her door and see she was awake, sitting at her desk. She'd say, "I'm just getting my homework done." Jennifer was self-disciplined and structured. Now we had a child who couldn't cope in school. This was like having a different child. It was as if one day we opened the door to find someone else had moved in.

Jennifer started saying to me, "Mom, can't somebody just give me something to make me feel better? I want to feel normal. I want to feel better."

I was crazy, crazy researching during this whole time. What was it? Was it depression? Was it PMDD?[3] Bipolar? Anxiety? I was looking for anything to help me understand. Her counselor from freshman year, who we found when she was first cutting, had recommended a psychiatrist. Before Jennifer had met with him, he sent an eight-page questionnaire to get background information about her behavior and aspects of her moods. My husband, Doug, took her to that appointment and they were prepared with the completed questionnaire. First the doctor met with Doug for about twenty minutes and reviewed the questionnaire. Then he met with Jennifer for about thirty-five minutes. By the end, he prescribed an atypical antipsychotic,[4] a drug used for bipolar, and gave us another doctor as a referral because we indicated we wanted a second opinion.

Of course I immediately distrusted that diagnosis and went home and researched that medication for about four hours and found the FDA site with public information about drugs. It was there that I read, "This has never been tested on children under eighteen." She was a fourteen-year-old who weighed about ninety-five pounds. She wouldn't qualify as an adult to consider even a small dosage. I'm not a doctor, but I didn't feel right about that. I ran as fast as I could and didn't go back to a psychiatrist until her senior year when we started seeing a doctor who was recommended by a friend. That doctor asked Jennifer to track her moods, and then he did a physical and blood test. Other than some vitamin deficiencies, nothing concerned him. He wanted to monitor her for a couple of months. He made it clear that he wouldn't diagnose or prescribe medication.

By the summer of 2010, shortly after we'd seen that doctor, I somehow found out about borderline personality disorder (BPD), though it wasn't *his* diagnosis. I am baffled as to why I can't remember *how* I learned about BPD, but as soon as I read the list of symptoms used to diagnose it, I knew immediately. I didn't even have to dive into forty-five pages of documentation. It was right there. I immediately bought books and started reading.

I'll never forget the moment I shared it with Jennifer. The morning after I first found out about BPD, I was up early because, as usual, I couldn't sleep. I went downstairs to read more. When she woke up, I asked her to come into the office, and I said, "There is something I'd like you to read." After reading the list of symptoms she looked up at me from the computer with sad eyes and said, "Mom, this is *me*. Why didn't anybody tell me?" I said, "I don't know the answer to that question, but I think now we have some direction."

Up until Jennifer's senior year, there had been no definitive diagnosis, no meds, three or four ER trips, three counseling periods across two doctors, outpatient treatment, and no one mentioned that borderline personality disorder could be a possibility. That was one of the most frustrating things for me, to think that the medical community had let me down. I know that is a strong thing to say, but that's not what *I* do for a living. That's what *THEY* do for a living.

As soon as we got the diagnosis, we made appointments. We met with the doctor at the hospital who confirmed Jennifer had eight of nine symptoms for borderline personality disorder. Again, I was so frustrated, thinking that after all those doctors and hospitals, not one diagnosed her so that she could receive proper treatment, and by then she was eighteen. If I'd had any inkling that BPD was her diagnosis, she could have had better therapy earlier. It may not have solved anything, but she would have had better tools sooner. Maybe she would have graduated because that year was the toughest—hearing all my friends' kids talk about college plans, watching them graduate and throw parties while I had to explain that Jennifer wasn't going to college. I didn't tell them she had dropped out of high school.

Once I learned the diagnosis, I studied and researched and read books and blogs and websites and found programs designed specifically for patients with BPD. When it became clear school wasn't working out and Jennifer wasn't going to finish her senior year of high school, we tried to get her engaged in a program. Luckily we have the means. Whatever we probably would have paid for college, we said, "We'll divert it to her care, because that's going to be her college for the next six months to a year."

But she couldn't commit herself to a program, and by then she was eighteen. There was nothing I could do. Nothing. She couldn't commit to a program, and because of the expense involved and the way she anticipates guilt, she wouldn't risk committing then failing. That was the most crushing moment for me, realizing it was too late. Realizing at that point there was nothing more I could do other than continue to be there, love her, support her in whatever she wanted to do, and guide her. But there was no treatment I could impose. I would have had more influence when she was fourteen or fifteen or sixteen. If I'd had the tools, if I had gotten her into a program before she was eighteen, I think she would have had a different outcome when, in the fall of her senior year, she broke up with her boyfriend and by March had dropped out of school. After we got Jennifer's BPD diagnosis, I had to talk to her first counselor. I told her we'd gotten an official diagnosis of BPD. I asked, "Did you ever consider that Jennifer had borderline personality disorder?"

She said, "No. We don't diagnose children under eighteen."[5]

I said, "That's surprising and unfortunate because what I have read, and I've read quite a bit, is that it *is* prevalent and it *is* real for children under eighteen, and for years she's had obvious symptoms. The cutting is a dead giveaway. Self-harm is number one on the list." I continued, "And also the main reason we came, the trouble she has with relationships and the volatile moods are signs of BPD." But diagnosing wasn't something this counselor did. "I'd like you to reconsider that perspective about diagnosing children under eighteen because had I known earlier, I would have been able to do something more, and Jennifer would have had a different life than dropping out of school with a 3.8 GPA."

I didn't mean to make her feel guilty but did want to make a point. I wanted her to reconsider her diagnosis policy because it could have helped Jennifer. When you hear those distressing, traumatic stories of parents who've lost their kids to drunk driving or something horrible and they stand in front of a camera saying, "I'm standing here talking to you, pleading so it doesn't happen to the next kid . . ." That's how I felt. I wanted to speak out so that what happened to Jennifer, her not being diagnosed, wouldn't happen to others. I also felt disappointed. Let down.

Another huge source of frustration is the privacy laws the government imposes. The doctor says, "I can't talk to you but you can talk to me." It's one-sided. Even *with* consent. It's possible Jennifer wasn't honest with the counselor she had at eighteen. Here I was, not knowing if Jennifer was telling her counselor about the behaviors I knew were going on that were more harmful than what the counselor could know, because

I *lived* with her. Certainly I understand a counselor is under obligation to report self-harmful behaviors. But it was so frustrating, especially during senior year, when Jennifer was going through that horrible phase of running away, dropping out of school, and experiencing depression and anxiety. I would call her counselor in case Jennifer wasn't disclosing certain things and say, "I'm feeding you information. I know you can't talk to me, but here it is . . ."

Here's another one. That counselor knew Jennifer had done heroin because she told her. What is wrong with telling a parent their eighteen-year-old is doing coke and heroin? I'm not sure why the government has to protect that. I understand privacy laws, except when it is self-destructive. Be sensible. Common sense has left our culture when it comes to mental health and privacy. Of course you don't think about it until it's relevant to you. You don't consider the impact.

But I was always open with Jennifer about what I told her doctors. I'd say, "I called your doctor. I said such and such." I would never hold anything back from her. Kids aren't stupid. Parents should never hold back information from them. They are sensitive and pick up a whole lot more than one may think. They know more about what a parent is feeling than sometimes the parent does. They are good at that.

I try to always communicate clearly with Jennifer. But one time I didn't inform her in advance that my husband and I would be attending her counseling session that day. It was an absolute, sincere, honest—rest my hand on a Bible—mistake, an oversight. I work, I travel, kids, blah, blah, blah. But she was furious, thinking we were trying to deceive her. She threw a fit in her counselor's office when we showed up. She is a one-to-one person; any more than that is a crowd for her, and she felt like we were ganging up on her. I told her I wasn't trying to deceive her and I never have done that. I told her I wasn't going to hold anything back from her because it wasn't helpful and would not serve her well. If she finds me being untrustworthy, who else can she trust when she already feels sensitive about everything in the world around her? I needed her to know that I would always have her back and I'm always here for her.

The good thing is that through some of that early work she did with her counselor and discussions with her, she had become self-aware. When she wasn't in what I call her "states," her irrational type of states, we would talk and I would be able to get through to her. I'd say, "You need to recognize the point where you're feeling certain ways or when you know you're going to have anxiety or feel like you are going to explode," because that's what it would be like, these volcanoes would erupt out of nowhere. She became aware of her sensitivity, which has helped her through difficult times. She also became aware of her depression symptoms. I'd talk with her when she was open and ready. She'd expressed that she was lonely all the time and empty and none of her friends liked her. She had that constant feeling of being in her own universe.

Any parent knows when their child is hurting. You feel their pain. The powerlessness of not being able to help her frustrates me the most. Through all of this, I have been lucky to have always known to keep working to communicate with Jennifer verbally or in writing. We used to journal to each other. But again, that didn't continue for long because she has a hard time following through on anything.

In September, Jennifer didn't return to finish her senior year of high school or participate in a treatment program. I told her she needed to get a job because summer jobs are temporary, not real jobs. She didn't work during the fall. I said, "By October 31st, you're going to start paying rent. You need to make a decision about what you are going to do." She had money saved in the bank and was pretty good with money. We had bought her car and she'd offered to pay for it. I said, "Once you start working, you own your car insurance, any maintenance, and rent. It's time for you to make some choices in life." She finally got two babysitting jobs that worked out well: close to home, both the same day. She can't deal with pressure, and for her, being with kids is fun. For her, that's the ideal job.

But I felt I had to start drawing boundaries because of the disruption to the family and our inability to have any measure of control. Parents need control. I'm not saying excessive or autocratic, but control over a functioning household. I said, "October 31st, I expect rent." I said one hundred dollars a month or twenty-five a week. Nominal.

Then something happened on October 31st, Halloween. She was mouthing off or being disrespectful, and I said, "By the way, today is the day you owe me rent." I had given her a strict rule: *pay by October 31st.* "This isn't an option. This is what is going to happen, or you can't live here. You can't have it both ways," I replied, probably not as calmly as I often do. She said, "I'm not paying you rent then." I said, "You're not paying me rent?" That was it. I was tipped over. I went upstairs and said, "Get your bags and get out!"

She couldn't believe I was really drawing the line. She tried starting an argument, and I said, "There is no argument here. There is no scene. There is nothing. Get what you need. Right now. Get out. You knew the rules. I've explained it continuously over four weeks." Doug and I were on the same page. She tried to bring her sister, Laura, into the situation. I said, "No. Laura is not going with you. This is not her issue. This is your issue that you have to deal with." That upset Laura. But she had to understand that line, too, because she couldn't be involved in her sister's battles. Jennifer left. She stayed with friends at first, and then with her boyfriend who lived farther away, which meant she had to commute two hours a day to her job. I reached out to her, but we didn't talk for a while.

We always reached out to her, even after her explosions, her fights with us, to say, "We love you no matter what." It has always been the message we give her. I think that helped and made a difference for her to know that no matter how badly she behaved, we loved her. I have also made that distinction very clear: "*You are not a bad person*," because she's not. She's a great person with an incredible heart. She's fun and smart and really great to be around when she is not having her issues. I never liked the messages from my upbringing—at home and our church—that one *is* bad if one acts badly. I never agreed with that message. It especially wasn't healthy for her.

Jennifer got an apartment. She figured out her budget. She came to the house and said, "Okay, here's my budget. Anything else I need to think about?" She worked through it with us. She felt a phenomenal sense of accomplishment and self-esteem. "I moved out. I did it on my own." Her boyfriend, Kevin, moved in with her. Not my preference. I wanted her to be healthy before she engaged in that kind of a relationship. But at the same time, secretly, I was happy to know he'd be there with her.

I monitored her. She seemed to be doing okay throughout winter, and in January she quit her early job, which was the bulk of her pay. I was proud that she checked in with me about it first. "Mom, the father says to me, he implies that I am responsible for his daughter getting sick, and I know I can be sensitive, but I'm really trying to put it into perspective." Jennifer showed me messages he'd sent to her, which weren't very kind. I said, "That's your decision. If you feel you can't work in that environment given your sensitivities . . ." because the father was the one she'd always see. "But you have to replace that job," I said. She quit. The wife was horrified by what the husband had said to Jennifer and called to apologize on his behalf. She asked Jennifer if she'd be willing to babysit on occasion. Jennifer did, and the whole thing was a good lesson for her. She got through that.

But she didn't find another job right away. February came. Still no job. March came. No job. Then I didn't hear from her. On March 11, I got a call from her boyfriend. "I don't know what to do with her. She's threatening to kill herself. She doesn't want me to go to work." I'd just completed my therapy session. I went to her apartment instead of to work. She wouldn't let me in. I had to drive to her boyfriend's work to get his keys and let myself into the apartment.

The apartment was a *dump*. It was . . . ack! I can't even explain my feelings when I walked in. I was thinking, "This is how my daughter is living?" Jennifer never goes out of the house with a hair out of place; she's fashion and appearance conscious. That goes with her self-esteem issues. I know the symptoms those unclean conditions represented.

She went into a rage and was uncontrollable. The building manager came down and said, "You have to keep it down." The police were called and arrived, but I had no intention of leaving because this was the first time she had threatened to kill herself while not living at home. I didn't know what events had preceded or what state she was in, how serious it was, or if her threats were her way to control Kevin. I stayed with her and eventually we calmed her down. Through all of this, she's had hormonal issues. That day she had started her period after three months. We've tried to do something about that as well.

We got through that, too.

But then she wasn't calling. She didn't show up for work, and her boss was calling me. For days. When I got her on the phone she said she was sick. I said, "But you can't *not* respond to your boss. You're leaving her high and dry!" She got back to work but called in sick again the following week. The flu was going around, but I knew there was some depression going on again. It was that time of year. Like clockwork. She wasn't on meds because the psychiatrist had said, "I can't diagnose you, so I don't want to put you on meds." I was totally okay with that. The more we read about BPD, we learned there aren't meds that work.

I was traveling for work about a month later. I'd just flown in and was meeting with a new client when I got a call from Jennifer's boyfriend's phone followed by several more. I didn't answer but saw Kevin's name come up. I thought it was Jennifer calling because she often forgot to charge her phone and then used his. Finally, I texted, "I can't talk. In a meeting. Do you need me to step out?" Then he texted: "She's in the hospital. She OD'd."

I ran out of the meeting. I didn't know how serious this was at first. I called my husband, "You need to get to the hospital." The nurse was going to call me because Kevin couldn't advocate on Jennifer's behalf. When I spoke to Kevin, he was crying and hysterical. He said she had taken a pill and smoked marijuana, which I knew she did. Sometime during the night she was nonresponsive and he knew something was wrong and called 911. She was taken to the emergency room and was barely breathing. When I finally got in touch with the nurse, she told me that her breathing was still the issue. They put monitors on her and gave her medication, but once they took her off assistance, her breathing declined severely again. They were keeping her on watch and wanted to keep her overnight. This was nine-thirty a.m. on Thursday when I was having this discussion, from a thousand miles away.

Doug called and said, "I'm going to give it to you straight. She almost died. If Kevin hadn't called, we'd be planning a funeral because she wasn't breathing."

There was nothing I could do. There were no earlier flights. I had to sit through the whole meeting, frequently stepping out to take calls. After the meeting I rushed to get my flight, the only one, which of course was delayed. By then, Jennifer was refusing to stay in the hospital overnight. There was still concern about her breathing, and if she didn't stay, the insurance wouldn't pay for the visit, neither of which she cared about. She wanted out.

I want to say it was an accidental overdose. She'd taken Oxycodone. It was hard for me to hear that. I knew she'd tried heroin and coke in recent months. The Oxycodone was a progression for me that I understood to be quite scary. Earlier that day I had told Doug, "You need to ask for a psych doctor," because they don't provide it unless requested. "She wasn't suicidal," is what the psychiatrist determined. Therefore they couldn't admit or keep her. They couldn't do anything. I don't know how much more suicidal you can get than when you turn to those kinds of drugs. To me, using those drugs is not just about numbing the pain. I don't know.

But she wasn't going to stay and we couldn't commit her. I finally arrived at the airport an hour late. I said, "Don't let her leave. Let me get there!" Doug said, "Don't bother coming." But I insisted. "No! I'm coming." I made it from airport to hospital—normally about a two-hour drive—in an hour and twenty minutes. Yeah. Stupid. But I couldn't let her go without seeing her. I made it by about seven minutes because she'd already packed up her stuff, put her clothes on, and gone out the door. The nurses and Doug convinced her to wait until I got there because I was on my way.

I immediately hugged her, asked her how she was feeling, and told her I loved her. She had been raging at Doug the whole day, saying, "Get out of my room," and starting that whole scene. I said, "I think the doctors know better, and I think for your health and safety it's better you stay." But she said, "No. I don't want to. I can't stay here. I have to go home." I said, "Okay." But while saying goodbye I made a point to thank Kevin directly and said, "I appreciate the call this morning and that it wasn't a call to plan Jennifer's funeral." I had to make that point in front of her because she wasn't grasping it yet. She wouldn't talk to us about it and still hasn't. And won't. I said to her in parting, "You need to get help. This is not something you can do on your own, and this is evidence of that."

I tried to speak with her over the next weekend. She wouldn't come around, wouldn't respond to texts or calls. On Monday, she came by but wouldn't come into the house, so I went out to talk to her and pressed the issue, probably too much. But I knew I had to because I wasn't going to have another opportunity. Again, I said, "You need treatment. You need counseling."

Over the next few months she had the usual roller coaster—ups and downs. The following January, almost a year later, at age nineteen, her moods were disruptive. She was fighting with her boyfriend and police were called. In whatever version of the story you want to believe, the fact remains that there was an altercation, police were there, and she was arrested. We now have had a run-in where her behavior has affected her life with serious consequences: a misdemeanor, "disorderly conduct and resisting arrest." In our state, there is a program called the Diversion Program that gives kids her age another chance. These are not problem kids; they don't have a background or criminal history, and it's designed to bring consequences to their attention. This program allows them to expunge their criminal records if they meet certain standards and commitments that include community service, regular meetings with a program and a drug counselor, regular testing, and staying drug free. But the challenge lies in her lack of follow-through, inability to commit, and severe anxiety that some days hinders her ability to even leave the house. We've struggled through the program. I finally had to say, "You need to make decisions."

Her having a misdemeanor is not where we wanted her to be. She could have prevented it, but she wouldn't commit. She gets a little self-righteous, you know, "I'm sick, so I shouldn't have to be held accountable for that." She definitely expressed that. She wants a little bit of allowance, but it's like, "You only get so much allowance. When you break the law, you cross the line and that's it. It's done. You've used it up."

The winter was really tough. She hadn't worked since the previous fall. Kevin, who was living with her, lost his job because her anxiety was so bad she couldn't be alone and wouldn't let him leave her to go to work. My husband and I supported them: apartment, food, rent, car—all of her expenses.

Jennifer was having trouble driving distances because of anxiety. She was smoking pot to get relief, especially at night when it was especially bad for her. She didn't sleep and got totally anxious. Jennifer knew she needed help and started seeing a psychologist who she loved. Best counselor I've dealt with so far, and she's been an amazing advocate and committed to Jennifer. Jennifer feels this person is invested and has her interests and her back. She was seeing her regularly. That was all positive, so we agreed that when this psychologist diagnosed Jennifer with bipolar and anxiety, in addition to the BPD, we said, "So be it."

The psychologist said, "We've got to get her on a mood stabilizer first and foremost because I can't treat her with the volatility that she has." We spent months searching for a psychiatrist or someone who could administer medications. After two months we found *one* psychiatrist who was on our plan and was located reasonably close to Jennifer. We were required to have our primary care doctor send paperwork, and the psychiatrist's office would get back to us and schedule an appointment upon receiving the paperwork. That would take three weeks from that point.

But practices wouldn't take her because she smoked pot. They said, "We can't administer medication because you are using. As long as you're using, we cannot determine your baseline to be able to know how to treat you." Jennifer explained, "I want to *stop using*. That's why I want to get on medication to treat anxiety." Four phone calls like that and we couldn't get anyone to treat her. Then we had an experience with a psychiatrist near me. After an hour of Jennifer sitting and spilling her heart and soul, baring everything, how she behaved, and by the end was totally vulnerable, he said, "I'm sorry. I really can't help you."[6]

I don't think I was ever so angry. She got up and stormed out, for which I didn't blame her at all. Her storming out of the room was justifiable. I felt the same way. I wanted to do the same thing. He turned to me and said, "Does she always behave like this?" I said, "She sat here for an hour. Couldn't you have explained better? You set me back weeks! I've been trying to get her help." It was an awful experience.

About six months later, around June 1st, when she was almost twenty, Jennifer had an argument with her boyfriend, which meant my husband and I had to pick her up late the night before an early appointment she had with her primary care doctor whose office is near our home. She stayed with us the next day and didn't have a car. She was in a bad mood that day. While I was at work, something set her off and she went ballistic and left the house. My husband was beside himself and called me crying, "I've never seen her like this! This is the worst I've ever seen her. I don't know where she is." He was genuinely afraid. I left work. By the time I got home, she'd been home, had another episode, and left again. I found her walking down the street.

She looked awful. She got in the car, but I said nothing. She said, "I think I want to kill somebody." I said, "Okay. Do you think you want to go to the hospital?" She said, "Yes." I didn't know what I was going to do, but I needed to change the direction these behaviors were leading her. I called my husband. We were only three doors down the street and I said, "We're coming home and we're going to the hospital. Meet us outside."

By then, we'd been through the drill enough to know what was going on and how it was going to happen . . . Even my husband Doug said, "What do you hope to accomplish? Why are we here?" I said, "She can't go on like this. We're at a crisis point and she needs to be in a hospital. She needs medication."

The stars were aligned because there was nobody in the waiting room. We were there five minutes. They had a bed. The psych counselors came over within thirty minutes. Usually it's an hour and a half to two hours, but there is a psych unit right next door to that general hospital. The counselor who came over had previously worked at a prominent teaching hospital that has expertise in treating all psychiatric disorders, including borderline personality disorder, so she very much understood Jennifer's issues. I said, "I know how this works. I know you can't talk to me. I get it, unless she gives you permission. But let me give you some background so you have context." The counselor was open and gave Doug and me an opportunity to inform her about the course of events, what had happened in the last couple of months and several years. Then she left to speak with Jennifer who said all the right things, you know, not the right things by normal standards, but the right things like, "Yes, I'm afraid I could hurt myself. I couldn't say that I couldn't hurt me or somebody else."

I said, "Awesome. That was the right thing to say because that is what the insurance company needs to hear." You know the game. If she'd said anything different we would have walked out of there. But we managed to get sanctioned by the insurance company, and she got to stay one night in the emergency room while we waited for a bed to open. Then she went into a psych facility.

Jennifer was immediately put on a mood stabilizer. They also put her on antianxiety and sleeping medication. We visited her while she was there, and she was discharged four or five days later. She's been on the medication, at least she tells us she's on it, and they set us up with a psychiatrist at that hospital. She's been driving down for appointments, committing to stay with it. That's why I say, "Right now, we're good!" You know, that's today!

The good news about her horrific raging episodes and moods getting progressively worse is that she ended up in the hospital and was forced into treatment. Leading up to that incident, her anxiety had been worsening; she wouldn't drive, not even to visit us at our house an hour away. Jennifer has been on a mood stabilizer since the hospital stay and it has been wonderful for her. She's seems genuinely happy. When we visited her in rehab one evening, she said, "Mom, this is going to sound weird, but I looked at myself in the mirror today and

I thought I looked pretty." I said, "I know, honey, because you *are*, inside and out." She's a very, very cute girl. Anybody would say, "Oh, she's a cutie," but she can't see that. She never has. Her self-esteem isn't there.

Through all of this, I was so consumed by everything that when we finally had Jennifer's diagnosis, I felt like I could relax a bit and finally have a plan. We put a plan in place, and that's when I woke up and said, "I have been neglecting my other daughter, and my husband and I were not on the same page with the parenting."

My husband and I have different parenting styles. I grew up with mental illness in my family, and there was chaos and volatility in my upbringing. I was used to the idea of being adaptive, and he's more black and white: "This is the way she is supposed to act." I was constantly in the middle of their relationship and it started to wear on us, especially by Jennifer's senior year. He was demanding things of her: to behave in a particular way, to abide by a rule, to do the cleaning, pick up after herself after she'd eaten because it would be like a pigpen. But again, I don't think she did it deliberately. She didn't have the concept. She knew she should clean up after herself; it just didn't occur to her that she should do it right then. Often something distracted her so she went on to the next thing without a thought of cleaning up after herself. It was a constant state of friction, and I think it was symbolic of his frustration over how to parent. For me it was, "So what? She left dishes. Have her pick them up later."

Managing our daughters' chores was a source of friction. We would have chore charts. I worked and couldn't be home to enforce it. I'd come home after a very stressful twelve-hour day as a manager of a team having had hours of meetings. Doug would start barking at me, "She didn't do this!" and "What's the point of having charts?" On and on and on until I finally said, "I'm not here to enforce it. I don't know what you want me to do." There was an expectation that I should follow up on that because he knew he was not as tolerant and wanted things done by a certain time. That's how *he* is. When he has a task to do, he does it. He's methodical. That's okay. But I'm like, "Yeah, well, I'll get to it when I get to it, and if it doesn't get done, it's not the end of the world."

Then he would say things about her that would hurt me. I know he didn't mean them. He's a sensitive person. He is so good at talking to her, communicating better than I can at times. Many times. But he couldn't get past this thing of feeling lied to, being disobeyed and disrespected constantly. That was too difficult for him. He would constantly imply or outright state that Jennifer was lying, and he was right. I didn't want to believe it because through all this we still had a relationship and communication and we always, always, always made a point to say that we may not like her behavior but we loved her unconditionally.

Finally, I had a difficult time hearing him say, "She's a liar."

I said, "You know what? She's not a liar. Calling her that cuts me deeply, because if she's lying to you, she doesn't mean it. You have to understand the difference in that behavior. I can't play the middle." I packed my bags and went to my parents', which I had planned to do because at the time my dad needed 24/7 care. I had sent my mom on vacation to get away for a few weeks. I was going to take care of him and work from their home. But I said, "I don't know if I can come back because I can't do this 'in-the-middle' anymore." It was straining. I was starting to get resentful. We've had a great relationship. Married twenty-seven years. Bumps and everything else like any other couple, but we're very close. But this was hard. I always felt the burden, the expectation that I was supposed to control her behavior.

Then, as I started researching and learning about BPD, I felt like *I* was the one doing all the research. I think Doug had too much of it and couldn't absorb any more, whereas I needed to learn as much as I could. For him it was devastating, and he was worn out. It was difficult for him. He started experiencing anxiety and had difficulty managing his parenting style, at least reconciling it to what Jennifer needed. It was constant friction for me. I was in a difficult position. He didn't open up to friends at first like I did. He thought his friends wouldn't understand or they were just golf buddies and probably don't talk about things at that level other than what their kids are *doing*, sports or school or whatever. He had less of an outlet. It was difficult for him to cope.

But we resolved that by really trying to step back and take away the frustrations around parenting, or recognizing that if he was emotional or upset, venting about something, I needed to let him. I would see him being critical of Jennifer and that was a sensitive point with me because I didn't feel that critical outlook was fair. You can't be critical in that way. There are certain things you have to accept and give allowances, and you can't parent these kids in the same way. So it hit a sensitive button, and I had to realize that, okay, he needs to vent and then I'll vent. We have an understanding now that we're each going to reach a point where we are spent and that doesn't mean we're giving up. It means we need to lean on one another and be a sounding board for each other to express frustrations. Recently he said, "She should be able to do this now . . ." I try to be the rational one and say, "Baby steps." And he'll do the same exact thing for me.

I can't imagine single parents who have kids with these conditions because at times when I'm at the end of my rope, my husband steps in and can be the pacifier; when he is at the end of his, I step in. At least we have each other to balance and be able to express frustration, anger, and the hurt. The hurt is the hardest part: to think that your child would deceive you in such ways.

Jennifer's behavior also began to make things difficult for her sister, Laura. When Laura entered eighth grade, there was so much chaos in the home. It was already a hard time for Laura because she had changed schools and didn't know many kids and we were somewhat new to the town. Laura is even-tempered and calm, very empathetic and forgiving, but the chaos in the house affected her because she does not like conflict in the least and that is all she experienced because of Jennifer. At that time, Jennifer wasn't abiding any rules and was creating friction in the family. She takes things without asking. Not because she is trying to be malicious. She doesn't think to ask and doesn't understand it's disrespectful. She has gone through my laundry, everything in my room. You mention it; she's been in there. She started doing that to Laura, who was beginning to stand up for herself. That started conflict between them and they'd always been very close.

On the night that Jennifer was threatening suicide and the police came to the house, I didn't know Laura had heard it. My husband went with Jennifer to the hospital and I stayed at the house. Laura woke up crying, so I went to her. She let out a lot I didn't know. She keeps emotions to herself. One incident she told me about was when kids at school said to her, "Hey, I hear your sister cuts." Laura said, "Mom, how do I respond to that?" I said, "It's none of their business and you don't have to discuss anything." I knew then that Jennifer's illness and behavior had started to affect Laura. After that incident in which police were called to Jennifer's ex-boyfriend's house because she was raging, his parents found out. His parents are neighbors to a boy who was Laura's good friend. But shortly after that incident this boy informed Laura that she was no longer welcome at his home.

That hurt a lot too. But I understand, because people who don't deal with mental illness don't get it. I wouldn't expect them to. It's hard for another parent to understand. Because of what I have experienced, I am able to not judge other parents, but I don't expect the same from others because it's human nature to be judgmental. I'm sure people have judged me as a parent for things Jennifer has done or how she has behaved. I've never had anyone say things to me, luckily. But my friend whose daughter also has BPD was judged. If I had lived in a small community all my life, I think it would have been different for me.

I'm a private person and also the type of person who doesn't really care what other people think. It's not their life, and good for them they don't have these problems. That's the way it is. I was hurt, but there was no action I could take other than console Laura who had by then been affected more than once by the community because of Jennifer's behavior. That's what stung the most. At that time Laura was starting to experience depression, which was also crushing. We definitely never intentionally ignored her, but we *did* ignore her because we missed cues that could have informed us of her well-being, and we shouldn't have. It was accidental because we were focusing 98 percent of our attention on one child.

Laura's a talkative and congenial kid who can make friends and find a way to feel comfortable in most situations. But her behavior definitely changed after those two incidents with the kids and the parents in our community. She became more guarded and protective. I don't think that's necessarily a bad thing for her personality. That's what she had to learn in this family environment, like what I had to learn in mine. It shapes you differently.

With Jennifer out of the house, it has actually been better. I hate to say it, but my husband and I have talked about her coming home, and we both look at each other and think, "Gosh, of course we would love that, but it would be . . . *intense* . . . and we wouldn't have the peace we have now." My younger daughter feels the same way. She would never admit it because she adores her sister. But Jennifer has hurt her. Jennifer would call and say, "I'll come down and we'll do this . . ." and she'd never call; Laura would have arranged her life around her sister, and she'd be a no-show.

I've been learning to have balance and spend more time with Laura when her social schedule allows. When she was taking driver's education I'd spend time in the car with her.

We take moments. "Let's go have dinner, just you and me." Or, "Let's go driving for an hour and stop along the way and go into shops . . ." Anything to steal a moment so she feels connected.

It takes every bit of strength for a parent to love unconditionally when a child is behaving in ways that one could never imagine would be exhibited by a person of one's own flesh. But a parent must love unconditionally and be supportive because, ultimately, the parent may be the only person in the world for that child. This is true even when a child rejects the parent, which I know happens often. The parent is the only person a child has.

Jennifer is the first thing I think about when I wake up in the morning. We worry about her every day. It's so hard. She is better off than most, but she's still volatile and fragile. She's still a child emotionally, in many ways. She's impulsive. She doesn't have the ability to not be impulsive yet. I'm hoping she'll grow out of that like a lot of people do. I used to have nightmares about her cutting. I'd wake up in the middle of the night. It's tormenting.

So. That's where we are. It's day by day.

⸙

*Esme's persistence in getting help and staying connected to Jennifer regardless of her behaviors was key to gaining her daughter's trust. Esme also possessed a deep understanding of her daughter's mental health. Despite the chaotic home life, Esme managed this difficult balance of staying connected while setting boundaries and realistic expectations such as requiring Jennifer to maintain employment and later demanding nominal monthly rent. Esme knew her daughter was capable of these responsibilities, but pushing Jennifer to finish school at the time, Esme and her husband determined, was not in their daughter's overall best interest. She knew that expressing unrealistic expectations would likely result in failure, stress, and a damaged relationship, all of which would prove to create crushing long-term consequences.*

*Of course, parents sometimes see events and behaviors more clearly in hindsight, and readers may question Esme's other assessments about Jennifer's suicidal threats. When Jennifer threatens suicide over the phone to her boyfriend and police arrive to intervene, Esme says, " . . . her threats were more about her expressing how she felt." Was Esme in denial about the seriousness of Jennifer's suicidal behavior? Jennifer had made threats before when she overdosed on aspirin, and there were also cutting incidents, including one that was "near fatal." After each of these events, Jennifer received counseling. Counselors didn't suggest that Jennifer's behaviors indicated more serious issues or suicidal ideation. Still, even before Jennifer was diagnosed with borderline personality disorder, which includes behaviors such as manipulation through drama and threats, binge drinking, and impulsivity, Esme was well acquainted with her daughter's manipulations.*

*Esme had to trust her instincts because efforts to help her daughter were often undermined by an inability to communicate effectively with Jennifer's counselors. It is possible that counselors were not actively listening to or placing value on Esme's input. Also vexing was that no counselor would provide a diagnosis that could have provided a starting point for treatment even though Jennifer had clear signs of borderline personality disorder. Statistically, those who live with mental illness have a greater chance of recovery when supported by family or loved ones. With the exception of cases involving abuse and violence within the family, counselors would serve the young adult patient best by including family in the recovery process. This doesn't mean parents sit in on therapy sessions. But parents can and should participate in learning about their child's diagnosis, which is what Esme did. Counselors can and should work with patients to obtain consent and therefore be permitted to disclose destructive behaviors such as substance use to parents. Disclosing such information in a nonjudgmental setting enables parent and counselor to have a more complete picture of a patient's mental health. When an adult child refuses to sign a release allowing communication between professional and family, language within the HIPAA law allows for the counselor to use her best judgment about disclosing destructive behavior.[7] Though a counselor may not want to give a formal diagnosis for a minor, she can work with the family more effectively by conveying, for example, "Your daughter exhibits symptoms of _____ and we will treat accordingly until we know more."[8] It is not uncommon for a diagnosis to change throughout the process of treatment, especially when substance use is involved, but having a starting point from which to work can be beneficial so that treatment may begin in early stages of detection.*

*Parents want only what is best for their child.*

# CHAPTER THREE: KERRI AND THOMAS

*Will anyone believe what I'm going through?*

*My hands were tied; I had warned the school,*
*he had a history, and nobody was concerned.*

*Kerri's first interview took place at her home, a 1960s-era house in a leafy suburb shared at that time by her husband, daughter, and son, Thomas. Kerri is hospitable and has a comfortable presence; her efficient nature was evidenced by her clean and uncluttered home. While showing the way to her dining room, Kerri indicated the door to the basement where, in that late afternoon hour, Thomas was still asleep. At the time of this first meeting, Thomas, who was born in 1991, was twenty.*

*In the process of navigating toward a diagnosis and through treatment options, parents become frustrated by HIPAA[9] laws that obstruct communication with their child's doctors. And yet, parents are usually their child's best or only advocate. A parent is vigilant for symptoms as subtle as an altered speech pattern or facial expression that may indicate an impending health crisis. It is usually the parent, not the medical professional, who holds the full health history of her adult child, and she can prevent a critical error in drug treatments. It is often the case that a person with a mental illness trusts only a parent enough to be guided into treatment compliance.*

*But a person experiencing psychosis, delusional thinking, and/or anosognosia (see Glossary of Brain Disorder Diagnoses), may become temporarily distrustful of those they'd previously relied upon for their care. A person in mental health crisis may feel loved ones are trying to control them, and may act out of fear. In these cases, parents need support in getting treatment for their child because when a parent enforces treatment, the critical parent-child trust is at risk, thereby endangering the path to recovery. Even when a parent knows their child is unwell and at risk of endangering himself or others, effective treatment can often be elusive.*

*This is Kerri's story.*

**KERRI:** Thomas was first diagnosed with OCD and general anxiety disorder at eleven years old. During those early years—eleven, twelve, and thirteen—I kept thinking, "He's going to get better. He'll get this under control." I really thought he could have a pretty normal life and he'd be able to graduate high school, go to college, you know, get a job, maybe get married. But then he seemed to get worse; he was hospitalized in eighth grade for being suicidal. His anger and OCD prevailed and his grades began to fall. One of his good friends avoided him, and he didn't make many new friends. We did what we could and took him to several psychologists, including one in the city, which was a long drive after work in rush-hour traffic. My coworkers would see me talking on the phone with my son and therapists all the time and leaving early for his appointments. Finally, there came a time where one psychologist said, "I can't help Thomas anymore. It's more than OCD."

Thomas's angry episodes and verbal abuse continued through his teen years. He was out of control. When he was fifteen, just when we were getting him diagnosed, he called his dad at work to ask for help with his iPod or something, but my husband was in a meeting and told Thomas he couldn't talk right then. When Thomas persisted, his father hung up on him. Thomas flew into a rage, tore up the kitchen, smashed wine glasses, water glasses, and a vase on the tile floor. If he doesn't get what he wants, he threatens to break his phone. And then does it.

I think Thomas suffered a lot of brain damage from meningitis when he was an infant and again later from psychotic episodes. At seventeen, Thomas's mood swings became severe and he experienced psychosis. When he looked into his sister's room he thought her stuffed animals were talking to him. We tried to get him into a private hospital that specializes in treating adolescents and teens, but our insurance wouldn't pay for it, so we got him into treatment at a local public hospital. He went back to school, but that wasn't going to work. He was psychotic at school despite the meds. Our public school system didn't hesitate to pay for his evaluation and admitted him to a school affiliated with a psychiatric hospital. But again, he became psychotic and was put back into the hospital. After three weeks, we took him out of the hospital so he could be with our family for a vacation to Italy. I guess he was mostly okay, but he had strange ideas about the religious statues. He slept in our room because he thought the Virgin Mary would come to him at night.

When Thomas exhibited psychotic and manic behaviors it was very scary for me because those behaviors were not the Thomas I knew. It was difficult for me to hear him saying crazy, irrational things, and I would wonder if he would ever go back to his "normal" self. When a loved one is in one of those states, it feels disorienting for family members. It is uncharted territory, and I felt isolated because none of my friends could imagine what we were going through. It's like we had all fallen down the rabbit hole.

Thomas managed to finish high school, even took community college courses, and held down a part-time job as a bagger in a grocery store. He never advanced beyond bagger, though, because they didn't think he was capable of more.

Thomas was accepted into a state school. My husband and I both knew this was not a good place for him—too big—but we didn't want to spend money for a private college because we weren't sure he could hang in. Once he was there, he'd call me about eight or ten times a day to check in, which was not surprising. When he's home he doesn't want to let me out of his sight. It's a little creepy, yes. When a week passed and he didn't call me from school and his debit card was out of money, we knew something was very wrong. We drove to the college, which isn't far. When we got there, we learned that Thomas's roommate had convinced him to move out and live with another guy who "was weird like Thomas."

When we found his room, we saw Thomas's side was completely trashed—things thrown everywhere, his cell phone broken in half, and his computer shattered. We found him wandering the campus. He'd been smoking a lot of weed and was psychotic. He was then eighteen, was hospitalized again, and took a medical leave of absence.

Thomas was discharged from the hospital and moved home, which was a challenge. We all felt like we were walking on eggshells around him. My daughter had enjoyed the time when Thomas was away at college. She had felt free to bring friends around, not worried her brother was going to do something weird. While living at home, Thomas worked again as a bagger at a grocery store and, though he didn't see anyone for therapy, he was on meds. We warned him about using recreational drugs.

Thomas returned to State in the fall of 2011 and was seeing a new psychiatrist whom I wasn't crazy about. We had gotten a new psychiatrist, because for a long time he'd been resisting going to Dr. D—, the doctor he had since he was fourteen. He thought Dr. D— was overmedicating him. At that time Dr. D— had him on anxiety medication, and in addition, Thomas was taking a mood stabilizer, an atypical antipsychotic, and an antiseizure drug. Thomas felt he was on too many medications. The drugs caused weight gain and made him feel like he wasn't his true self. He also felt when he took medications that he acted less smart and too nice and people took advantage of him. He thought the meds made it hard for him to think clearly— affected him cognitively—and his true personality couldn't come through, etc., which is a very dangerous way to think.

This new psychiatrist started Thomas on an antidepressant for his severe OCD. He had tried that same drug two summers before and it may have triggered some manic episodes. I question if that antidepressant played into his behavior that arose shortly after he started taking it again.

Then Thomas quit all his meds cold turkey. I think that going off his medications abruptly put him into a manic state where he was very angry with me and blaming me for being overmedicated. He'd be up all night and call at three or four a.m. to rant and rave about what a horrible mother I was, that it was my fault he had been overmedicated, that he had lost out on the last six-plus years of his life with these medications. It was directed at Dr. D— and me. He said he was going to sue Dr. D—. It went on and on. He was very angry about being put on so many meds and how they had affected his cognitive processing and made him "stupid."

We visited him a couple of times at school. He was obviously going down a very dangerous road, and in January and February I knew he was drinking excessively, staying up all night, and sleeping part of the day and then just hanging out. Another issue was this one friend, Abel, whom he met through Rick, another student, during freshmen year. Rick and Abel were childhood friends and grew up in low-income housing. We met Abel, who hung around campus even though he was a high school dropout. We knew that Abel had been or still was a drug dealer on campus. Rick was no longer socializing with Abel, but Thomas was with him regularly. We often told Thomas we didn't want him to see Abel and that he was a bad influence. None of Abel's friends were in college; they were very different from Thomas's childhood friends.

At the end of January, beginning of February, I called the counseling center director at the college to tell her Thomas had gone off his medication and that I was concerned. Of course I got the whole speech about privacy laws and HIPAA. If she were to check up on him she would have to tell him I had called. I said I was very concerned and reminded her that she had been the one who'd called me the year before when he was hospitalized and that she should be aware of his history. Then she agreed to find out how Thomas was doing.

She spoke with a counselor in the disabilities services department who Thomas met with and who checked on him periodically to ask if he needed help with classes. She also spoke with Andrew, the resident director with whom he met periodically. She called back and said, "Andrew says Thomas seems fine. They haven't seen anything out of the ordinary." At that time he was still attending a couple of classes.

My hands were tied; I had warned the school, he had a history, and nobody was concerned. But Thomas was passing his classes until the end of February despite everything. "No red flags," were the words his counselor used. There was nothing more I could do. I even met with the psychiatrist to see whether he could help me enforce hospitalization. He gave me a legal form that I could take to the police and they would forcibly take him. But if I forced the issue in that way I would lose Thomas's trust completely. I'd heard they'd only keep him forty-eight or seventy-two hours anyway because he was an adult. There was a time limit. I almost wanted Thomas to hit rock bottom. I wanted him to end up in the hospital but not because *I* made him. Because out of the five times he'd been hospitalized, I had taken him to the ER all but once, when the school committed him.

In mid-February, on the Friday of President's Day weekend, we were on the road with our daughter heading out to look at colleges when our cell phone rang. Thomas was in the hospital ER and asked us to pick him up. The day before, Thursday, he had become intoxicated and blacked out. He had been outdoors somewhere and his friend Abel realized he was in pretty bad shape. Abel must have dragged Thomas while passed out because he had cuts all over. Abel had called 911, and Thomas ended up in the ER. Thomas said, "I almost died of hypothermia!" He'd spent the night in the ER, had been discharged, and needed a ride back to campus. He was really weird, acting like it was our fault. We said, "Sorry, but we're hours away on the highway and there's nothing we can do." I was fed up with him. I wasn't going to turn around. I said, "You got yourself into this; figure it out."

I've always felt he's ruined things for his younger sister. Here we are, trying to look at colleges and had planned a whole weekend. I wasn't going to run and rescue him. Our daughter, who's a great kid and good student, was having health problems, and I always wonder if it was connected to the stress of her brother's illness and all the uncertainty he has caused. She was first diagnosed with Lyme disease then later with chronic fatigue syndrome with fibromyalgia. We'll never know her diagnosis for sure, but she became depressed from not feeling well, always feeling tired and run down, and it finally got to her.

I contacted Thomas's case manager at the department of mental health and told her things were getting worse. But he was over eighteen and I couldn't force hospitalization. I was shocked to think that he was brought unconscious, with alcohol poisoning and all these issues, and he supposedly had hypothermia, *and* he'd been hospitalized at *that very same hospital* before. Don't they keep records? He'd been brought into that *same* ER one year and two months before when he'd had that manic, crazy episode during final exam week and had been hospitalized in *their* psychiatric ward. I'm thinking, "I can't believe they actually discharged him." I was aghast. I was surprised that once they found his wallet and his insurance card they didn't recognize him in their own system. I was hoping that if he had no way to get out of there, maybe they would take him back.

I was hoping, "Oh gosh, this is the perfect opportunity!" But it wasn't as if I could say, "Get evaluated." Because if I did, he'd be like, "No, I'm fine, I'm the best I've ever been! Nothing's wrong with me. I don't have bipolar disorder. I've been misdiagnosed . . ." and all this stuff.

Spring break was coming and I thought, "There is no way he can come home for spring break. I *don't* want him at home." I was concerned for my safety because he had so much anger and was not medicated. I felt it wouldn't be safe. During other episodes, I was scared of him as I felt that he could lose control and destroy objects in my house.

It all culminated in March when I knew my son was in pretty bad shape. He'd started out with four classes. By March he had dropped two, and by spring he wasn't even attending the other two. The first week of March, we called Thomas and told him he could not come home for spring break. His plan was that I'd pick him up that Friday and he'd be home for the week, chill, and I would take him back. I said, "This is crazy because you've already dropped out of two of the four classes and you're not even going to the other two. You are failing. Why would you go back to school to party and stay up all night and sleep part of the day? The party's over." He said, "No, no, I want to go," and had grand plans about getting an apartment with Rick so that the next fall they would live off campus near other friends. I said, "I'm not paying for another semester if you're failing." He said he'd get a job. It all sounded crazy.

That Friday, my husband took the day off from work, and he and the case manager met on campus and together confronted Thomas in his dorm room to try to convince him to get evaluated. She had called the crisis team in advance. He kicked them out of the room and said, "Leave! I'm not going."

My husband came home and then Thomas started calling using a friend's cell phone because he'd broken his again. "Oh my God, I'm going to be homeless." He said, "You need to bring me home. You're horrible parents . . ." We had to be firm, "Unless you're willing to go to a hospital, that's it." He hung up. That whole night we didn't know his whereabouts. The next day he finally contacted us.

He had called Abel, who was homeless and lived part of the time out of his car or slept on different people's couches. Abel's mother had once had a restraining order on her son but allowed Abel and Thomas to spend Friday night in her apartment. When Thomas realized he had run out of options, he called us. "Okay, come get me. If you want me to be evaluated, you can take me to an ER. But if they think I'm fine, you have to agree to let me come home." I said, "Fine. I'll let the crisis team decide." I knew they would definitely commit him. He wasn't suicidal and I knew how the system works, but I'd called the crisis team in advance and told them what was going on.

At the beginning of his evaluation, Thomas was acting normal and he almost didn't get committed, but then the person from the crisis team convinced the on-call psychiatrist that he needed to be hospitalized. That made Thomas pretty upset.

After the crisis team helped us get him committed, we were told to leave though we didn't yet know where he would be placed because of availability and where our insurance would be accepted. By the afternoon of the next day, a Sunday, somebody from the crisis team was nice enough to tell us where Thomas was being sent, but it was unofficial because supposedly with HIPAA we weren't even supposed to know that. He was assigned the head psychiatrist at a transitional unit. But it was at least a couple days before we talked to Thomas and only because he finally called us. There was nothing we could do. We couldn't call there and say, "I know my son is there," because of HIPAA privacy laws. He hadn't yet signed HIPAA papers allowing them to keep us informed. When he called us, he asked for clothes. I said to him, "Make sure you sign something so I can talk to the staff." But he didn't at first, and that same day I called the hospital trying to get the name of the case manager assigned to him. I couldn't get through to anybody because Thomas hadn't signed the paperwork, and I couldn't call him to say, "Thomas you haven't signed the release . . ."

It wasn't as if he was trying to keep me away. He's forgetful that way and not always the best at doing certain things. I finally had to say to someone, "Listen, I'm paying the insurance. You may not want to tell me anything but please give my phone number to his case manager. Maybe she can get in touch with me. My son wants me to visit and bring clothing." A woman was kind enough to put me through and I talked to the caseworker.

When we went to visit him that first night, we'd gotten lost on the way and there was only a half hour left of visiting hours. We didn't know which unit he was in because Thomas had forgotten to tell us. The receptionist wasn't going to tell us. And then there were only twenty minutes left. It was the most hysterical thing. I wasn't mad because, you know, it gets to the point where there are so many things going on that you have to laugh. Finally this other woman felt sorry for us and found out where Thomas was and we got through. There were all these roadblocks.

Thomas was in the unit for a week and he met with the psychiatrist *once*. Even after a *week* he wasn't on any medication and the psychiatrist was going to discharge him. The guy never bothered to get any information, didn't do any research, and wasn't returning any phone calls. Even Thomas was frustrated because he was trying to talk to him. That's a terrible hospital. It's a terrible institution, and I was mad at myself because I should have been more proactive to get him into a better facility or refused that particular hospital. Instead of leaving him at that first hospital where he got evaluated, I should have figured out the system and insisted he stay in the ER there until there was a bed available in a better place . . . Maybe I should have. Unless you have a lot of money and don't have to worry about insurance, or you have people in positions where you can say, "I need him here," you're at the mercy of insurance. Unfortunately, we have awful insurance.

I complained and got Thomas assigned a different psychiatrist who was much better and who finally got our history. Thomas was adamant he wouldn't take meds, but this psychiatrist convinced Thomas to start taking five milligrams of an atypical antipsychotic, which is really nothing. They also gave him an antianxiety med. He stayed a month at that hospital because we had to declare him homeless and say that we refused to take him home if he was discharged. Then DMH (Department of Mental Health) tried to get him into a group home but there were no openings, so the new psychiatrist filed paperwork to say he needed to stay longer because they were still working out the medication.

Thomas was still very angry. He felt abandoned and said we were horrible parents, how could we do this to him, we didn't love him, etc. . . . . Eventually, once he got more stable and was on a low dose of the antipsychotic, he started to understand why we had him committed and we were able to have sort of good visits and were visiting him just about every day. Thomas's sister visited. My brother visited him at Easter with his wife. My in-laws, his grandparents, came. My mother in Florida couldn't visit but would call him. He realized we had done it because we loved him.

We learned there was an opening in a young-adult residence nearby, but his case worker from the department of health, who was not the best and who I had tried to get replaced but couldn't because the department is very understaffed, messed up the paperwork. Thomas would have been out within two weeks but instead was discharged from the hospital after thirty-six days into respite care in a psychiatric facility that wasn't a hospital. The patients were adults, and some were there for months because they were homeless. We couldn't bring Thomas home because the moment we did, he would have been taken off the waitlist for a better facility. It's bureaucratic BS because he'd become stable enough and I was willing for him to stay at home until they found a group home, but then he wouldn't have been considered "homeless" and would have been ineligible. It was really hard because Thomas didn't understand that. I mean, he did but he didn't.

The respite care place wasn't as bad because at least he could come and go during the daytime as long as he returned by ten p.m. He would walk into town and take the train into the city and visit his best friend, Scott, whom he grew up with and who's always been there for him. Scott goes to the university in the city, and Thomas could visit him during the day. He'd take the train home and I'd pick him up at the nearby station. I tried to make it palatable for him to stay there. My father-in-law would take him out for lunch or dinner and visit. Thomas stayed there for three weeks while paperwork was worked out.

Finally he got into a better group home in April, but it was mid-May before he moved into this place in N— where the treatment is dialectical behavioral therapy-based.[10] It's a house with roommates and there's a living room, dining room, and kitchen. He has his own bedroom. There's an assistant manager who's there about four days a week, and different staff there 24/7. If you're not in school taking courses or working, you have to attend their day program. You can earn up to seventy checks a week, ten a day. If you get a minimum of fifty-seven checks, then you earn Level II and have certain benefits. For example, on Level II he can go out at night with a friend or come home for a weekend. He can be gone only every other weekend. There's an incentive for keeping one's room clean, for example, and for doing the job assigned that week, which could be doing the dishes for a week or making the group's dinner for a night or two. There are different jobs. They also receive all their services there; a therapist comes once a week and meets with Thomas one-on-one for an hour. A psychiatric nurse comes once a month to do meds. They have other group meetings he has to attend. He can go to the Y once a week to work out and to the library. They may go to movies as a group.

I'm not happy with this place, to be honest. I like the staff. They're well meaning, but it's frustrating that there's no psychiatrist overseeing them, just a psychiatric nurse. Thomas has been depressed. She was going to prescribe an

SSRI antidepressant,[11] and thank God Thomas told me! Because she only comes to that place once a month, I had to call her office, "Let me tell you about his history: he has tried that same antidepressant twice in the past—both times with a mood stabilizer—and became manic." Thomas cannot be on *any* SSRIs. It activates him.[12] I said, "On every class of antidepressant he has become activated." She was like, "Oh, gosh. Thank you for telling me. I'm definitely not going to give him an antidepressant!" Then we talked about getting him to take an antiseizure drug that is sometimes prescribed as a mood stabilizer. He's been on it before but he still refuses meds. She's working with him on that. The only thing he's willing to take is an antianxiety medication because he realizes how anxious he is.[13] That's basically it. Sometimes he takes a sleep aid if he can't sleep, but he's not willing to go back on the antipsychotic. But recently he decided to stop taking his meds, which is out of compliance, so he doesn't get a check at the group home.

He started doing research and decided he doesn't have bipolar disorder. He definitely knows he has GAD, general anxiety disorder, which he thinks causes OCD. At one point he was positive he had borderline personality disorder and he sent me links from different websites that showed the definition and wrote a long email with attachments telling me which symptoms of borderline personality disorder he had. There was another time when he thought he might have a condition supposedly caused by having PTSD. Then there was a time where he thought he had antisocial personality disorder and some other thing. He's always finding the newest thing, but he doesn't want to accept that he has bipolar disorder. He's okay with having anxiety or depression or OCD. He can accept anything but bipolar. He will never again go on a mood stabilizer, ever. More recently he has admitted that he knows intellectually that he could benefit from some medication but that he is too afraid they will start to work and then the dose will need to be increased in order to continue its efficacy. He is so afraid of trying again and failing.

He was always a thin, skinny kid. When he started on the mood stabilizer during high school he gained some weight but then lost it and was pretty normal. When he was hospitalized freshman year, they put him on an atypical antipsychotic, a different one than he had recently been taking, and it caused a ten-pound weight gain in about a week, all in his stomach area. He gained more weight and got stretch marks. He got to a high of about 169–179 pounds. He's probably lost at least twenty to twenty-five pounds. It's coming off slowly. By the time he was hospitalized this last time, he'd lost at least fifteen pounds. Now he's at about 142. But even though he's lost weight and he's really thin, he's self-conscious and obsesses about these red stretch marks on his middle caused when he gained a lot of weight from the antipsychotic. Now he's getting too thin because he doesn't want to eat much, and he doesn't want to go on medication that causes weight gain.

Looking retrospectively, I believe he was overmedicated by Dr. D—, his original psychiatrist, because at one point he was on 900 milligrams of mood stabilizer, 350 of an antiseizure, twenty-five milligrams of an atypical antipsychotic, and then we were adding the antidepressant. That's a lot of medication considering that he was at his most stable taking only five milligrams of an atypical antipsychotic with some antianxiety and was acting pretty normal. Maybe it's due to having recently turned twenty-one and his brain has settled a little bit because at fourteen, fifteen, sixteen he was out of control, having rages. Maybe now he's able to control that—his hormones are not as wacky—and we got to high levels of medication because that was the only way to control him. I was surprised, because after a month of having his medications reduced, he seemed functional. His biggest issue is extreme anxiety, which can be debilitating. He also has sleep issues, which I believe are tied to the mood disorder. Two separate times, for a short period of time, he became dysregulated and was up all night and slept part of the day, which made him cranky. He has been mostly calm for the past year, and I don't fear he will be destructive or verbally abusive like he was in the past. I don't know if it's a lull and he'll get a manic episode again. I don't know!

The biggest issue with mental illness is that the medications have so many side effects, and that is why many don't want to take them. If there were better-targeted medications, there would be better compliance and better outcomes. I try to believe anything is possible if more money were put into mental illness research. Just as now it's possible to perform a heart transplant, it would have been mind-boggling a hundred years ago. Someday there will be, if not a cure, better treatment with better outcomes. I am hopeful for the future.

---

*A vigilant advocate isn't always heard, as we see in Kerri's experience in which she warned her son's school that he was increasingly unwell. Kerri's evidence included her witness to his destroyed room, lack of communication with him, and her own experience parenting him. Sadly, school mental health professionals relied on different criteria, namely, his attendance in classes, grades, and how he "seemed to be doing" by those who helped him manage his coursework.*

*It would have been understandable had Kerri thrown her hands up and felt there was nothing more she could do to protect her son. But had she not pursued assistance in getting her son hospitalized, it is very possible he could have endangered himself or others, particularly given his history of anger, verbal abuse, psychosis, destructive behaviors, and his history of medication noncompliance and substance use that led to binge drinking. There is a higher incidence of death by suicide or violence when people with mental illness use a substance.[14]*

*But Kerri did pursue treatment for Thomas, thereby*

*protecting him from unknowable harm to property, self, or others. Her persistence is giving him a better chance for long-term recovery. Advocating for our child doesn't always mean we can control their behaviors. It is notable that Kerri, as do many parents in her situation, works harder at getting treatment (and protection) for her son than he did, so her efforts seem more directed at saving his life than getting him into recovery. But Kerri must hold the hope for him until he can grasp it on his own.*

# Chapter Four: Bianca and Miguel

*Looking for the little bit of normal.*

*There was this one moment of normal and
that's what matters.*

Though our only previous contact with Bianca had been via
email, she appeared immediately at ease for the interview, filling
the room with her warmth and humor. Miguel was born in
1987 and was soon to be twenty-five at the time of Bianca's first
interview.

Parenting and advocating for a person with a brain disorder
can be all consuming. Accepting a diagnosis of a serious mental
illness presents a significant emotional hurdle. But there are
also the heavy burden of grief and the complicated logistics of
managing another's treatment along with the exhausting moment
to moment vigilance in keeping a loved one functional and, ideally,
engaged in life. Daily life becomes centered on accommodating the
ill person, and even decisions parents make about their own work
and personal life are dictated by the limitations set by their child's
illness. Parents find they spend a strange amount of time discussing
and thinking about the person who is ill. Such focus on the most
troubling issue within the family dynamic results in increased
spousal conflict, and siblings suffer from diverted attention.

Experiencing grief is common for family members of
those who suffer with a brain disorder because of the seemingly
sudden change in personality, thought processes, and cognitive
skills. Parents and siblings also experience depression brought
on by the emotional intensity, chaos, and grief associated with
managing and living with another's persistent mental illness.
Grief, emotional exhaustion, family disruption, and stigma are

*all factors that drive family members behind a wall of isolation.*

*The unending demands create high stress for parents, and yet one often puts their own needs last, believing there isn't time for them, or their child's needs are more immediate. The demands are more profound for single parents, particularly those whose efforts are not supported or understood by the child's other parent.*

*As a result of the intense stress, grief, and chaos, parents have difficulty remembering select details while other hideous images or moments are burned into their minds. Events that require action and stir up the deepest emotions happen all at once. Perhaps for some, forgetting is a gift. It is remarkable that every parent admitted at one point during their interview that there were many more events that had happened or other details they were unable to recall because during the worst part of their child's illness, "It was all a blur."*

*Like many who seek relief from challenges that a loved one's mental illness brings, Bianca looks for moments in life that are "normal," a coping mechanism she learned as a nurse from a mother whose son, one of Bianca's patients, was profoundly disabled by cancer. Finding "normal" has been no easy task. Bianca is expressive and became visibly sad while telling her story and used her formidable wit to recover. By the end of the interview, she appeared emotionally spent.*

*This is Bianca's story.*

**BIANCA:** My two sons, Arturo and Miguel, and I were invited to my niece's out-of-town wedding when Miguel was twenty-four. Beforehand, I was really worried because I knew it was going to be stressful for Miguel with so many people. He has sheltered himself, and this was a large wedding. We'd never attended a large gathering like that. I said, "People are going to introduce themselves to you. Claire has only two cousins, so the other two hundred and fifty guests are going to ask about you. They're going to ask things like, 'What do you do?' I'm trying to prepare you. What are some answers you'll have, ones that will work for you?"

Miguel said, "I'll just tell them I'm crazy."

"That's a real ice breaker!" I said. "Or . . . you can say you're . . . between jobs."

We planned and talked about, "If you get overwhelmed at the reception, it's okay to go for a walk. Just tap me so I know what you're doing and that you'll come back. Let me know if you need to leave."

Whatever he did, he handled it well because he was engaging, charming, laughing, joyous—the way he used to be. It was wonderful to watch him. When we came home I was actually mad because I thought, "Are you faking it?" I sat him down and said, "What was different?"

He said, "I was drunk."

"Well, I hate the drugs I give you. Maybe I should give you a fifth of rum!" He didn't look drunk! He didn't act drunk! He acted what we remember as normal. He was so impressive that friends of my niece and her new husband said to them, "I want to be like your cousin." He was outgoing, he danced with every person there. He was the second one to dance with the bride. He was wonderful!

Then he woke up Sunday morning and didn't talk for forty-eight hours.

His diagnosis at about age twenty was very clear-cut. The hardest part for me was not to question it. But I *did* question it. Are you sure it's not just bipolar? Are you sure that's what it is? Are you sure he has schizophrenia? Maybe he's just having a hard day. Are you sure it's not just burnout from, I don't know, maybe he smoked too much marijuana?

Getting to the point where one can matter-of-factly accept it is a challenge because it's got such stigma. People who I thought would step up to the plate, shied away. They're afraid. "Are you sure you're safe? Is he going to murder you in the middle of the night?"

"No," I say, "he's not."

Every time there's a shooting, I cringe. *Cringe.* The pain the family must be going through. The pain the kid must be going through. But that doesn't mean that's what *my* son is going to do.

Oh, God! Mental illness: it's not the club you want to sign up for. It's not what I ever thought my baby would turn into. And it's painful because it hurts my kid and I can't fix it. There's not an easy fix. It's not what I signed up for at all or what that little boy signed up for either.

I got the diagnosis, and I thought maybe Miguel just had a bad day, and then I'd look for the little bit of normal. "Look! He's getting better. Maybe he's bipolar." Then I started choosing which mental illness sounded better: "Oh, bipolar! I really like bipolar." Because bipolar is socially acceptable. Nobody cringes from bipolar. Schizophrenia: *that's* a bad one. Everybody ducks for cover and thinks they're going to get murdered at night. It's catchy, or whatever. But bipolar . . . "Well, maybe it's schizo-y tendencies, so he doesn't *really* have schizophrenia."

It's hard for Miguel, too . . . coming to grips with his illness. On his good days, he's great. On the bad days, he's not so great.

Now, at almost twenty-six, he's good about hiding his symptoms such that others perceive he's improving. But when you really make him talk, you see he's better but he's not well. It gets discouraging for him, too. He says, "It's been five years and I just want to be like I used to be." That may not happen. He says, "I can't wait until I can come off the meds." That probably is not going to happen either.

As a family, when the boys were growing up, we moved constantly. The agreement my then-husband, Carlo, and I had was that once my oldest son, Arturo, entered high school, we wouldn't move for six years. I said, "I will *not* pull them out of high school. That's a terrible thing to do to them, and I won't do it." He agreed to not take another job that required moving.

Arturo was a junior when Carlo took another job and moved out of state. I commuted five hours with both boys back and forth every weekend. We made that drive every weekend and every holiday to spend with him.

Arturo graduated high school and Miguel was entering his senior year of high school when out of the blue Carlo said, "I'm done with all of this." He dropped us entirely. Carlo even withdrew all college support for both boys. I believe stress adds so much to mental illness. I read somewhere: "The diagnosis is the gun, but the environment pulls the trigger." Miguel was sixteen or seventeen when his father kicked us out, and we didn't see it coming. I went into a major depression. My oldest son flunked out of college. Miguel started acting up that year. That's the first time I saw him with marijuana and I busted him for it. He got arrested for having an open beer bottle in the car. His grades started slipping. He was grounded almost his entire senior year.

Miguel's dad has stressed him out. For instance, during freshmen year of college Miguel wanted to spend Christmas vacation with his dad. I said, "That's fine. Call and make arrangements. I'll pay for gas; you drive." This was not unusual; over spring break of his senior year of high school and during the following summer months, Miguel had visited his dad. Typically, Carlo would tolerate Miguel for maybe three days and throw him out and then maybe two days and throw him out. When Miguel went to Carlo's that Christmas break of his college freshman year, his dad pulled out a gun and threatened suicide in front of him. Miguel laughed it off, and the new wife thought it was hysterical. I said, "You're not going back there ever again."

Miguel continued to get into trouble when he was in college, which is in our town. The police got to know me from my sons. Actually, once I met a police officer that blinked at my last name, and I said, "Yeah, they're both mine." Miguel kept getting busted for underage drinking. I finally said, "I'm not coming to court anymore. That's it. Your dad's not coming. No matter what you do, he's not going to come. Stop doing this to me. Just stop! I can't make him come, and all you're doing is making life really, really hard for the two of *us*." After that Miguel kind of stopped getting into trouble.

Miguel never had a serious girlfriend until he was in college. It was spring quarter of his sophomore year at college when he met Cassandra. I believe this young woman was quite influential in triggering and feeding his psychotic behavior. She was unbelievably charismatic. From an eighty-eight-year-old man to a four-year-old boy there was one common response when people described her: "Hot!" Miguel fell head-over-heels in love with her, and she did not love him back. Miguel was really into being able to prophesize, to predict the future. She claimed she could predict things. He was not raised in a religious household, but his delusions centered on religion and she convinced him she was the Messiah. Together, they were going to establish a new religion.

Starting Miguel's sophomore year, Arturo, who had dropped out of college, had taken the very small inheritance he'd received from my mother for tuition and used it to pay Miguel's instead. Unbeknownst to us, later that year Miguel withdrew from college and donated the money to a church. That was one of my original clues that something was not right.

Miguel was twenty when he took off with his friend and came back around Christmas. At that time, everything was a sign to him. If he saw a word, it was a sign. He was frantically reading the Bible to look for signs—not to understand religion—but to look for signs. He became more and more garbled. I called his father and said, "I will not make this decision to commit him without you."

The following February, Carlo drove from his home, and the four of us sat down to talk through what was going on with Miguel. Carlo was not helpful. But I was surprised by the way Arturo stepped up to the plate. Miguel even accused his father of sexually abusing him. But I had never let that kid out of my sight. I know beyond a shadow of a doubt that his accusation was part of his psychosis. That was not real. But his father flipped out and wouldn't talk to him anymore and left. We didn't hear from him again.

I called every treatment place I could find. I got an appointment for Miguel to go into a treatment facility though he was resistant to help at that time. The people at that facility recommended I wait and tell Miguel the plan on the day I was going to bring him in. I knew I could negotiate and reason with him using the "stay in my house" and "do it for me" pleas, because we had that kind of relationship. Unfortunately, the facility called the day before to confirm the appointment and, of course, Miguel answered the phone. Miguel felt he'd been lied to and betrayed. The people at that facility told me they wouldn't do that. But they did. And he took off.

He hitchhiked to Virginia. A church group found him and sent him home on a bus. I was furious. I said, "You took their money! You lived in a homeless shelter. You took money from people who need it and you don't, so you'll earn money and send it back for the bus fare."

From that February meeting with his dad, he slowly kept going downhill. But to get committed is really hard because he has to be deemed a danger to others or himself. And he wasn't. But he had started fasting. He wasn't eating or drinking anything at all. This is a five-eleven kid who was down to a hundred pounds. I convinced him to go to the doctor, who said, "I don't really think it's enough to commit him, but I'll sign the papers." Miguel took off hitchhiking again. I was like, "I can't physically hold you back. I can't stop you."

Then the police showed up. I thought he was dead: police at my door, my kid not in the police car. I could only imagine they were going to tell me he was dead.

The police had seen him hitchhiking, and since he looked

fifteen, they asked for his ID. They saw him get into a car and then came to our house to verify his age. They told me they'd also just been informed that the car he was in had broken down and had been towed to a gas station. I explained everything and told them I couldn't get him committed. They said, "This will qualify as a 'danger to himself' and we will call ahead. If you go now, the judge will sign the papers and we will pick him up." I went and signed the commitment papers. Incidentally, my mother had passed away and all this was happening the same day my mother was being buried on the other side of the country.

I was told the police would pick him up and take him to the university hospital. After that, I couldn't find out if he was in the ER or where he'd been placed because he hadn't signed HIPAA papers. I worked in that hospital and had to work that night after being up all day. There is a way to find out where he was without anybody getting in trouble. I couldn't look it up, but the charge nurse can look at the entire census, and she confirmed he had been admitted. At least I knew where he was. He was there for six weeks. The first ten days I went every day to visit, but he would not allow me to see him. He was very angry. When I finally got to see him, he was still really pissed. I said, "I understand. I hope one day you know I did this *for* you and not *to* you. I can't stand by and say your behavior is normal. I can't accept it anymore."

At that point, they were forcefully giving him shots of an atypical antipsychotic. But he wouldn't eat. He wouldn't do anything. His liver enzymes were astronomical. Doctors thought he might go into liver failure, or he had hepatitis. He had been taking some kind of supplement that jumped his enzymes off the chart. His body was wasted. He'd gone *months* without eating.

For years, Carlo had insisted I exaggerated about Miguel's illness. Even after Miguel was committed that first time for six weeks of treatment, Carlo blamed me. But Miguel was committed without me being present. I didn't exaggerate anything. When Miguel was first committed, I called his father and said, "Don't talk. Just listen. Don't call the hospital, or if Miguel calls, don't you dare tell him *I'm* the crazy one. Don't do anything to stop this. You're not going to help us, so just don't stop this." Because that's what Carlo usually did. Later I urged him, "You have to visit. Miguel needs you here." But Carlo wouldn't come. Never came. Instead he called the staff to tell them I exaggerated.

Another time during Miguel's hospitalization, I walked in and found Miguel on the floor in his room curled in a fetal position, crying, "The demons are tearing my heart out! I can feel them tearing my heart out!" I begged the staff. "Give him something! Why is he on the floor by himself because demons are tearing his heart out? Why isn't someone here with him?"

And then he cried out, "Why won't he come see me?"

The job I had until very recently at a cancer hospital was really hard. It was consuming. Intense. When Miguel was in the hospital for those six weeks, my older son wasn't settled either. Life wasn't going along easily. It took a second commitment hearing to keep Miguel in the hospital. I had to take a lunch break from work to go to the psych ward and testify in front of the judge to keep him there. I didn't want to do it again. I thought, "No, *you* guys do it. He's here. You know he needs to be recommitted. Don't make me be the bad guy again. It's taken me four weeks to get him to talk to me and trust me again, and in the long run, he really needs me."

I don't remember what I said, but afterward the attending physician said they'd never heard such an eloquent, impassioned plea. The judge gave him a commitment of six months, which I thought was wonderful. But it wasn't legal because he was over eighteen. Within sixty days they were required to go back to court again for more commitment. I said, "I just can't do it again. Right now I can't honestly say that he's harmful to himself or anyone. He's eating. He's doing what he needs to do. Does he still have the diagnosis? Absolutely, but I can't do it again." That was the hardest thing in the world to do. I was like, "*You* guys do it." A social worker from the facility did testify. Miguel got angry, but the mental hospital had the right to give him shots, keep him on an antipsychotic, and if he didn't show up for his appointments, to put him in a halfway house—none of which they exercised. He had been committed through December, but by the first of October, that was it. Nothing.

Miguel tried different psychiatrists. His psychotic thinking is all around religion, God telling him what to do, and his belief that he's not good enough because of not accepting God as his Savior. He would think he was a bad person for doubting God, and fasting was his penance. His views on religion are nothing like what I taught. It's also important to him that one doesn't mock or challenge his religious beliefs. He wants a counselor who will accept that he truly has a religious belief, is also a fundamental Christian, and accepts his religious outlook, which they're not going to do.

When he was twenty-one, he voluntarily committed himself to the hospital. He thought God told him to commit himself because he'd come off all his meds again. For a while he had an outpatient psychiatrist. When he came out that time, he was stabilizing. Then out of the blue, Cassandra, the young woman, reappeared. She called and said she had a thirteen-month-old child and needed babysitting help. In spite of my warnings, he up and moved to be her babysitter. I kept asking, "Is that my grandchild? I need to know if that's my kid." Because timing-wise, it was really close. Miguel lived with her mother and stepfather and was doing door-to-door sales of alarms. Finally, a few months later, he said he wanted to come home. I said, "You can live in my house only if you are medicated. You don't have to have a job, but you *have* to be on medication."

When he came home he planned to fast, but I said, "No. Not acceptable." We compromised: he could drink instant breakfast shakes as his way of fasting. I told him he couldn't lose weight. I said, "If you stop eating, I'll send you back." He started going to our family doctor because it's difficult to find a psychiatrist for him. She called dozens of psychiatrists trying to find someone who was religious based. A friend helped him find a psychiatrist whom Miguel actually liked. But the doctor fired Miguel. I was livid. I said, "Why did you take my son on at all?"

He said, "I think you'll do just as fine with your family doctor."

I said, "Why did you do this? You have no idea the damage you caused! It took me *five years* to get him to see a psychiatrist. And just like *that*—all gone!"

For years I tried to get him into cognitive behavioral therapy (CBT).[15] It takes so much energy and I have no support from anywhere else. It's really, really overwhelming to plod through it.

One problem with Miguel is he's sensitive to all medication and we've gone through everything. He's never been on therapeutic doses of any drug because of side effects. Eight milligrams is a therapeutic dose. Four milligrams keeps him in limbo. He doesn't crash and burn, but he's not normal. The last time he got to six milligrams with an antipsychotic, he lost his vision. So he can't take a therapeutic dose of that drug. He tried an atypical antipsychotic and gained nearly thirty pounds in a week. He had another one that made his blood pressure bottom out and he got so tachycardic they didn't think his heart could handle it. On another drug his cholesterol jumped almost a hundred points. Now he has normal cholesterol. The one drug he agreed to take is an atypical antipsychotic. He said that's the one he likes.

When he went back into the hospital at twenty-three, almost twenty-four, the doctors wanted to start him on an older-class antipsychotic, which has so many lethal side effects it scared the hell out of me. They actually started him on his first dose without informing me. They began discussing it with me and I said, "That is a *last ditch* drug." Up to that point, he'd never been on *any* medication for six months, long enough to give anything a committed trial. I refused that older drug that had dangerous side effects and demanded they switch him back to the antipsychotic he had been taking. I couldn't accept a drug that has so many more severe side effects. Miguel already had a permanent tremor from antipsychotic medication. This is my cellist. He can't play anymore. He can't feed himself soup anymore. The tremors won't go away. Some of the other side effects from the older-class drugs, like impotence, are horrible. I'm not going to leave my son impotent if I can avoid it.

That drug I refused when he was in the hospital is the one he has yet to try. It *could* be a miracle drug. At this point the worst that can happen: it would work but it would drop his counts and he'd have to go off it. This may be the best we get. It's not really what I want. But I don't want to kill my kid. Not worth dying for. I say, "Miguel, it's *your* decision . . . there are side effects . . . you'll have to get blood work done . . ." I don't know if it'll work. But there aren't other meds out there. That's another reason why I'm really afraid: he's had every major side effect to a drug.

I feel like I'm his therapist, which I don't really want, but there isn't anybody else. I'm hoping we'll find somebody. I've said, "I don't want to be your therapist. I want to be your mom." I tried to convince him he needed a therapist. "You need to get a therapist and give up on considering whether or not the therapist will discuss your religion or their religion. That has nothing to do with the fact that you need a therapist." I would tell him, "You need to be aware you're not doing so well right now."

There was this time when he was twenty-four; he was in the shower trying to wash away his sins for over *six hours*. I said, "You have to come out." He said, "No, I'm almost there." I said, "Nope. This is psychotic behavior, and if you don't come out, I'm going to call the police." He got out. I said, "Miguel, I have to be the one to monitor you if you can't monitor yourself, and this is not acceptable behavior. You need to see Dr. A— and figure out what you need to do with your drugs. Have you been taking your drugs?" At that time I was still working twelve-hour shifts. I couldn't always be there to give him his medication.

Our family doctor, whom he trusts, tried to tell him he needed someone like a neuropsychiatrist, who knows the meds, because he doesn't do well on them. Bless our family doctor. She constantly called people, studied up on his illness. I totally trusted what she did and her opinion.

There was a two-month period where Miguel quit talking. I was like, "Okay, that's going to make looking for a job real easy!" But his doctor rolled with it. She addressed the schizophrenia. She'd say, "You have schizophrenia. You have to take the medication. This will be lifelong. We'll find the right drugs for you . . ." She's open and matter-of-fact. "Yup. It is what it is. If you run away and hide from it, you really can't deal with it."

Miguel responds to me because I don't sugarcoat. I try to be factual. Communicate. When he'd say, "I'm stressed right now," I'd allow him to do a fast if he wanted as long as he was drinking something. I'd say, "You need exercise. Go walk the dogs. You need to sleep, but then it's time to go see the doctor. Do you need me to make the appointment or can you do it?" Our family doctor once told me that Miguel respects me. She said, "He has a tight bond with you." I said, "I don't lie to him."

Adding to the difficulties in getting proper treatment for Miguel is that, when he was twenty-five, our family doctor, the only one who would take him, closed her practice. This was devastating. I spent over ten hours calling more than twenty-five doctors, including those at universities, trying to find anyone who would take him so we could get his drugs renewed. We finally found someone at the university who cancelled on the day of the appointment. I went hysterical, "No! You absolutely cannot do that! I am desperate. I have nowhere else to go!" Miguel was psychotic at that time. He was functional, but barely. I refused to let that university psychiatrist cancel and brought Miguel to his office. They talked and Miguel got on meds. He upped his antipsychotic medication a little bit, which I think has helped him a lot. The doctor said, "I don't know if I'll still be available and in the psych department because of the study I'm doing . . . ," but he promised he'd see Miguel again. If he couldn't see Miguel, he said he'd find someone who would treat him.

I don't know what I would have done differently for Miguel except maybe tried to get help for him sooner. Although I was blocked. It's so hard. I tried. I couldn't get treatment for him until I got him committed, and it was really difficult. I understand HIPAA. *But give me a break.* Really! I wasn't out to harm him, but because of all the laws, I wasn't allowed to *help* him.

The treatment isn't always what you hope you're going to get, either. While Miguel was hospitalized for the six weeks, I went one day and there were six people standing in a line outside his room. He was doing therapy with them, one at a time. Oh my goodness, he was so good! I heard him asking, "Why do you say that? What exactly did you say? What did she say? Well, have you done this . . . What do you think would help you not be so stressed when your mom calls?" Then the next one would come in. *He* was conducting therapy! The nurses thought I was a patient too. Frequently nurses came up to take my vitals, which he loved. It was funny, but I'm a nurse. I worked at that hospital. I thought that he would get great care! It's a big fantasy! That still makes my skin crawl when I think about it.

Until recently, I had physically demanding work. I found

another job because I knew no one would hire me once I hit sixty-five, and what I was doing was definitely more than I would be able to handle. The advantage of the job I had for most of Miguel's illness was that, though I'd be gone for twelve hours, I only worked two days one week and three the next and I could be flexible around Miguel. But I could afford only so many days off a year or else I wouldn't get raises or bonuses. Or I could get fired. I have a friend who will go see Miguel during his hospitalizations. If I asked for family leave and couldn't get it, my friend would take a day off and stay with Miguel. My older son talked to his boss so he can sometimes cover for me; he will work from home to be with Miguel if he's in a really bad psychotic state. Some people pull through to help.

There were times, especially when I was working twelve-hour shifts, I'd get irritated at Miguel for not helping me. This one time I worked three twelve-hour shifts then went out of town to a funeral. I returned to find my house a complete mess. I said, "You're not broken! Pick it up! I work too hard to come home on my days off and clean up this house!" As soon as I raised my voice, which at the time didn't seem like a bad thing to do even though now a part of me knows I shouldn't yell, I could see him visibly shrink. Then, seeing him recoil, I felt like saying, "And don't do that either!" I felt guilty about getting angry. But on the other hand, "Pick up your dirty dishes!" He's not broken. He's tougher than he looks.

The summer he was twenty-four, Miguel told me his dad had called and was going to be in town and wanted to take him and his brother to dinner. I said, "Fine, whatever. Just don't bring him here. I don't want anything to do with him." But as it happened I ran into him at a restaurant. A man came up to me and started talking to me. It seemed like he was hitting on me, so I said, "I'm going to my table." Then he said he was there to take Arturo and Miguel to dinner, and as soon as I said, "How the hell do you know my sons?" I realized it was my ex. I didn't know him! He didn't sound like himself.

I'd never seen him without a mustache. He had glasses on and was dressed differently and I wasn't expecting to see him. It was disturbing.

It was then that he said he wanted to get disability for Miguel. I said, "Don't do it in the state where you live because it won't do me a bit of good here. I don't think you're going to be able to." Then I added, "He has a lot of disabilities. He can't read now. He doesn't have the attention span. He's got a permanent tremor. When you take him to dinner, don't get soup because he'll spill all over himself. You know none of this because you haven't been involved." I was nice. I was low-key nice. Then he said, "I know it's been really hard." That was the wrong thing to say because he has not been involved or helped, and really doesn't know what it's like.

The medical bills are astronomical. I don't have a spare ten thousand dollars to pay them off. I can't claim Miguel as a dependent because now he's disabled. I paid off the first hospitalization, but I said, "Miguel, you have to ask the hospital for help on this one. I cannot pay another ten grand." They told him he didn't get his application for financial aid in on time so they've turned him over to a collection agency. Come and get it. At this point I'm so angry about it. I know what kind of care we give away at that hospital. If he ever gets on his feet, we'll deal with his credit rating then. I don't have it. His dad was in town saying, "I'm going to pay for the lawyer to get him disability." I said, "Fine." But even that makes me angry. He won't pay a penny for medical care. He won't find a place for him to go and yet he's a physician, a pediatric specialist. It's not as if he's illiterate or inexperienced in medical care and treatment! It's like, "Why can't you help with his care?"

I didn't want Miguel on disability because I thought there was *something* he could do and tried to convince him to get vocational testing. I didn't want him to give up. But he didn't want to mess up eligibility for disability. I said, "I don't want you to give up because I see you make progress when you really try." I almost had him in a yoga meditation class, then his dad offered him disability and he just quit. You know, you can't quit. You've got to keep trying, keep working on it. You can do better than *this*. At that time he was in a slump, sleeping all the time again. That's the other thing: he takes the meds and he sleeps twenty hours a day.

But at twenty-five, he did finally receive supplemental disability (SSI)[16] and was paid a lump sum for the seven months it took to process. He used the lump sum to rent an apartment that's an hour away. He still spent 75 percent of the time with me. I said, "It's a trial. It's a transition. Keep the stress low."

He takes his meds. He joined a church group near his apartment. I went to talk to his church group to make sure they were not trying to tell him they would pray for him and he could stop taking his meds. I couldn't say, "He has schizophrenia. Do you guys know that?" I think they recognize he has some needs. I found them to be different from any church I'd ever attended, but he found solace in it and they were very kind. I felt better about that.

He doesn't fast, and no more standing under the shower for six hours and then ten hours. He said, "I really thought that was going to help me." I said, "Do you understand that is not what rational people do? You need to have something to compare yourself to so you can monitor yourself. If you're going to be living on your own, Miguel, when you do something like that, you need a person who can tell you what is not normal." I'll have to keep a close eye on him. We'll be going there to see him a lot.

Arturo used to be really angry with Miguel, thinking he could control his behavior. He now acknowledges it's a really crappy disease, a crappy thing to have happen to you. Not long ago Arturo said, "Mom, you're almost sixty-five . . ." I said, "No, I'm not there yet! But thank you for noticing I'm getting old!" But then he said, "I don't think I can take care of Miguel." He didn't say, "It isn't fair," he said, "*I don't think I can do it.* I can't financially do it. What are we going to do? How am I going to take care of him when you're gone?"

I was grateful for that. I said, "At least you realize that at some point you're going to step up."

I told Arturo that I would find an attorney. I don't have a huge estate, but I said, "We'll see how we can set things up." If Miguel gets too much money, they'll pull him off disability. Yet he can't work. Years from now, who knows how politics will change the system? How do I set up money for him to continue to get disability? It's a crazy system and draining to try to get things arranged. I can't figure it out. I don't see how he could ever do it on his own.

I have approached another family member, who has a good relationship with Miguel, to ask if she'd be guardian of a trust fund for him and, in essence, kind of watch him. I wrote to her because I didn't want to ask her face-to-face and make her feel like she had to say yes. If she says no, then we'll find somebody else. I don't want Arturo to be his caretaker. I want Arturo to be his brother. I want somebody else, if one is needed, to be his caretaker. Maybe he needs to be in a halfway house. There isn't any place to send him. There are very few resources.

In high school, Miguel had friends who, at the time, gave me gray hairs. They were not the friends a parent would pick, but these young men have stood by Miguel. The one who I'd see and would think, "Please God, get him out of my life," has been Miguel's best friend. He's accepted his diagnosis, is open about it. When Miguel's jaw starts clenching, Evan calls it "his nasty face" and says, "Miguel! Think about upping your drugs! That nasty face is coming back." Some friends won't have anything to do with Miguel, but Evan and a few others will put up with anything that Miguel does and understand Miguel is a really good person.

Recently, a friend of Miguel's moved into my house. His parents kind of kicked him out. He cleans my house. The day I came home and my house was spotless, I was like, "You can stay for a long time!" He takes care of my dogs and works at a market so he brings home groceries. He's always been supportive and good to Miguel. Miguel has another friend from high school who invited him to the beach. He spent time with those friends who are an incredible group and who support him fully, where he is. One time I thanked them for sticking by Miguel. I said, "You guys have no idea how unusual this is. But I do, and I truly appreciate everything you do for Miguel." Instead of saying, "Thank you," and disappearing, they stepped up even more. That is a major blessing for Miguel.

But Miguel's brother, Arturo, doesn't have a lot of friends and doesn't tell people his brother has schizophrenia. Maybe he doesn't want others to treat his brother differently. At first I didn't want to tell people because I didn't want people to look at Miguel oddly. It was wonderful how he acted like his old self at that wedding. People were in awe of him, but they wouldn't have been if they had known about his illness.

People who I do tell would not treat him differently. I told people at my previous job. They probably understand better because they are health care professionals. I haven't told anyone else because I don't have many friends outside of work. I told my sister and a cousin who was quite close—at the time she was in her eighties. His cousins know, but my mother never knew She was old and frail and we didn't feel she needed to know. I don't advertise his illness because he has a right to privacy. I am very open if someone asks me, "Why isn't your kid in college?" I say, "He has a diagnosis of schizophrenia." It's amazing—when you're open about it, many people respond with, "Oh, my brother or my sister, my aunt, my uncle . . ." And then they seem like, "The burden is off, it's okay to talk about it." It's common, but people are afraid to say anything.

When I finally came out and said his diagnosis at work, I learned there were a number of people who had siblings diagnosed with schizophrenia. Within a span of four years, two of my coworkers had lost their only sons; one died in a car accident and the other died by suicide. I just say, "My son has schizophrenia." You know, *you* guys deal with it. I'm not going to hide it. That's what it is. He's not going to kill anybody. He's a great kid. He's a great person. Once someone said to me, "How do you handle Miguel?" There have been some terrible times, but I said, "I look at these two women and I'll take what I've got." Because they'd trade places with me in an instant. But it shouldn't be like that. My son shouldn't have to work so hard to be sane. And there isn't a magic pill. And there aren't many resources out there for us anymore, either.

His illness consumes my life. Sometimes I have to leave. I have a new hobby! I ride motorcycles. I'll go away for a weekend if I know he's stable. If he's not doing well, then I'm around more. What concerns me is that he might wander or have a break and not be able to find help, like the time I caught him taking a shower for six hours. That's not healthy. I do worry. But I worry whether I go or stay. And his brother and his friends will show up when I go. They know I need to leave so they will have dinner with him. They alternate so someone sees him every day. I don't want him to become isolated.

I have to get a break from him because I tend to hover. I try to interpret every behavior, looking for something "normal." That was a lesson I learned from an eighteen-year-old patient I had one summer who had a horrible, tragic diagnosis. As a result of being ill and being on a ventilator, he had lost his hands and his feet. His mother was always there. One day I walked into his room and saw he and his mother playing a game. I thought, "With all of this cascading down on them, there was this one moment of normal and *that's* what matters."

I try to quit looking at Miguel as if he's sick or disabled and try to find what's normal and go for those "not-sick" moments. After years of this now, that takes so much energy. You can't find it easily. But you can find it.

———∞∞∞———

*Clearly, it is not easy to be sole caregiver and advocate for an adult living with persistent mental illness, work full time, and also grapple with personal issues such as divorce or the recent death of a parent. How does Bianca manage? As she mentions in a later chapter, she has "ripped a few pillows" and sometimes allows for self-pity. But then she remembers how hard it is to be the person who lives with mental illness and how much her son has lost. Or she reminds herself that she is blessed to still have her son. It's all a matter of perspective.*

*Bianca is also practical and realistic. Though the logistics of caring for her adult child are demanding, she is well aware of the realities regarding long-term care and advocacy for Miguel. The question of "What happens after I am gone?" is for her, and the many parents in her situation, a serious issue. While some adults in later career stages make final plans for retirement, Bianca must include logistics of her son's long-term care within her own financial planning. Even her employment choices are influenced by her son's needs.*

*Bianca is honest about Miguel's illness with herself and both of her sons. This approach helps her cope and comprehend what "normal" means for them now. She has come to know that limiting stress is an imperative for Miguel's health especially, as well as for her own. Bianca knows that what can be most healing for her family is to find and create "normal" moments where Miguel's illness is not central and to express gratitude when this is achieved. What Bianca also relies upon is a healthy dose of humor, which is possibly the one salve useful for managing any illness.*

# Chapter Five: Tessa and Riley

*Parents shouldn't have those thoughts.*

*Because when I'm gone, I don't know who's
going to be here for him.*

Born in 1978, Tessa's son, Riley, was thirty-three at the time of
our first meeting. Over the twenty years she had witnessed her
son's evolving illness, Tessa developed strong opinions about the
mental health system and motherhood. From our first interview,
her maternal ferocity was apparent, "Like a mother bear," she
says. Despite her busy schedule of work and caring for her son,
and perhaps because of it, Tessa is straightforward and practical
yet compassionate about the suffering that afflicts an individual
living with mental illness and his loved ones. There is no aspect of
her journey that she doesn't address, and often seems to challenge
herself to consider the worst, and to make admissions that would
be unbearable to most.

Perhaps Tessa was always this way, or it was the journey
with her son's illness that defined her thus because it is one marked
by challenges, unpredictability, and often crisis. For many parents
like Tessa, the time period between obtaining a proper diagnosis
and recovery is particularly ugly. Parents experience events they
never before could have imagined to be associated with their
own child's life narrative. Even years later, parents seem to be in
disbelief over a hideous event or series of events that took place.
Parents marvel that they survived the pain of witnessing a son
or daughter's suffering, particularly when their child deliberately
puts themselves in danger. Witnessing and sharing their child's
unimaginable suffering raises realistic concerns over the child's
fate should a parent precede him in death. Many parents worry,

*"Who will care for him when I'm gone?" Because a parent knows what can happen if their child doesn't have a loved one advocating for him.[17] Tessa is brave enough to give voice to this very real and practical concern.*

*Adding to the complexity of managing mental illness is substance use. Of those living with a brain disorder, 60 percent are dually diagnosed with substance use. Although substance use has been defined as a brain disorder in the DSM VI, the standard diagnostic manual that defines brain disorders and associated symptoms, it is not always addressed directly by patients, parents, or even doctors when coupled with secondary (or more) brain disorders. But substance use complicates the process of diagnosing mental illness and impacts the efficacy of medication and may possibly impede brain healing following a psychotic episode.*

*The subtext in the telling of these particularly horrendous episodes is that parents have moved through the most harrowing of challenges and now have the strength to talk about them.*

*This is Tessa's story.*

**TESSA:** About two weeks after Riley's eighteenth birthday, I awoke around two or three in the morning and found he still wasn't home. Usually if he didn't return home it meant I'd get a call from the police or something bad had happened. By then he had a history of getting drunk and getting into fights.

My concern that night intensified because I was thinking of the two young men Riley had recently brought home and introduced as "friends." After they left, I had said to Riley, "I don't like the looks of them. They look hard and criminal." He brushed me off. "Oh, Mom!" I said, "I mean it. I don't like them and I don't trust them." A mother knows in her gut that something isn't right. They were not from his high school. They were older and got on campus to deal pot. Riley had met them through a high school friend. Shortly after I'd warned him, Riley got into a fight with one of them. It was stupid. Riley had said, "The only way to God is through Jesus." One said something back, and Riley punched him in the nose. The other kid punched back, but no one got arrested.

I got the dreaded call at about five a.m.

"We have your son at the hospital. He's been brutally beaten with a baseball bat. He has a head injury but is doing better now. They're going to release him soon."

I was stunned.

But this wasn't the first head injury he'd ever suffered. This was the fourth. Between the ages of three and five, he'd fallen off the monkey bars and gotten knocked out, smashed the back of his head in a car accident, and had gotten smacked by a friend swinging a golf club. Each time the ER doctor had said, "He'll be fine." It was the eighties then, and each time I had inquired, "But I'm concerned about a concussion."

The fight had happened around midnight and he'd been at the hospital for six hours. His friends brought him home and told me the police had treated it as a fight, but Riley was brutally beaten, assaulted, and his head looked like Frankenstein's monster. His eyebrows were swollen over and blood was coming from his eyes. His shirt was saturated in blood. His friends helped him into the house, and I gasped, "Oh, my God!" The doctors had wrapped an ace bandage around a pack of ice to hold it against his head. He was misshapen. I was shocked.

He was clearly still a mess, so I took him right back to the hospital and demanded to speak with the doctor, who said, "It looks like a level five concussion. It's a bad concussion, but we checked and we don't think there's anything wrong. I think he'll be okay."

This was 1997. I said, "You *think* he'll be okay?"

He said, "Listen, Ms. S—, there's nothing we can do right now. Take him home and watch him, and if there are any changes, bring him back."

Every day that week I rushed him back to the emergency room. He was still bleeding through the eyes. One night, while I was helping him to the bathroom, he collapsed and screamed,

"Someone's sticking a knife in my head!" He didn't know what had happened.

I had good insurance at the time, thank God. I took him to a neurologist, Dr. M—. He did a battery of tests and asked a dozen questions. Dr. M— said, "He seems fine." Now it's a blur, because at that time I was in shock and terrified I was going to lose him. But I recall that after pressing him further, the neurologist said, "I have to be honest: he's fine right *now*. But with head injuries this severe, we won't really know anything for six months to a year."

Well, he seemed fine. He still had anger issues, but not nearly as bad. I thought maybe the whole incident was a wake-up call for him because he stopped drinking for a while.

Riley's troubles started at thirteen, after we'd moved to California to be near his dad. He didn't always get along well with Ted, his father. After Riley ran away a few times, Ted and I agreed that, although we were not dating one another, it would be good for us to co-parent under the same roof. It worked well and was helpful when Riley was fifteen, which is when I began to see significant changes in him. He got mixed up with the wrong kids—wealthy kids who drank and partied when their parents were away. These kids didn't have curfews. I was the only mother who allowed kids to hang at our house while I was there, and doing so made it possible for me to meet his friends. Riley also wasn't sleeping and often stayed up late playing video games. He'd sneak out of the house and go drinking. He'd get into fights and get arrested and had to go to juvenile hall. Things spiraled out of control. Surprisingly, Riley still did well in an honors program that was hard for most to get into.

At sixteen, Riley was more frequently angry. *Really angry.* I was an angry teenager, but this was *rage* over the smallest trigger. His dad, who at the time was a counselor working with troubled teens my son's same age, just said, "He's a teenager.

He's rebelling." But I thought, "Eh . . . I rebelled. No. This is too much anger." But both of us agreed, we needed to get Riley into therapy.

There was an incident around that time when Ted was out of town and I had to be up for work by five-thirty a.m. Riley was blasting rap music at three in the morning. It was as if he had trouble processing what he had understood at twelve and what had been easy for him to understand as a child. He couldn't seem to process what he knew before: there are rules and regulations in an apartment complex. You can't play loud music late at night!

I went into his room and said, "That's it!" I unplugged his boom box. I started to take it from his room when he grabbed me and yelled, "You're not going anywhere!" He didn't strike me, but the act of grabbing me was enough for me to suspect something was terribly wrong. I didn't know if he was using drugs. I didn't think he was using pot because I knew the signs from my teen years, and I didn't smell alcohol. I thought, "He must be on coke or who knows what?"

I called the police because I was really angry and didn't know what was going on with him, but I knew it wasn't good. I felt, "How *dare* you touch your mother like that!" He'd never acted that way with me before. *My* mother would have knocked me across the room if I'd behaved that way. The police came and talked to him. Immediately, the sight of law enforcement calmed him.

He was sixteen and that was the first of his big rages. I was blown away.

Shortly after that incident, Ted and I took Riley to psychotherapy. Riley was late getting home from school that afternoon, and in the car on the way to therapy he said, "I'm really sick. I'm gonna throw up. Let me out of the car." We pulled over and he threw up. At the therapist's office he sort of melted into the chair. I knew then he was doing drugs, but I still don't know what. Maybe it was heroin because recently he said he'd tried it once and didn't like it because he couldn't move. His drinking persisted.

The psychotherapist asked my son to talk and he said, "I have nothing to say." She said to us, "You're paying for nothing. If he's not going to talk, there's not much I can do. Obviously, *you two* are having issues from a long time ago, so let's work on that." She asked Riley to leave the room. We went back twice more, but we couldn't drag Riley to the sessions, and if he did go, he wouldn't talk.

The therapist pooh-poohed Riley's behavior. I said, "No! You don't understand. The anger that I've seen!" I told her how Riley and his father argued and got in each other's faces and veins would be popping. They'd be arguing and Ted would say, "I'm walking away. I'm not going to be involved in this childish behavior." I saw rage. His anger was to the *n*th degree. The therapist said, "*You two* have issues, and he has hormones and teenage rebellion." I said, "I can tell you numerous stories of *my* teenage rebellion, and never was it like what I've seen in Riley."

I left the therapist's office angry with her. There was never that kind of rage with my brother. She said, "I'm sure it's just a phase." About the video games she said, "Kids do that: stay up late and play video games . . ." I admit, I was relieved, thinking his behavior was a phase. I thought boys must be different. But as time went on, every month he was in juvenile hall for drinking and getting in fights.

And then his father and I got a letter from the state court declaring we were unfit parents and we couldn't control our son. I felt like a total failure. His father, who was helping young people Riley's age in a group home, did too. He left the psychology field. It affected him that much. It still affects me! Thinking about it now, I feel the same emotions.

We laid down the law for Riley. We said, "This is how it is: straighten up or the court will take you away and put you in a group home. We won't be allowed to see you. We have no control over you." Somehow he straightened up. He was still drinking; he just wasn't getting arrested. At least not for a while.

When he was seventeen, he dropped out of school. He said, "Everything they're teaching me at this school, I learned in fifth grade in Colorado. It's pointless." We said, "Fine. You have to work or go to community college or get your GED. *Something*. You *cannot* sit around." He became an assistant manager of a bagel place. He was handsome, had a girlfriend, and was popular. He had friends who drank and smoked cigarettes and pot. He's still handsome. But in a picture I have from that time, I now see confusion in his face.

Riley earned the State Proficiency Degree, which is not useful everywhere. But it is more difficult than the GED, which he got later. We celebrated with his father on his eighteenth birthday. Riley had gotten all As in the science, math, and reading sections. The test results indicated he was in the top 2 percent.

Around that time, my father died, my work hours were cut, and Riley's father decided he was moving back to New Orleans. I said, "Oh, great! I uproot and come out here and then you leave! Riley still needs you."

His father said, "He doesn't need me."

"But *I* could use your help," I said, but it didn't matter.

I was again a single parent, on my own to care for Riley at the time of that brutal beating. Only a few months later I gave Riley the option to either continue living with me and get a job to help pay rent, or move out so I could get a roommate. After Ted moved out, I could not afford the apartment on my own. Riley did seem fine. He was functioning. He was working again. He chose to move into a shared house with kids, but he soon grew to hate it. My son can be neat, and that place was always trashed. Once I was there and he was doing the dishes. I teased him, "You're doing the dishes?" He said, "I gotta get out of here!"

But since I had a roommate by then, he went to live with his dad. Worst possible decision. His dad lived in the French Quarter in New Orleans. By December, I got a call from Ted.

"Riley is in the hospital."

I said, "What do you mean? What now?"

He said, "He had a break."

"What do you mean, *he had a break?*"

That night his father had awoken suddenly because Riley was standing naked, wielding a knife over him. Riley threatened him. "Go to the roof." Nothing Riley said made sense. Ted was scared to death and called the police. They took Riley to the psychiatric ward at a hospital in New Orleans, which is odd because his father had been hospitalized in the same ward and even the same wing at eighteen when he overdosed on LSD.

Back in California, I waited for the doctor to return my call. I asked if Riley was on drugs. I was hoping it was a temporary drug-induced psychosis like what his father had experienced. But the doctor said, "No drugs or alcohol in his system. We believe he is schizoaffective."

I broke.

I didn't know what that meant. I knew what schizophrenia meant. I'll never forget what he said. "He is partially bipolar and partially schizophrenic." I didn't know the term "bipolar," but the doctor informed me, "The old term for it is manic-depressive." I knew that term because my mother was manic-depressive for years. Then the doctor added, "And it's actually good." At that, I wanted to go through the phone and scream and kill him. I said, "What's good about it?" He said, "Because it's not full-blown schizophrenia or full-blown bipolar, we can make up a cocktail that will work better for him." I didn't understand, but I was trying to hold on to anything positive.

I went the following week to see my son, and it was really bad. He was catatonic. He didn't know who I was. At nineteen, they had to help him walk because, neurologically, he couldn't do it on his own. It was horrible seeing him be a zombie. The doctor said, "We had to give him a shot because when he got here, he was thrashing."

That was a rude awakening. I questioned, "Why? How? I must have done something to make him sick."

They put him on different medications: an antipsychotic and an antiseizure medication. The following week he was better but not normal. He was able to talk a little, was functioning to a degree, and he knew who I was. I stayed for two and a half weeks, as long as I could get away without losing my job. Because who was going to support him if I lost my job?

He stayed in the hospital for three months and was stabilized. I wrote and called every night and eventually the staff knew me.

Of course Ted said, "I can't take him. There's no way, not after what happened." I'm sure it was traumatic for him. I arranged for Riley to live near me, but I couldn't care for him either, because I had to work. I found a live-in program an hour and a half away. There was nothing near my home or work, and this one was close enough for me to be able to make regular visits. He was there a month when they called to tell me he'd gone off his meds. He was young, only nineteen and a half, and didn't know any better. Everyone resists accepting mental illness, but especially when young. Everyone *else* is crazy.

He was put in the hospital but not for long. Again, Riley was catatonic. The administrator told me they couldn't take him back into their program. I scrambled to get him a caseworker through the county and arranged for him to get a spot in D House, a really great supervised group home near me where I could visit regularly. The plan was for him to go there after he was released from the hospital. I couldn't take him into my home because by then I had a roommate.

He didn't like the hospital, but while he was there he became so stable on medication and treatment that he had the wherewithal to hire a patient advocate to get him out. He can be very clever. Riley was released and went missing. Obviously, since he was not on medication, no program would take him, and he lost his spot at D House. He was twenty. He was homeless. I was freaking out because I didn't know where he was. A month passed and I still hadn't heard from my son. I didn't know where he was, what he was doing. I was a wreck.

I was on my way to see my psychologist and stopped at Starbucks for coffee and saw one of his old friends from high school. He said, "Hi, Ms. S—. How are you doing?" I said, "Hello," and then, "Hey, have you seen Riley around the neighborhood or anywhere?" All of a sudden, *right* as I spoke, I saw what appeared to be a grizzled, forty-year-old man who'd been living in a cave, eating locusts. It was Riley, who was twenty years old and nearly unrecognizable. He wore gray sweats, which he'd never before owned, and wasn't wearing a shirt or shoes. He was scratching like an old man from the Bible who crawled in from the wilderness. Riley saw the friend talking to me and yelled, "Leave my mom alone!" Riley poked the friend in the eyes, thinking I was in danger. Luckily, the friend was fine.

The Starbucks manager called the police, and Officer F—, who was part of a psychiatric crisis unit, arrived with two other humungous police officers. Officer F— said, "Stay back!" I was freaking out, and Riley was wild-eyed and tweaked like he was on drugs. His system was clean; he was psychotic.

Officer F— said, "Riley, how are you doing?" He knew my son from other incidents because Riley had been off and on his meds and by then had been hospitalized six times. Officer F— had helped me get Riley into a program after his first bad break. He sat and talked to Riley. "Why don't you come with us? We want to help you." I don't know what triggered Riley, but a second later there was a scuffle. Riley and Officer F— were wrestling on the ground. Officer F— stood, and a huge officer as big as Arnold Schwarzenegger put his foot on Riley's neck, smashing his face into the cement. Another officer held Riley's arms and legs so he was immobile.

Riley was psychotic; adrenaline and paranoia took over. Riley was afraid they were going to hurt him, which they did. But not like he'd be hurt later. He went away in an ambulance. He was a 5150.[18] I got him on a seventy-two-hour hold and quickly got conservatorship.[19] These days you have to jump through all kinds of hoops to get a conservatorship on your loved one. His caseworker and I arranged for Riley to be transferred to a home where he stayed for a year. I didn't have the means to take care of him, and that break was bad.

He was released around Christmastime of 2000, and finally got into the D House. I have a picture of us then. He was doing really, really well until he went off the meds. He figured, "I don't really need these. I'm doing so well." He ended up back in the hospital. I can barely count the number of times he was hospitalized in the years that followed. He's been in every hospital that I know exists within a two-hour radius of my home. Every time he went off meds, he'd wander the streets homeless and eventually land in the hospital. Once, high school kids beat him because he was homeless.

Between the ages of twenty-two and twenty-five he left the state. I didn't know where he went, but occasionally I'd get a call. In New Orleans, he was pistol-whipped and robbed in the French Quarter. He got seven stitches in the back of his head and spent the night in jail. He went to Georgia and Colorado. A friend called me and said, "He can't stay here. He's nuts." I said, "Yeah. I know."

My life was difficult during that time. I had become a personal trainer and immersed myself in work and my own physical training. I was seeing a psychiatrist and taking antidepressants. Had I not been seeing a psychologist and psychiatrist, I probably would have been in the hospital too. I began to understand that I had absolutely no control over anything but myself. All I remember from that time is praying every day and night. I kept trying to find out his whereabouts through friends and acquaintances. I learned he was in Mississippi because he landed in the state hospital there.

Riley would go off meds because *he* didn't think he was sick. He had a doctor at a city hospital who told him, "There's nothing wrong with you. You're just a lazy drunk." My son would sound logical, and he'd say, "They don't know what's wrong with me. How can I believe they know? They're crazy! One doctor says I'm a drunk. Another says I have ADHD. A third says I'm rebellious."

It made me think, "Gee, what if it's depression and they haven't picked that up?" He is smart and sometimes manipulative. During the first five years of his illness, I didn't know if he really had a mental illness or doctors were just labeling him. My trust in doctors isn't 100 percent. I've had relatives who died while under a doctor's care. Professionals had told Ted and me our teenager was rebellious and going through a phase, and others said he was an alcoholic. He had several diagnoses; the first was schizoaffective, then ADHD, schizophrenia, and then bipolar.

I knew there were genetics involved and that my mother was manic and that Riley's father, who most people said was "crazy" and a genius, had had his own drug-induced psychotic break. But, for years, I wanted to believe that my son's first signs— the anger, rages, and staying up all night—*were* part of a phase. The first diagnosis he got in New Orleans—schizoaffective— was the one that stuck. Later, it was finally confirmed after ten years and twenty-two hospitals and I can't tell you how many stints in and out of jail for being drunk in public.

Once I accepted it, then his world got better.

The first time I really accepted it was when I spoke to the nurse at the Mississippi State Mental Hospital where he stayed a few months. By that point, he'd been sick for five years, in and out of hospitals, and wandering, homeless. The nurse said, "I've been a psychiatric nurse for over twenty years and have family members with mental illness." She listed his symptoms and evidence that confirmed Riley's diagnosis. I realized also that he'd been on medication for six weeks and I'd gotten my son back. It started fitting together like a puzzle. "My God! This has been going on five years!" And where was I? I was in denial.

That's when I woke up and began researching, reading books, and constantly searching online.

I'll never know how Riley made it back home alive, but when he returned, I had a roommate, who is now my husband. I convinced my boyfriend, "Yeah, he's on medication." I offered Riley our extra room. Well, I don't think he was there three days before he started drinking and smoking pot and went off meds. He was up all night. Manic. I thought he was doing speed or methamphetamine. But it was alcohol and pot.

Riley came home one night at two in the morning all a mess and disheveled. I said, "What's going on?" He just yelled, "Ahhh!" Nothing he said made sense. I said something and he punched me in the nose! It was weird because I felt as if I was watching from outside of myself and I didn't feel anything. I was more in shock and awe over watching his mental state than feeling what was happening to me. I called the police but didn't want him to go to jail because I knew a mentally ill person doesn't get treatment in jail; they often get mistreated. At that time, law enforcement advised parents to kick them out of the house and they would be picked up and taken to a psych ward.

The police came. I said, "He's crazy. He needs to be placed in a hospital. He's a 5150." But he straightened up as if nothing had happened and we were sitting and talking! He said, "My mother and I just don't get along."

The police looked at me and said, "Sorry. We can't take him because he seems fine."

We kicked him out of the house because he wasn't fine. I knew he'd been drinking, and I wasn't going to put myself in danger. The police did not pick him up, and Riley was on the street and disappeared again. This time he went to Colorado. I got a call from a friend whose daughter is Riley's childhood friend who, incidentally, is bipolar. My friend said, "I don't want my daughter with your son." I said, "I totally understand."

Later, Riley told me that he was off meds the whole time, sleeping in the Rocky Mountains, working every day through a temp agency. I don't know how he did that. My doubts about his illness came back. "How could he work? How could he function with full-blown mental illness?" I couldn't figure that out and still can't.

Many things happened to him, but he returned home when he was twenty-eight, having been all over the country. During that homeless stint, I never got called. Probably he didn't want anybody to call me and didn't give out my number. Upon his return, he needed a place to live and stayed with us. I got a caseworker, and I got him back on SSI.

He went off meds again. This time, nothing happened. He agreed to go to the hospital. I brought him to the hospital and got a conservatorship on him again. He went to another treatment center for about six months and was doing well. After he was released he went to live in a supervised group home in our town, but he didn't like it and I don't blame him. He was twenty-nine, a young person, while most of the residents were fifty-year-old zombies. That's enough to depress anyone. I saw the room he shared and it wasn't nice. A rat that lived in the closet had died in his laundry. Riley said, "I woke up and my roommate was talking over my bed!"

Riley went off his meds again when he was thirty. I remember his caseworker told me you have to manipulate a mentally ill patient to keep him medicated. He said to Riley, "If you get back on meds, we'll get you into a better program." A small manipulation, but he started doing well for about four months when his caseworker called and said, "It's not working out. Riley is not getting along with others." Really, he wasn't getting along with only *one* person, who happened to be his roommate. I still see other residents from there because I donate time. They always ask about Riley, but my son says, "I don't want to associate with those people. They're nuts!" Yeah, okay.

Riley was out of that house. Dylan, the caseworker, and I had to work something out. We made a deal: stay on meds and clean and sober and we'd help him get a place. He got a great apartment with a roommate who was a very kind, older man with a dog. Riley enrolled in classes at the nearby community college. He excelled and was at the top of his business law class. Once he showed me his teacher's comment that said, "Riley, keep going and I'll have to hire you for my practice." He finished the class with an A.

Around December 2008, eleven years after the illness had begun, Riley was having side effects from the medication. He was on seven different medications.[20] He didn't know whether he was coming or going. It didn't happen until the nurse added another one to help him sleep. He'd gone from three medications to *seven*. He said, "Mom, look!" Riley was on an antipsychotic known for causing a shuffling walk. I thought, "Oh, my God." I said, "Let's talk to your doctors." I started researching medications. He said, "I'm getting off *all* of them." I said, "No! Not a good idea! We need to talk with your doctors to wean you off so you don't suffer withdrawal. You can't go cold turkey!" He said, "If they don't put me on alternatives and take some of these away, I'm going off all of them."

We met with about seven mental health professionals at once. I said, "Is there an alternative? Can we reduce them?" Questioning the medication to his doctors in front of him was a huge mistake. That stuff needs to be in private because a mentally ill person is black and white and their brains start going, "Hmm. My mom supports me. The doctors *are* nuts!" All of a sudden my son became adamant and said, "No! I want off *all* medications right now!"

In hindsight, I see he'd gone off his medications a couple of weeks prior. He was talking fast. He seemed like a sharp-witted person if you didn't know bipolar mannerisms! But not one of those seven mental health professionals could convince him to stay on meds. There is no logic for a mentally ill person who begins to cycle. That's why I wanted court-ordered treatment without involvement of the criminal justice system. Dr. P—

said, "Riley, why don't you come to my office and we can talk more?" Riley said, "No!" I said, "Riley, they're willing to work with you." But there was no logic. Riley said, "I don't want to talk to you either, Mom!"

I did everything I could to keep a low profile with him and stay in touch. I called every day to check in with him. It was fun talking to him. He was sharp and witty, but he was talking really fast. He was still living with his roommate, who, luckily, was out of town on a business trip for a couple weeks.

About six weeks after we'd sat down with the mental health staff, it was Christmas and my son was at my house. Generally around Christmastime he's happy to be with us. But this time he couldn't look my husband or me in the eye. Scott and I had gotten married about nine months before. I pulled Scott aside and said, "He's losing it. We need to get him into the hospital before something bad happens. I'm worried."

I said, "Riley, are you taking your meds?"

He yelled, "I don't want to talk about it!"

"Are you going back to school?"

"Ah! Those people! I'm not going back to school!"

"Okay. How about we eat dinner and exchange gifts?"

"I'm sick of y'all!"

Nothing he said was very connected to anything we said.

"I gotta go! I got things to do!"

"What do you have to do?"

"You don't understand! I'm joining the army!"

"What?"

"Yeah, for your information, I've had a recruiter come and pick me up." And he did, three times, in fact. He said, "I'm going to Iraq."

I thought, "Oh, God, that's not good to put a gun in his hands right now."

A couple of weeks passed. Riley wasn't at his apartment and wasn't answering my calls. I went looking for him all around town, the county, everywhere to try talking some logic to him. I thought I could get him into the hospital, something, anything, before something bad happened because I could see he had been getting really bad. It was the worst I'd ever seen; the *worst* in terms of psychosis and not making sense and speaking gibberish like he was on speed.

I couldn't find him because he *was* with the recruiter. I finally reached him on the phone. I said, "I don't believe you are with a recruiter," because I knew Riley would say, "Oh yeah? Here!" And then he'd hand his phone over to the guy. Which he did.

The recruiter had a low voice. "Hello, ma'am."

I said, "Listen, you don't understand. My son has a sickness. He can't join the army."

He said, "Your son seems fine to me." At that time, they wanted bodies.

Two days after that, I drove to Riley's apartment. I had my little Chihuahua, Milo, who Riley *loves* and vice versa. But Riley said, "That freakin' dog!" And then he spewed more profanity. He was talking to things and people that weren't there. His face was so contorted I barely recognized him. It was clear his psychosis was bad. I started to cry. I said, "Please listen to me. Come with me. I'm going to get help for you. Please come. Please!"

"F— you!"

I was helpless. I thought, "Oh God, please intervene. Please let a cop come. Somebody come!" I wanted a big scene so I could get help and get him committed. But wouldn't you know, the day I needed somebody, no one was around—not his roommate, not a soul. And we were outside. I was scared. Not for me, but for him because I knew that the way he was acting, if he did anything, the police would kill him. They'd shoot him on sight. He was clean; no drugs were in his system because he seemed to be aware that he would be tested by the army. But he was off his medication and severely psychotic.

He said, "I'm waiting to hear back from the army. I took

the exam for the Army National Guard and all I need now is the physical," which I knew he wouldn't pass. Seeing him as he was then, they'd definitely get the signal! He was way too far gone. I started to argue with him, and he said, "Forget it! I'm doing what I'm going to do!" He took off. He just ran away! I was like, "Where is he going?" He ran across the street. Disappeared.

I drove through town bawling. I almost got into an accident. I was praying, "Dear God, please intervene!" I'd heard horror stories while in NAMI and knew what could happen. I went straight to see Dylan, his caseworker at the county mental health department. He threw his hands up and said, "Tessa, there is nothing we can do." I said, "Can't we get the police?" He said, "You know the story. They've got to be a danger to themselves or others." I said, "Trust me . . ." I was crying. He said, "Our hands are tied."

Days passed. His father had visited for a few days after Christmas. They'd gotten into a major blowup, which I didn't know about. It was January tenth and I called Ted. He said, "I don't want to talk to him anymore. He seemed fine to me." I said, "He seemed fine to you? You don't have a clue because you don't know him! You don't know the illness." I continued, "Trust me. He is *very* sick right now, and I'm afraid he's going to hurt someone. He's not in his right mind."

I cried and cried and prayed. I looked all over town for him. I went to his apartment again two days later. I looked online at the public booking log on the county sheriff's website because that's what I'd done in the past when I couldn't find him. It would say, "Drunk in public," and his name would be there because it's public information.

Well, I found him. He had a $50,000 bail and a felony charge, "criminal intent to terrorize." When Homeland Security tightened, all you had to do was be psychotic and screaming, and if someone is scared or terrified, that's a terrorist charge and a felony. Another charge was "resisting arrest," because he ran from the police. Of course he was going to run from police. He was psychotic. He ran from me!

I went directly back to speak with Dylan. He said, "Oh, you didn't see? It's on the front page of the paper." I said, "What?"

The paper reported Riley had attacked a girl. I became sick. It felt like someone had punched me in the gut. I threw up. I said, "What happened?" He said, "He was screaming at everybody." I said, "Of *course* he was screaming at everybody! He's paranoid!" He was highly schizophrenic.

The police had tasered him, hog-tied him in cuffs, and took him to jail. I couldn't talk to him for three weeks because *he was out of his mind.* They locked him up in what is called a safety cell, a padded cell. He was naked. For three weeks at the county jail, I couldn't see or help him. I called the public defender's office. I called everybody. "I've got to be able to talk to my son!" I called the county jail. "I've got to know! I know he's sick. He needs to be in the hospital!"

I finally found out who I needed to talk to at the jail to see him. Riley was still out of his mind. He was in an orange jumpsuit. "I don't know what I'm doing here! I joined the army! I'm going to be in the army!" I said, "You're not going to be in the army. You committed a crime."

The DA prosecution's job is to throw the book at them. I figured out who was DA for his case and contacted her. I said, "Is he on medication?" She said, "No, he won't take medication." I said, "Does he even know he's crazy? How does he even know he's supposed to take medication? He didn't know who *I was* when I saw him a week ago! Can't they give it to him?"

"Only if he's a danger to himself."

"He's incarcerated because he's a danger to others! That makes absolutely no sense!"

He'd been switching back and forth for six months. Then, in jail, he'd seem fine while I was talking to him through the glass, and the next moment he'd be back in the army. That's how I knew he wasn't getting medication or at least the proper medication. I had to fight tooth and nail. I sat on the doorstep of the jail's mental health director to get treatment for him while he was in jail. I had to get people from NAMI to help. Or else he was facing prison.

Finally, the DA convinced Riley that if he took medication he would look good in court and would get out. It was a little manipulation, but it was true, too. He needed to be stable to defend himself. He had no rights. I had no rights.

It had been reported in the newspaper that Riley attacked a girl. But according to the public defender, he never attacked the girl. I called the reporter and said, "Your story is wrong." He said, "I'm going to follow this trial." I thought, "My son is not going to be competent to stand trial. He's way too far gone." It was a nightmare seeing him in court in an orange jumpsuit and bound with chains around his ankles. His hair looked like it had been fried! He was mentally incompetent to stand trial. I almost broke right there. The judge would say, "Do you understand what I'm saying?" and he didn't. He didn't have a clue what the judge was saying.

Riley was treated as if he'd committed murder or rape! Not even close. He was charged with "child endangerment," which sounds like he put a cigarette out on a child. It was nothing like that. The public defender told me that he was downtown, walking and screaming at everybody, "Get out of my way!" He was haughty and not making sense. "If you come near me, I'm gonna get you!" Then a teenage girl, about sixteen, walked directly at him. I don't know if she didn't know any better or she thought, "Pshaw, I can do what I want." He said, "That's it! I'm going to get you!" He chased her. She ran into the street, and a car stopped inches away from her. Thank God the car stopped! But that was the "child endangerment" charge. You'd have thought he'd held a knife to her, did something deliberate. It wasn't deliberate. I'm not saying it didn't terrify the girl.

Later we learned that the girl's father was a well-known lawyer and well connected with the DA. The public defender told me that if it had been anybody else walking by, he would never have been charged with child endangerment. Instead, it was six months of hell. All during Riley's incarceration I was always thinking, and so was the public defender, that since he didn't do anything he'd get out soon. But because the girl's father was so connected, that was not the case. I wrote letters to the public defender and the judges. He had two different judges in the case. I wrote to the DA's office, the DA's assistant, the head of the public defender's office, the mental health department . . . everyone I could think of. I was at the civic center every day. I sat outside the court waiting for his public defender while she was in court. She came out and I said, "I've got all day. I need to know what's going on with my son. I need to help him." She started to walk away and I yelled, "No, no, no! I need to talk to you *now*!"

After six months, in June 2009, I convinced the judge I'd take him into my home. The DA imposed a three-year restraining order even though Riley doesn't remember the girl. "What if I run into her and she sees me and I don't know her?"

While in jail, Riley was allowed out of his cell for only a half hour to call me— usually at three a.m.—and I had to get up at five-thirty a.m. for work. The inmates with mental illness were not permitted to be among the general population because of staffing shortages. I had to constantly stay on top of the jail mental health and monitor whether he was getting proper medication. He didn't know what he was getting. I'd say, "What are you taking?" but he didn't know. I contacted the jail deputy and said, "I want his records sent there." He said, "Riley doesn't have a release for you . . ." You know that story. It was always a runaround.

The public defender worked with me and told Riley, "Your mom is trying to get you out of here, so sign the release." After that, he finally started getting proper medication.

Riley was traumatized from that experience. My son was tasered three times. He told me the taser is the worst pain. "I felt like my brain was going to explode and my body was on fire. Inside out. My blood was on fire." When I visited him in jail, he had bruises and burn marks down his back. His shirt was ripped. His eye was bruised. He'll still go through periods where he can't sleep because of nightmares from that place. The first six weeks he was home he had to sleep with the light on. If I went to shut the light off, he thought my hand was a gun because of the sheriffs in the jail.

Riley told me about a guy in jail who was homeless and mentally ill. He was a really skinny black guy with a funny accent my son imitates. Riley says, "It's funny, but it's not funny, Mom." This one day, the man was scheduled for release at eight o'clock that night. Riley was watching from his cell and couldn't believe how the deputies treated the man. For some reason they electronically opened the door to the man's cell on this day though it wasn't yet time for his release. The man came out of the cell and the deputies said, "Get back in your cell!" It seemed the man thought he was being released because in a few hours he would have been. The deputy said, "Get back in there! Okay, that's it! I'm gonna call my boys on you!" They were playing with him. Then the man said, "Go on, shoot ya gun!" Riley watched as they kept tasering him. Then that guy had to stay another 180 days because he was charged with resisting arrest and striking a police officer. It was supposed to be his last day. He's out now. Riley pointed him out to me on the street. He was abused, and my son witnessed it.

After he was released, I fought to get him into the STAR Court program, which provides a whole team to support the mentally ill person newly released from jail. The team consists of forensic caseworkers, psychotherapists who work one-on-one, a probation officer, a career counselor, and his community mental health advocate. The team monitored each mentally ill participant who also had to go to court each week to prove they were on course. They graduated in phases. It was a good program.

Riley has relapsed since then, but he's now convinced he *has* to stay on his medication, at least his biweekly shot. That's huge. For the longest time, he wouldn't admit he had a mental illness. But now sometimes if I ask him, "What do you think about this or that?" He'll say, "Well, I have a mental illness, you know. I don't have a normal brain, so I don't think the way you think." That's huge.

I always worry. For a whole year prior to his arrest and incarceration, I had been thinking, "Wow! Look at this! He's med-compliant! He's on his own and in school! He got an A in business law! Recovery!"

Well, recovery is daily.

You never think something like what happened to Riley could possibly happen: getting sick, getting thrown in jail. When my son was incarcerated, I couldn't eat. I went down to ninety-five pounds from my regular weight of 106. I couldn't sleep for those three weeks that I couldn't talk to him. My husband said, "I don't think you got up off the couch." What was the point? I lost my son. They locked him up and were going to throw away the key.

I fooled people into thinking I was doing fine because I was actually getting to work on time. But I was a complete mess. I was close to being put into a psych ward myself. I didn't know what was going to happen to my baby. It was really hard. My last name was in the paper! "Is *that* your son?"

I had recently started working at a women's gym, and my coworkers and clients knew my son. That was overwhelming because while some women would say things like, "My sister has a mental illness . . ." or "My husband has a mental illness . . . ," there were others who acted afraid because they didn't understand. I heard people talking. "Did you hear what her son did?" Once, this woman came up to me after my son's name was in the paper and everything was twisted about what had happened and she asked, "Has he ever hit *you*?" I looked at her and said, "Are you out of your mind? Do you know what mental illness is?" I thought I was going to be fired and didn't care. But then a couple of women said, "Why don't you leave her alone?" I ran to the bathroom.

People don't know that Riley was a good kid. Even in high school, if he saw some guy picking on a girl he'd step in and say, "Back off." When my father had a stroke and Riley was sixteen, we had a family reunion because we didn't know how much longer my father would be around. Riley would help his Paw-Paw get up and walk, and asked, "What do you need, Paw-Paw?" I didn't ask him to do that. People don't know his character. The worst my son had done before that was being drunk in public and getting in a fight. He's never carried a weapon. He doesn't believe in guns and never has. My father always said, "If you have a gun, someday you're going to have to use it." My son believes that too.

I am thankful and grateful that now Riley can sit and have conversations with people. He was telling me about a show we watched one night and we were laughing! I feel joy that he can live a pretty normal life. I'm grateful he's no longer in jail, he's getting help, he's home, and he's safe. I see his happy person come out now, which I haven't seen in years.

But there were times when I thought, "God, if it's your will, take him in his sleep." I felt that way after he was incarcerated, and beaten, and when he was sick. Because when I'm gone, I don't know who's going to be here for him. He doesn't deserve to suffer. He'd be better off with God than down here in this cruel world. That's hard for a mother to think that way, and I've beaten myself up over it. But parents of children with persistent mental illness are not alone with such thoughts. *Even* those thoughts. The motives of my heart are not because I don't want him around. I cannot bear for him to suffer again like he has, beaten down by society. It sounds terrible for a mother to say such things. It does. When I spoke to my sister about it she said, "No. I know exactly what you mean."

In jail, he was in a cell where he couldn't move for

twenty-three-and-a-half hours of the day. The incarcerated are treated worse than animals, especially those with mental illness. Any person who sits for twenty-three-and-a-half hours a day is not able to go to the bathroom, and toxins back up in one's system. After he got out of jail he was hospitalized for two weeks with severe colitis. He was in a lot of pain and almost died. Part of me still thinks, "Why didn't you take him then? Gracefully?"

I hope he goes before me. Parents should never have to think that. I never thought I would ever say that. But I'm sitting here in this room and I know that not his father, not his step-dad, not anyone cares about him the way I do. Once I'm gone, even if I leave money and a will for him . . . I think about that. I'm scared.

He has relapses. One night, while he was still on probation, he was out walking around. He wouldn't take his meds. He got drunk, and I prayed he wouldn't get picked up and thrown in jail. He was found unconscious on the road and brought to the hospital, then jail. He had alcohol poisoning and fell and hit his head. Long haul toward recovery once again. Sadly, relapse is part of recovery. Wish it wasn't, but it is what it is.

In May, early 2012, he was doing well because after fifteen years, he reconnected with his high school sweetheart. They had been looking for each other, and he found her on Facebook. He thought it was destiny. She had moved out of state and they talked every night on the phone. He saved money for two months and then visited her for two weeks. She's a single mom with two kids from different fathers. Hearing this I thought, "Two little kids!" That's a lot of stress for anyone. Whenever he'd call from her house I'd hear a two-year-old squealing. I thought, "I couldn't take that."

She knew he had an illness and had a head injury, and every day in front of the kids she'd ask, "Did you take your vitamins?" instead of, "Did you take your meds?" I thought, "This might be great! This might answer my prayers!" On the flip side, I knew that if one thing went wrong . . . relationships could be devastating.

I was in the process of making arrangements to take leave from my job to be able to travel with him, change his insurance, and obtain a caseworker when the whole thing fell apart at the end of May. It didn't work out. She called and said, "I think he's gonna be really upset when he gets home. We broke up. He smokes too much and he can't handle kids." I said, "He loves children, but a lot of people can't handle kids. Kids can be stressful!" I had to get real with her.

He came home and didn't want to talk about what had happened with his girlfriend. He received his SSI check on June third. We had only recently decided to switch the whole payment over, making him the total payee, which amounts to almost $1,000. Before, I was payee and used a portion to cover rent, leaving him with $338 to live on. But that month, he got the whole check and went to his girlfriend's to see if he could make the relationship work. He didn't take a cell phone charger nor did he take any meds. He had $938 but was paying $200 a night for a hotel. I couldn't reach him. I was freaking out. This went on for days. I didn't want to call his girlfriend because I thought that would really make her not want to be with him. I finally called her and said, "I didn't want to call you, but I'm worried about my son."

She said, "Actually, he just showed up at my door." She doesn't know much about mental illness obviously, because she yelled and screamed at him and told him he was selfish. He left and got drunk. He was gone a week and wasn't answering calls. I was thinking, "I don't know where he is. God only knows what can happen. He's in a place where nobody knows him."

Even though he didn't call me back, I texted and texted. "Everything's okay. You have a home here. If it didn't work out, don't worry about it. Momma's been through a divorce. That's life." Finally, after a week, he called. He hadn't slept. He was drinking and walking around town. He was not in contact with his girlfriend or stalking her. That's not who he is. Who wants to be with someone who doesn't want them?

Ted and his fourth wife were, by then, living nearby. I had talked to Ted and told him Riley hadn't called me. A week later, at two a.m., Riley called Ted from the bus station. Riley had no money or cell phone charger and did *not* have his meds, and he was due his biweekly shot. Thank God he called. I told Ted I was furious with Riley and asked if he could stay with him and his wife. Ted said, "Yeah, he wants to stay with me." Even though I had all this anger toward Riley, I knew that arguing with a crazy person and someone who is in crisis is useless. I said to Riley over the phone, "I am not angry with you. I am sorry all this happened. Stay with your dad. Get some sleep." Riley stayed there two days and slept and ate and slept and ate. That was it.

He arrived home on the bus at midnight. It's never a normal time! I trod lightly because I knew a relapse of that magnitude can take anywhere from a month to a year to heal. And he was emotionally devastated. Relationships have devastated me in my life, and I don't have the challenges he has. He came home, and I did everything to keep him on track. He had no money.

He was home. But wasn't, really. The following three weeks he went on binges, coming home drunk. Once, I came home from work and found cigarette butts smashed into the carpet. I said, "We gotta talk." He said, "I know, I know . . ." This went on for a month. Until July.

I was dog sitting for six weeks and had planned to spend the Fourth of July at the dog owner's home in the mountains. Riley came to the mountains because I knew my husband, bless his heart, had never dealt with anything like Riley. Riley is not his child, and Scott was disturbed by Riley's behaviors. He's known my son for ten years—before we were married—and knows Riley's a good person. He's not a criminal. My husband tries to support me but he's frustrated. I can't talk to him about

Riley or he gets angry with my son, and I'm in the middle. I have said, "Don't ask me to choose between you and my son. Forget it! It's not going to happen!" When Riley is clean and sober, he is my husband's ally. He likes my husband. That's good. But when Riley's drinking, he doesn't like anybody.

We all went to the mountains. Everything went well at first, except for a fight I had with Riley's father when I challenged him for telling Riley it was okay to gamble online. And also, Riley was still on a drinking binge. I had no idea that while we were sleeping, he'd walked a mile downtown to gamble. He won fifty bucks and spent it on alcohol and came back. I awoke at four a.m. to noise. He was dancing on the deck and I'm thinking, "Oh God! I don't own this place! What if somebody . . . and worst of all . . . What are you doing?" I lost it. I said, "Enough of this!" Then my son threatened, "I'll effin' beat you, bitch!"

Scott was ready to jump him. But I knew his anger was fueled by the alcohol, that he wouldn't hit me, and that he was just imitating stupid gang talk.

We returned from the mountains on July fifth. Riley got his check and guess what? He went back to his girlfriend. Again, no meds. Fortunately before he left, I'd managed to make him get his antipsychotic shot, which is the only thing that keeps him from going full-blown psychotic. I didn't know where he was, what he was doing. I didn't hear from his girlfriend. I was texting, basically saying, "I'm here for you. You have support. Remember 2009. You're in a state where nobody knows you and nobody cares. You could end up in jail and I can't help you. I love you."

That went on for three days. He called the second week in July. He was on the street sleeping with bums. He was freaking out, which was good. I wired fifty bucks for him to get food. He said, "Aren't you going to send money for the bus?" I said, "No. You can pick the ticket up at Greyhound. You're *not* getting more money."

He came home. I didn't yell, I didn't scream. I gave him a hug and said, "Thank God you're okay. But we need to talk. Now go to bed." He went to bed and again, slept for two days. He was out of it. Then we talked and he said, "She rejected me." I said, "I know it's painful. But you left without your meds. You left without your phone charger. Think! Think about what could have happened!" It worked out okay for a couple of days.

For the rest of July and all of August he didn't try to leave town again because he'd spent all his money. But he was still designated payee for the whole SSI check, which meant in the next few weeks he'd get another check for nearly a thousand dollars. On $338 he can't do much, but on almost $1,000 he can get a round-trip ticket, which I knew could endanger him. I talked to the caseworker right away. I said, "Change it right now so he can't get all the money." Then Riley called the caseworker, "That's my money!" But his caseworker said, "Riley, you're unstable right now. I'm not giving you a dime." Thank God for the caseworker. I again became the designated payee and could use the money for rent even though it doesn't really cover rent or food. But at least it wasn't in his hands.

There was this time, several months later, when Riley again demanded changing the payee over to him. I had said to Dylan, his caseworker, "There's no way Riley can have that money right now, and I don't know if he'll ever be able to manage money." Riley made a big mistake for which I'm grateful: he called Dylan and chewed him out, "That's my fucking money!" Dylan didn't know Riley had been drinking. Dylan called afterward and said, "I'm giving you a heads-up. He's an angry man right now." When I got off the phone, Riley came storming through the door. Angry. Anyone else would have called the police because he looked scary. But it's frustration. Alcohol makes him a different person. I knew he wasn't going to hurt me.

Riley yelled, "I want you to change the money over to me. Write the letter!"

I said, "Okay. I'll do it." I knew damn well I wasn't going to do it. I was thinking, "Over my dead freakin' body!"

Riley went on and on. I have come to realize that arguing with Riley when he is angry or unstable, or showing him my own anger, could turn him away and I would lose touch with him forever. If I lose touch, it is inevitable something bad will happen to him. When Riley was angry about being denied as sole payee, he threatened me with, "I'll go away and you'll never see me again!" It was manipulative of him because that is my one button. I panicked and called Dylan and said, "I think this is going to backfire on me. Keep the checks going to him!"

But Dylan said, "I'm not allowing Riley to get the checks because he's angry and unstable."

Even though their hands are tied for other things, caseworkers know I am the caretaker, the intervention, the good cop, the bad cop, the everything to Riley, and I'm not going to let anything slide. I've driven around this county for eight hours looking for Riley. I don't ever want anything like that 2009 thing to happen again.

Later that night, Riley calmed down. He came into my room and apologized. I said, "I'm your mother. I'm the only steadfast person who has been there for you through thick and thin. You hurt me deeply. I don't know if I can look at you right now because I'm so hurt."

I was hurt but I was laying on the mom guilt while he was calm and still thought he was going to get full control over his money. I wanted him to see that he wasn't ready to manage money. I said, "By the way, where is your $1,100 from financial aid the last two months?" He said, "Oh, come on. You know I spent that." I said, "That's too bad. You could have put that money toward an apartment." He said, "You're kicking me out!" I said, "You're the one who wanted out. We made a goal for you to become independent by January. If you can't find the right place, we're not going to kick you to the curb. Stop stressing. Get your act together. Go to school because that's your future.

All I was going to do is take your checks and put away the money for you."

He hit a point of clarity and he was ready to defend himself but instead let out a big sigh and said, "Why don't you keep the checks in your name."

The rest of July, without much money, he wandered around drunk. He'd hang out at a cemetery where homeless people live. Often he'd come home drunker than a skunk. He'd pass out on his bed. There was nothing I could do except pray and stay in control of his money so he wouldn't put himself in more danger. When he came home in the morning to sleep I'd see him and think, "Thank God he's okay." Then I'd go to work. What could I do? Really? I had no help from the police. The only help I had was from his nurse and the caseworker he'd had in 2009 when he went to jail. I said, "Can you just call him?" They said, "He doesn't call back." I said, "Trust me. That doesn't matter. It's a psychological thing because you were his caseworker when he was on probation, and hearing from you triggers memories of jail and probation. It may sound cruel, but it makes him think, 'I don't want to go there again.'" I said, "He may not respond, but he sees your call." Meanwhile, I texted 24/7. Later, Riley called me and told me he'd gotten their calls.

He went missing for a week in late July. I didn't know where he was. I texted and prayed, texted and prayed. One night, at midnight, he called, drunk. "Mom? I'm at the bus station. Can you come get me?" I packed up the dog. He was ten minutes away, thank God. He looked like hell. His shoes were off because his feet were swollen. He told me he'd been walking around town. I said, "Don't you realize yet it's not working? Come home and sleep." I let him sleep. I fed him. I said, "I gotta walk the dog." When I returned home he was gone again. Then it was August.

He was getting alcohol from friends; well, not friends. Bums. Homeless people who were kicked out and knew Riley from his homeless days. He'd get drunk with them and, ironically, lecture them about staying on their medication. It was the second or third week of August and his drinking binge was still going strong. It was the same thing. He'd come home, go to bed. I'd see him maybe two days. The rest of the time I didn't know where he was. I prayed. I know I have no control. You must relinquish to a higher power. I'd pray and non-stop text. Even though he didn't respond, I knew he read them.

I managed to convince him to get his shots even though he didn't take his other meds. The shots he gets every two weeks keep him from going full-blown psychotic and getting into big trouble. But this was a three-month relapse that was quite significant, and he was damaging his brain further by being off meds that help him keep clarity. Still, he was confused and drinking and self-medicating. I texted him, "Obviously this isn't working. No judgment. How about we meet and talk? I love you. You can overcome this!"

His birthday is on the eighteenth. On August seventeenth, he called at eight o'clock at night, surprisingly, not too late. He said, "I thought about what you said. Meet me at the water park," which is where he and his friends used to smoke pot as teenagers. I met him there. He was barefoot. His feet were beat up, bruised, and swollen. He was pretty out of it and exhausted. No sleep for a week. He looked at me and tears welled up in my eyes.

I said, "What do you want to do?"

He said, "Well, you're right. All these years I've been doing it my way trying to make it work, and you're right. It's not working. I'm willing to do what you say."

He's never said anything like this to me before. I cried. I got him in the car and said, "Let's go home, get you cleaned up." He slept for two days. We got him a birthday cake. Nothing fabulous this time, because I barely had any money.

*It may seem shocking to learn Tessa's wish for her son to predecease her. But harboring this sentiment is not uncommon for a parent whose adult child lives with persistent mental illness, and it is one borne from genuine compassion. Who can bear the thought of the many scenarios in which an ill person will undoubtedly suffer without the caring advocacy that only a parent or loved one can provide? In many cases, there is but one responsible adult who holds the medical and personal history, and the trust of one who lives with mental illness. For Riley, that person is Tessa. After all that Riley has experienced, it is understandable that she wants always to be there for him. One can only imagine what may have been Riley's fate had she not advocated for his release from jail, insisted he continue to receive his shots, and been the one to make the calls and arrangements for all of his treatments, and the list goes on.*

*Though Tessa is blunt about most things, it hasn't been easy for her to be honest about her son's mental health. As she confesses, she was initially in denial about her son's diagnosis because no one ever wishes for a mental illness diagnosis. Maybe it was because she didn't want people to judge her or her parenting. Her fierce mettle does emerge later as she recognizes her denial, accepts his illness, and advocates for him. For many caregivers, these stages of denial and acceptance are part of the long journey with serious mental illness. It is a testament to Tessa's character that she acknowledges her denial and the ways it may have hindered her ability to help Riley.*

*Readers may feel that Tessa is still in denial about her son's drinking and aggression. She says Riley would never hurt her, yet he has a history of aggression and verbal abuse, some of which has been directed toward her. An example of contradiction can be noted when Tessa tries to emphasize to his father the extent of his illness and psychosis and says, "I'm afraid he's going to hurt someone." In fact, Riley has often been verbally abusive, always coincident with drinking and medication noncompliance. It is likely Tessa underplays his violent tendencies because she knows that even when provoked, he is more likely to be victimized than to harm another. She also makes the distinction between behaviors of the non-medicated drunk version of her son, "that's mental illness" or "that's the alcohol," from the person she knows him to be when he is in recovery and sober. Many parents are justifiably sensitive about their child's violent behaviors for fear of stigma, and specifically societal misperceptions about the confluence of violent behavior and mental illness.*

*Tessa knows she cannot control her son, only support and encourage him. In Riley's case, any step toward ongoing recovery is progress. She is realistic he will likely have relapses. Most remarkable about Tessa is that she carries the hope for him until he can on his own volition.*

# PART II

*From a parent's worst fear to hope,*
*recovery, and coping.*

*Parents of children who live with persistent mental illness grieve*
*the loss of the person they once knew. Severe brain disorders tem-*
*porarily or permanently rob talent, skill, and personality traits*
*that once defined a vibrant individual. Treatment may restore*
*some qualities over time.*

*Sadly, self-inflicted violence is a painful reality for those*
*living with brain disorders. Though many believe a person with*
*mental illness is likely to inflict violence, statistics indicate that*
*a person with a brain disorder is more likely to be victimized or*
*endanger himself. In 2007, the most recent year for which there*
*are statistics, there were almost 35,000 suicides, nearly twice the*
*rate of homicides.[21] Suicide rates are highest for those whose risk*
*factors include mental illness and substance use.*

*But while a parent of a child diagnosed with mental illness*
*must move through a challenging journey that evokes grief, one can*
*also find hope and gratitude. In the stories in Part II, Catherine*
*tells her devastating story. A loving, doting mother, she does the*
*best she can for each of her twin sons, from making a family din-*
*ner every night to creating one-on-one time with each of them. But*
*without the support of family and community, she cannot save her*
*son. Nathalie and Delia found hope with appropriate treatment for*
*their daughter and their family. Dan and Rebecca work together,*
*exemplify parental patience, and find their own individual ways to*
*cope. In their own ways, they each find gratitude.*

*Meet the parents.*
*    **Catherine** is an accomplished scholar in her field and a*

*clear and direct thinker in other aspects of her life. Even while grieving deeply, she is warm and forthcoming and is a thoughtful and caring mother. Catherine possesses a lovely speaking voice. Her son Philip, a fraternal twin, was born in 1991 and died by suicide in 2010.*

***Nathalie and Delia's*** *more than twenty years together is evidenced by the manner in which they sit angled toward one another on the couch and occasionally hold hands during emotional portions of their interview. Nathalie, a pastor, is neat, professional, and dressed conservatively. She has a practical, even-keeled approach, which she may attribute to her Midwestern upbringing. Delia, a nurse, is slim and fit, and when she communicates with others, she is fully engaged, connected, and visually expressive. Both share a glowing complexion that seems to come from a place of inner strength. Gianna is their daughter.*

***Dan and Rebecca*** *are a formidable team. Both are hardworking and accomplished and laugh easily. Dan is practical, a deep thinker, and a little fidgety when talking about himself. Rebecca, a teacher, is intelligent, thoughtful, and outgoing. She is warm and responsive to others. Together, they are supportive and generous. Stella is the younger of their two daughters.*

# CHAPTER SIX: CATHERINE AND PHILIP

*Remembering Philip and the isolation
of mental illness.*

*1991 – 2010*

*We contacted Catherine after another family member directed us to the poignant obituary written for Philip. What drew us all to this announcement were the copious accomplishments that showed intelligence, compassion, and worldliness for a young man of only nineteen, alongside mention of his mental health struggles. We were struck by such honesty. It seemed to us that inclusion of all the facets of Philip's life was a beautifully genuine tribute to his life and reflected that he was well loved, which turned out to be true even if those who cared deeply about him were challenged as to how to help him.*

*We also saw the mention of his struggle to be an indication that one of his parents may be willing to speak about their experiences with Philip. We knew that hearing their story would be deeply insightful. We approached Philip's parents by postal mail with a promise we would not follow up on our request and that there was no time limit to respond. Catherine's email response came surprisingly soon, and we set a time to meet at her home shortly thereafter.*

*We arrived early for our first meeting with Catherine and were kept company by one of her friendly cats as we waited on her porch from which we had a lovely view overlooking the immediate neighborhood and a portion of the vibrant city. Catherine appeared minutes later carrying a grocery bag filled with fresh apples, oranges, and tea biscuits she later served with hot tea. It was a late afternoon in March when we met.*

*She warmly welcomed us into a large sitting and dining area of her beautiful, family-worn, 1930s-style home that, despite an open floor plan, was dimly lit without direct sun and made darker by the mahogany wood mantel and trim throughout the room. The living area was festooned with photographs of her late son in frames, loosely pinned or arranged on poster boards. She waved her arm indicating they'd been put up during the funeral that had taken place only two months before and welcomed us to view them, narrating the significance of a few. Many photographs showed Philip with other family members, mostly his twin brother William, from toddlerhood to young manhood.*

*We settled into one end of a sturdy, family-sized dining table covered for our benefit by a cloth. Despite her deep grief, Catherine made us feel immediately at ease. But her sadness was palpable. As she began to tell her story, we were mesmerized by the warmth and clarity of voice conflated with her expressions of deep longing and loneliness. As the hours passed, without our notice, outside and in the house it had grown colder, and by the end of her story we were sitting in darkness.*

*This is Catherine's story.*

**CATHERINE:** We did a lot of family things.

My poor son.

Philip's diagnosis was schizoaffective disorder. Schizoaffective disorder has a big dollop of depression, which I think he had. I mean, who doesn't? He clearly had problems with reality. He was never manic. Doctors didn't want to go all the way up to schizophrenia. Since this was new to me, I didn't know what the subtle criteria were in that spectrum. Now I think he was more schizophrenic.

Everyone said if I could get him to twenty-two or twenty-three, he would get better. When they're younger, they can't see a way out. They can't see if their minds are going to get any better.

Philip turned nineteen in November and killed himself in January. Two months.

For his funeral, we put up pictures from when he and his twin were little tots in England. He was a young, angelic lad. There's this picture, taken by a colleague's wife, where I'm holding Philip and he's holding a picture and looking at the photographer. I love that one. The picture of Philip in the red sweater was taken last summer at my sister's farm. He's looking a bit more disturbed in the face. That picture is an example of him not doing well. He looked like that a lot in the last six months.

We thought Philip and Will were identical twins—one sac, one cord, and everything. But Philip, throughout his whole life, was different than his brother. Philip had a larger frame, more like his dad. William has a smaller frame like me, and he doesn't show any evidence of schizophrenia.

They went to English schools for three years. In kindergarten, in England, Philip kept to himself on the playground. Skipped around by himself. We thought it a little odd that he didn't muck in with the others, but he seemed very content. He had friends and went to birthday parties. They shared friends because they were twins. When friends came over they were always together, but it became clear throughout his youth that his twin fronted him, that if they walked in the room, Will did the talking. Many twins have an extrovert, one who does the talking. We just said Philip is the quiet one. So that was okay.

Philip did well in school. He did fine wherever we put him. He used to say he was a slow reader, but he always did well in school. His handwriting was dreadful so we had him do little handwriting exercises. We taught him how to type. I gave him books to practice letters, but his handwriting was still almost illegible. Will's handwriting wasn't that good either, but given I had twins, there was a developmental comparison available to me. Will's handwriting did get more legible, whereas Philip's

117

did not. In fact, his got worse and ended up in a scratching-like shorthand. He could read it, but nobody else could. Though we were in the States during their middle grades, we returned to England for their ninth grade where the teachers really dinged him on penmanship. He got a lot of points off in high school for his handwriting. He seemed not to care. Or maybe that was another signal that he wanted to do his own thing. He was very much into being an individual. He didn't seem to have the same social pressures other boys had. He had some friends. One friend who was also new that year was a chorister. He went to chorister events with that friend, which he enjoyed, but he was always reserved.

Things started going bad in ninth grade in England. I didn't think he was mentally ill, but I did think something was up because he would be *angry. Really angry.* One time I was picking him up at school. I rode my bike to get him and we had stuff to carry. It was early December, the beginning of the holidays. In England, you have all this PE stuff to carry. I was struggling to carry it all in the basket. He was ahead of me. I said to Philip, "Could you help me?" He was livid. Inappropriately angry. I remember thinking, "My God! He's going to kill me! He's so angry and it's just not needed." It was uncontrolled anger. And he wouldn't help. He would also walk out of the room a lot. He seemed unhappy.

The twins had mutual friends from their all-boys school in England. I remember one time they were playing tennis with their friend, Simon. I'd gone off, and when I returned I saw that Philip was really angry with Simon. It wasn't like him. It wasn't like either of my sons. We weren't a family that got angry. At least, I didn't think we were.

We returned to the States after ninth grade and they went to a big public school with people of all shapes and sizes. Philip's friends from his previous American school, which he had loved, went there too. Philip had loved his second-through-eighth-grade school that he attended in the States. It was a small, kind of eclectic, very intellectual school where he fit in. It worked for him. When he was in high school, he kept saying, "I wish I could go back to grade school." But throughout most of high school he seemed fine. He seemed to have friends, although Will was always the initiator. Philip would watch soccer games with various people at their houses, but not a lot. He spent most of his time at home. He read a lot. He had these huge books from a twelve-volume set and he read seven of them—fantasy books or something. He read those and played video games. Will was never interested in video games, so Philip had a lot of alone time. He always got his work done and he was a good student.

But he didn't always help out at home. Every once in a while I would ask them to sweep or clip the hedges, and Will would help but Philip would say, "No! I'm not!" in a really adamant way. Setting his limits. I let him do that. It was only later that these incidents became more manifest and linked to his illness—the walking out on people, the yelling and saying, "I don't want to do things." Making up pronouncements about me or whoever happened to be around. Those incidents increased over time. By his senior year, during which he was seventeen, it was becoming clear he was having a hard time.

Because they are twins, they were always together, and I thought I'd take each boy on a weekend trip. Will wanted to hike and camp, while Philip chose to ski. Philip and I stayed in a large, communal dormitory-style mountain lodge. One night we were playing Ping-Pong and he couldn't cope. He sat down, put his head in his hands, and wanted to talk. But he couldn't get a sentence out. It was always half a sentence and then he would stop. That was really difficult for me. He would try to talk but he couldn't finish any thought. I tried different pathways and strategies to get him to talk. "Philip, let's try and talk a different way." I kept trying ways to get him to feel more comfortable. I kept trying. I'd say it different ways. I still never got a statement about what was going on in his mind so it was clear to me, if you could call it clear, that he couldn't express what was very emotionally important to him.

He also didn't want to ski with me. I'd watch him ski. Then I'd go by myself. We were skiing on the same slope, but we wouldn't ski together. He did a lot of these kinds of pushing away, which was sad. I would have rather been buddies and chatting and hanging together and playing Ping-Pong and having a good time. That was kind of disturbing.

We came back and he seemed sort of distraught. Will told me recently that he remembered Philip coming home very upset after that weekend. I am aware that in our family the subtext was that "Philip couldn't relate to Mom." That was the feeling I got, and I tried to take it in stride and told myself that's the way life is. Sometimes you're closer to some children than to others. It made me sad, but I hung on.

During his junior year, he wandered a lot. He'd go off in the middle of the night and ride his bike, into the fog, the high hills, and would come home at one or two in the morning. I didn't restrict his freedom because I knew he wasn't doing drugs or hanging out with gangs. I didn't want to cramp his style. But Philip wandered and went off on these bike rides more frequently. The summer before senior year, both boys applied to a series of colleges and universities. Later that year, they were accepted into most all of them and were accepted to the same ones. There was one college to which Will applied that Philip did not because Will applied at the very last minute on the deadline. It was clear Philip couldn't possibly join Will there if he were to be accepted. Interestingly, Will did choose the one school to which Philip didn't and couldn't have applied. Philip chose a college in the Midwest. Both schools were far away and small. As far as we were concerned, both were good schools. They were both accepted into nearby Ivy League schools, and both declined. Once they chose their schools, they each arranged to take a gap year; they'd have one year off before entering college.

During senior year, Philip was less and less together. He
was increasingly disturbed, erratic, and angry. He was missing
school. We'd hear that he was out riding his bike. He'd cut class
and go riding. During lunch he was never on campus. He'd go
off by himself, which I didn't think sounded good at all. Real
loner. I was increasingly asking Will to check on him, "Find
him at lunch." But Will was having his own struggles with
girlfriends or this and that.

I was worried because that winter of their senior year
the two boys and their friend, a foreign exchange student,
were making plans to travel around Europe the summer after
graduation. They were planning to backpack to youth hostels.
I'm an archaeologist, and that summer I was going to Bolivia
where I was doing fieldwork, and my then-husband, Nigel, was
heading overseas for his work. I was worried because, by then,
Philip would walk away from us all the time. During his senior
year he was so disturbed that we finally decided it wouldn't be
good for him to go traveling because he'd often walk off in a
different direction. If Will was looking for a train, for example,
not paying close attention, Philip might wander off and they'd
miss the train because they'd have to go find him.

Nigel and I sat Philip down and told him he could either
go with Mum or with Dad in the field for the summer. Later,
we'd see about what to do in the fall. They were all set with their
gap year plans that spanned from September to the following
August when they'd start college. We owned a house in England
that we rented out. A room had become available, and we
arranged for the boys to stay there during their gap year. They
were both going to work in Cambridge and they'd also be near
their half-brother, various family members, and friends they
knew from school over there.

But, for the summer, Will would travel, and Philip chose
to come with me into the field. When they were very young, I
worked a lot on my husband's project overseas when he first
started it so we could all be together. I did that until my husband

took a full-time teaching position. Then I stopped working on his project and went full time back to my own work. Will and Philip went with me to Bolivia bunches of times. Even when they were four, they traveled down there with us, rustic as it was. Philip chose to come with me that summer instead of traveling with his brother.

They graduated the fourteenth of June. The plan was: I'd leave first because I had to initiate my field project. Philip would come a week later with one of my students, and they would travel together. Nigel was going to his work site overseas, and Will was flying to England and then Germany to meet his friend. Everyone was doing what had been planned except for Philip.

Then, two days after I had left for Bolivia, my husband rang me there and said, "I told the boys last night and I'm telling you right now, I'm leaving you. I'm filing for divorce next week. I'm moving out tomorrow. I'm taking a sabbatical and going to live with my girlfriend who I've been living with on and off near the university for the last six months. We have nothing more to say to each other. I've sent you an email that says it all. Goodbye."

My then-husband had a history of erratic behavior and also had mental health problems, I believe. He was often irrational, and I always held down the fort to give my sons a stable life. He was always going away and coming back and going all over. So I thought he was just nuts again. Once, years ago, while I was in the field, he had called and said, "I'm giving our house to my father. I'm going to call you tomorrow and see what you think." At the time, I thought, "I'm going home because things are weird." I had an assistant that year that I left in charge at the worksite. I went home to calm Nigel down. His sons tried to calm him down too, and finally he came back. He said he was putting his ring on again. He said he was back and everything was okay again.

Now, my son was already quite vulnerable. He was at

home, alone, and wouldn't be meeting me for a week. So again, like the last time, I rushed home from Bolivia. My field team agreed to continue without me. I flew home the next day. It's a really long flight, and we landed at eleven at night; I got a cab and rushed home. The lights were all off. I stomped up the steps and opened the door. I found Philip as if his father had just left him—with one light on in the kitchen, hovering like a rabbit. Nigel had cleared out after he learned from Philip that I was returning.

Nigel was not only saying, "I'm leaving your mother," but Nigel was leaving Philip, too, which is heartbreaking for a son. Nigel and his girlfriend flew to Europe on June twenty-fifth without plans to return until September the following year. Without my knowledge, Nigel also had planned for my sons to be in England when he would be there with his girlfriend. The family would all be together without me.

Upon my return from Bolivia, Philip and I sat at home for a few weeks. We hung on. I got a lawyer. I had already rented out our house for the summer so we had to leave. The people working in Bolivia on my project suggested we come down there to the countryside. We flew to Bolivia. We clung to each other.

Philip would never before go to a therapist. Will had been going to one all senior year. The minute Nigel left, Philip decided he wanted to see a therapist and did for those few weeks. I worked it out that once we were in Bolivia, Philip would call once a week. Phones are kind of funky down there. We were in the countryside and you had to walk up a hill to get reception. On Wednesdays, at one o'clock, he would walk up the hill and sit on a rock pile by a field and talk on the phone for an hour to his therapist. It seemed to be a good thing to have a link to a therapist. He didn't really talk to me. I mean, he did talk. Mostly, he watched me fall apart. I cried a lot because I learned slowly about all the things that had happened during my marriage. Philip finally announced that he had realized his father was having affairs. There was a lot of pressure on Philip—added to that of having just graduated and figuring out college and all those issues.

Over that summer, Will was barely hanging on too, walking around Europe exhausted. I'd said to him over the phone, "You'll feel exhausted. This is really traumatic for you, darling. We'll be together soon." We all got through the summer and met in England. That's a traditional thing; we'd all come back from the field toward the end of the summer and meet up in England. Nigel would come from his work site. Well, obviously, that summer he was not going to come back. The boys had both decided they didn't want to sit in England by themselves during their gap year, so I booked them tickets home. My sons' stepbrother from my ex-husband's first marriage was getting married in September and they were going to stay until after the wedding and then come home. I had to come home to teach, because my university starts at the end of August.

I had booked my ticket to go to the wedding in England while we were at the airport in Miami right before Philip and I got on the plane to La Paz. Philip said, "Yeah! Yippee!" He was really pleased I was going to join them and go to the wedding. At least that was the happiest I'd seen him. But the rest of the summer, Nigel kept emailing me saying, "You're not coming to the wedding. You're not allowed. You've been uninvited. Nobody wants you." I replied that my sons said they wanted me to attend, as did my stepson who was getting married. Back and forth, back and forth. He said, "You can't touch me, you can't look at me, you can't do this or that." It was awful and I was a mess. Philip tried to call his father a few times and yell at him, and his father yelled back and Nigel blamed me. That was stressful for Philip.

Toward the end of summer, Philip and I met up with Will in England and tried to have a normal holiday there, doing fun things we always liked to do. The boys decided they wanted that. Philip was glad to be with Will. The boys joined their friend and left to travel for two weeks. Of course I was terrified, but Will was watching Philip. There are a lot of pictures from that journey and he seemed sort of okay. He wandered off a lot so they had to watch him. He had problems, but he hadn't had his psychotic break yet.

At least I didn't think he had.

But when I look back, I remember that while we were in Bolivia, he didn't want to dig with the team although he knew them. I would ask, "Do you want to dig with Mike?" Mike was this nice jolly lad. He'd say, "No! I'm making Mike mad. You can see that he is mad, you can see that I'm making him angry." Meanwhile, Mike's over there laughing. He was clearly not angry, but Philip thought he was. I thought, "That's really weird." When he did odd things, I'd think it was strange. But I didn't say to myself, "That's delusional." I didn't know the lingo. I didn't understand these were signs of not being connected with reality. That was what I saw happening that summer.

When did he have his big break? It may have been that summer. It may have been the previous spring. When he was traveling with Will and their buddy, I called them a lot. They would tell me Philip was saying crazy things. I wanted him back as soon as possible. I was so relieved when he returned I felt like I could protect him.

They came home in September and both got local part-time jobs. I was teaching. Philip was really low. We were all hanging on by our fingernails trying to work. We were all seeing therapists. That's when I started on antidepressants. Philip's therapist, Dr. C—, who he'd been seeing all summer and was seeing regularly—twice a week at that point—really wanted him on something. Philip wouldn't agree because his father was really not into medicine. I don't go 'round popping pills, but I needed something. I was a mess and I had to function. I had two kids, a job, and I had to function. Meanwhile, the newly estranged husband was on sabbatical in the fall in England, and for the winter he went to Paris so he was not seeing Philip's declining mental health.

I talked to Philip's therapist a lot. One night, she called me four times. There was a lot of communication between us. I had had a long talk with her that summer while they were in Europe and this communication continued because Philip was clearly coming unglued. But I didn't know it. And she didn't say it. She just kept saying, "We really want to get him on meds. This is getting to be a little bit more severe. He's very depressed. He's very angry."

I had asked Philip that summer, "What's the issue you talk about with your therapist?"

He'd said, "Anger. I'm angry all the time. I'm just angry at everybody."

"Are you angry at Grandma? At Will?"

"I'm angry at everybody."

His odd behavior continued to increase. He was wandering out of the room but also beginning a pattern of walking out while in the middle of a sentence. He'd be talking in the kitchen and then abruptly walk out. We finally got Philip on some drugs. He went to a psychiatrist who gave him something. I can't remember what, but they were meds I, of course, knew nothing about—so I researched them. The meds were hard for Philip to take. He didn't seem to do well on them, and eventually they switched his prescription.

It became a part-time job worrying about him. I'd rush home. Will was around so it was sort of okay. There was another kid around who was also on a gap year. They weren't totally alone. Philip was still playing soccer pickup games. He was sort of normal. He was doing jobs. But he was noticeably sinking, and the doctor was clear he needed to stay on meds. The psychiatrist thought that. But I didn't communicate with the psychiatrist much.

He was doing odd things. We had all agreed that the boys would cook dinner once a week. They weren't in school anymore. They could cook a meal once a week and I would help. That was my little plan for them to learn how to cook. Will's girlfriend would come over to help, and that probably made Philip upset. Then it was Philip's turn. He cooked once. He burned up two wooden spoons and things were all over. It was chaos in the kitchen. I tried to leave him on his own but it was nuts. He couldn't do it. I thought he was trying to be difficult. But now I know he was trying to cook. But he couldn't do it.

Will started working at an ESL school part time. Philip was working with a man gardening and landscaping. He'd come home with cuts all over. He popped his glasses off one day and they were never found. He was doing things you'd never expect of someone who is just gardening. Crazy things. His behavior didn't seem normal and the therapist called me a lot.

Once, in the fall, I had just gotten home from work and we were having tea. Philip sat down and said, "You know, I think we better call Dr. C— because I think I killed her."

I said, "How do you think you did that, Philip?"

"I said such true and strong things that if anybody heard them they would have been pierced by such a strong light that they would have realized their world was completely different and they would have committed suicide because it was so powerful. We have to drive to her house *right* now. We have to check to see if she is alive or dead."

I didn't know where she lived. "We'll call her," I said. "She's pretty good about answering her phone." I left a message, "Philip is worried that he killed you. Would you mind ringing?" She rang back pretty soon! I put him on the phone and they had a chat about that and talked about it the next day.

Later, she talked to me about it and asked, "Was he agitated?" Sometimes he'd do jittery stuff with his legs but wouldn't be up all night. He'd play computer games for three hours in a row or something. And he was doing odd things more frequently. Now I kind of know what was going on in hindsight. But it was clear to me by then that he wasn't doing well. But still, he was hanging in there, and I didn't realize he was mentally ill. Someone even said, "He seems sort of psychotic to me." I mentioned this to his psychiatrist, who said, "Absolutely not. He couldn't possibly be." So I thought, "Okay, I'm an idiot. I don't know. I'll say no more. I don't know what I'm talking about."

Then it was November. The plan had been that Will would go to Ghana in January to work in a school and then to India to volunteer there also. He would be gone for three months. He'd been saving money to buy his ticket and it was all planned. Philip wasn't going anywhere. That was quite clear. He kept going downhill in the fall and I didn't know what I was dealing with, other than the odd behavior.

December. My birthday is December seventh. Nigel decided and was emailing and calling the boys saying, "I can't live without seeing you. I want to visit you on the weekend of the sixth, seventh, and eighth. I'm in England and you're not here, and I want to come and visit you."

When the boys told me their father wanted to visit them during that weekend, I reminded them it was my birthday. "Do you think you could ask your dad, since he's not working, to come another weekend so you could be with me on my birthday? I'd really like you to be with me on my birthday." They said, "Yeah, we'd like that." As usual, it was always Will talking. Philip would sit there, he'd hear it, but he wouldn't talk. But this was stressful for them. Nigel made them have to say, "No, Dad." They were feeling pressured. I know Philip would feel pressured by that. He was always very sensitive about his father.

They went with their dad a different weekend. A rainy weekend. They came back and were quite low. Quiet. Low. After a few days, Will pulled himself up. He got back. Philip never pulled himself up again. Ever. He was low. Over that next weekend, after being with their father, they were quiet, did jigsaw puzzles. Then, the next weekend, we went to a cabin up north, on the coast. The three of us went first, then later Sophie, Will's girlfriend, and her mother had planned to join us.

The three of us—Philip, William, and I—went for a walk and looked at birds. I made sandwiches. We had eaten our lunch and started heading back. We stopped on the trail and I said, "Let's have a big hug! It's so nice to be with you two! We're off on an adventure—here we go!" Because it *was* a big new adventure: I was now alone, my husband had left me, and the boys were not in school anymore.

Then we continued walking. We were on this peninsula and there are cliffs along one side. There were no roads. The sun was going down early. It was December. The trailhead was three miles away. Philip asked Will for the water bottle. We stopped and Will gave it to him. I don't know if anything was even said, but Philip threw the bottle into the air. Really high up, and said something like, "Shit!" Then he took off running toward a cliff. He was wearing the red sweater [from that picture] so we were watching him and yelling. "Philip! Philip! It's all right! Come back!" He ran and disappeared. I totally panicked.

I went to the cliff and looked. He wasn't over the cliff. There were people sitting there, and I said, "Do you see him?" There were shrubs around. We looked for an hour. Then the sun was setting. We called for him. We looked through that whole peninsula. He clearly didn't want to be found. I was getting more panicked. We finally realized we'd better leave. So we yelled, "Philip! We are leaving! We are walking to the car now!" We shouted. We walked out, walking and walking, and suddenly we saw Philip off to the side and he joined us. He'd been ahead of us, actually. He walked toward us and we said, "Hi" and then left it.

Then came the crazy part. I had spoken to two people walking in. We didn't know them, but I said, "Did you see a guy in a red sweater?" They said, "No, but if we do, we'll let you know." We exchanged phone numbers. Ray was one man's name. I didn't know him, but I had gotten his name for emergency because there's nothing out there. After we saw Philip and we were walking out, I thought, "I better call Ray and let him know we found Philip."

Philip saw the phone and he became livid. He went ballistic. He yelled, "Give me that phone! Give me that phone!" I knew anything we'd give him he'd throw. A sweater. A water bottle. He ran away. I yelled, "Will! Grab him! Tackle him!" because it was getting dark. We both couldn't grab him, and we both fell. He ran and ran. We saw him way down by the beach, hiding behind a bush. I said to myself, "This is crazy. I'm not going all the way down there to coax him out." We yelled, "Philip! We are walking out to the car. See you there. We'll wait for you at the car."

We started walking. We could see, as it was getting dark, some movement, something red moved behind the bushes. We sat in the car and Philip finally got in, and we drove home and said nothing.

Later, our two guests, Sophie and her mother, arrived, and we made dinner together. That night, Philip went ballistic again. He screamed, "Will, if you leave, I'll murder someone! I'll kill you; I'll kill me!" He was overtly panicking about Will leaving in a month for his three-month trip. He threw things around.

We calmed him. We fed him. I was exhausted from the whole event on the cliffs. I called the psychiatrist and therapist. I'd been calling them whenever any incident happened, which around that time was quite frequent. They said, "As long as he's calm now . . . make sure he's taking his meds." You know, the usual riff. We've all heard it.

Then we went to bed. I slept through the night. But during the night Philip was awake, attacking William—physically attacking him. Everybody was awake, trying to take care of Philip. They tried to get me up but weren't able to rouse me. So I missed this. They were up all night. Philip was out of his mind. The next morning, we packed up and left. I called the therapist again.

That next night, at two in the morning, Will came into my room. "Mom! You've got to get up!" Philip was attacking Will again, throwing things at him and throwing *him*. Philip is bigger than Will. Philip was yelling, "You're with the wrong girl!" Philip was obsessed with a girl named Allison, who was in their class. Will liked Sophie. Will went to prom with Sophie; they'd hung out during the summer, and she had been Will's girlfriend for several months. Philip liked Allison and was furious that Will wasn't with Allison, which was weird. You'd think he'd be jealous.

I went into the room. "Philip! You've got to calm down!" But I couldn't talk rationally to him I thought, "What am I going to do? I can't control him!" I finally got him into bed. That was pretty scary. That happened before Christmas.

Another thing that was happening that year was that he kept wetting the bed. I had to work on his mattress, get all this cleaning stuff and get mattress covers. Some nights I was so tired. He'd wet the bed downstairs and wet the bed upstairs, so I'd have him just come up and sleep with me because I couldn't make up another bed. I spent a lot of time on the beds. He probably felt bad about wetting the bed. Anybody would. He was out of control.

Was that a psychotic break in December? I don't know.

We muddled through Christmas, somehow.

On New Year's Eve, I was in my sitting room. The boys were downstairs. Will was out with his girlfriend, but all his buddies were in the room downstairs. Philip would run up, and the boys would come up and get him and bring him down again. I think Philip was melted that night. He had gone on Facebook, and the next morning phone calls started coming in, saying, "You've got to look on Philip's Facebook page." I got a phone call from Nigel. "What's up with Philip? Look at his Facebook entries." Will showed me what he'd written. It was gobblygook. *I love Allison! Allison, I love you.* But the letters were wrong. It was like his fingers went in the wrong place. Fifteen, twenty, thirty entries. *World peace! We need world peace!* Allison saw it also and freaked out, didn't want to see him anymore, and cut him off. It was a big panic.

Again, I didn't get it. I didn't realize that was a psychotic break. But he was gone.

Then, January the sixth, I had two friends over, a man and woman, because it was Epiphany. Twelfth Night. We were sitting in the living room and Philip was upstairs. Suddenly, he started screaming. "You've got to get an ambulance! You've got to take me! I'm losing my mind!"

The next day, I had to give a talk at a conference. He was supposed to go to his psychiatrist at one o'clock that day. He had to go. I went to give the talk in the morning and then I called him. "Going to your psychiatrist? You have your bike, right?" It was just down the way, easy.

"Yeah, yeah," he said.

I had to go to a meeting, and afterward I called him again. "Did you go to your psychiatrist?" He said, "No, Mom, I didn't go. I called him up and said I was fine. But I figured something out. I killed my grandfather." He was talking about his father's father, Nigel's father, who had died two years before. He'd had a bad liver and was a mess physically and died. We'd been there the whole year before with the ailing grandfather during which the boys attended school in England. He'd interviewed his grandfather about his war years because they were studying WWII.

On the phone, Philip said, "I interviewed him, and the things I said to him made him realize he would kill himself." It was a repeat of this same kind of *I'm having control over other people.* I hung up and thought, "Oh shit! I don't know what to do! This is really beyond me."

I called my friend, Karen, who is a therapist. I told her what was going on and that I needed help with Philip because Nigel wasn't around to help. He was still in Paris with his girlfriend, Will was getting ready to travel, and I was going to start teaching in two weeks. I was scared to leave Philip at home alone because he was freaking out. There was no doubt about it. Ever since that weekend with his father, and that hiking walk by the cliffs in December, he'd been doing badly.

Karen told me there were day programs, and there was one nearby. I rang them up and asked for an appointment and got one on a Tuesday. I marched him in, filled out the forms, and they interviewed him. My health insurance covered it and they said, "Great, he starts tomorrow morning. Wednesday."

I thought, "Okay. This is great."

The program went from nine-thirty to three p.m. I took him there, and before I left, I told him I'd pick him up at three. I was in my office. It was the week before term, but I had to get ready for classes. They called me at one o'clock on the first day and said, "Philip has gone AWOL. He left. Just walked out." They called the psychiatrist and they called me.

"Oh, great," I said. I called Will at work. He had an afternoon job at a grade school. Philip was doing a lot of walking, running, and biking—all of it a frenetic expenditure. We drove around a while but figured he'd come home after a bit, and eventually he did. He walked in the door. We said, "Hi, Philip. How are you?"

The administrator at the day program said they would take him back but emphasized it wasn't appropriate behavior. I took him the next day and planned to stay an hour to talk to people because I didn't know the program. We arrived and Philip went into the room, and a social worker and a doctor took me into another room. "We need to talk to you," they said. It was the only time I met the doctor. They sat me down. "We think this is more. He needs to be admitted to the mental ward. He needs to be admitted *now*."

They left to talk to Philip. They came back and said, "Philip has agreed. What do you think?"

I burst into tears. I knew Philip was not doing well, but I didn't realize we'd really gone over the deep end. I mean, it was creeping up, all these things kept happening and happening. So I said, "Yes, of course! Clearly, if you think."

I talked to Philip briefly, and he said, "Yeah, Mom, those people in that group yesterday—I was *way* beyond them. That's where I was *months* ago."

I thought, "How perceptive is that?"

I walked out absolutely stunned. I went and got his stuff—underpants, T-shirts —and they told me the do's and the don'ts. I'd never been to a mental ward. They said, "You come at six-thirty. That's the visiting hour. You can bring his stuff."

I rushed over to visit him. There was a one to one-thirty and then a six-thirty to seven p.m. visiting hour, and I would rush to visit him every day. I contacted Nigel by email because I didn't have his Paris number. Nigel was only able to visit Philip in the mental ward one time during his three-day visit."

My son had crumbled over those six months. I watched him. I had been with him every day except for those few weeks in England. It was a gradual thing. I was not good myself, I can assure you. I was totally depressed because it was a surprise to me that my husband had been a philanderer and had left me. It felt like the whole world had known but me. All my colleagues knew about his infidelities because we were in the same discipline, and they'd seen him and hid it. They *all* hid it. I would hear another story, come home reeling, and end up in bed in a fetal position—and my son saw that. Philip was watching me fall apart, and I was watching him fall apart. He was clearly influenced by me, by my sadness. He'd see me crying. The whole thing was awful.

Philip had fallen apart and he was in the mental ward. He was in there for a month. Not, "He'll be there a week," like they said. He was in there for a *month*. He was bad. Really bad. I realized then I needed more information. The people in the ward told me I had to bone up on the illness, so I joined NAMI. I read books. I tried to learn all the medicines and about schizoaffective disorder, bipolar, schizophrenia, and the whole thing. I tried to learn as much as I could and to identify delusions. I talked to the therapist on the ward, and she told me that when he'd say, "I'm controlling everyone in the room," which he did in the ward, the therapist would say, "That's not reality. That's a delusion." They were aware he was having reality problems. But eventually the insurance couldn't cover anymore and they thought he was stable on his meds, so he came home and we sort of hung on.

Philip had new doctors and psychiatrists after he came out of the hospital and was in another program for three months. He was on an older-class antipsychotic and a newer-class one that also addresses depression. It was difficult. He'd still abruptly walk out of the room. He'd say really insightful things but then insane things. Like, out of context he'd say, "You're always so defensive. You're always so negative, Mom." All the things he used to hear his father say to me, like he was mimicking his father to me. That was difficult for me.

During that whole last year he wanted to go to church, so we went for a while. He used to meditate. While in high school, he'd go to meditation centers and had been very serious about that. We even looked online in the summer for him to go to a meditation place. Then it was the Episcopal Church. We're Episcopalian if we're anything—the Church of England to be more precise. Then he wanted to become a pastor and help people. He kept going from one thing to another. In the ward, he met a Black Muslim. He wanted to read the Koran. He was studying that. That was fine, cool. That was good. We accommodate.

Philip was living at home, with me. We got him involved in volunteering at a church garden. We got him on a program to walk dogs. He would ride his bike or I would drive him up the hill to get to his volunteer jobs or to therapy. He had something to do every day. That seemed to keep him. He was home, safe. Of course he didn't do anything else. He didn't go out with anybody. We used to watch movies a lot together, especially in

Bolivia. We used to have this little ritual of watching movies every night down there. I tried to get him to watch movies again, but he stopped doing that because he just couldn't get through a movie anymore.

His father visited twice during the spring. Once he stayed for two weeks because he was in town to deal with a legal matter. During one of Nigel's visits during that first year when he was living in Paris, he took Philip on a college tour. He made Philip tour around, talked about getting into the honors college and all this stuff. I thought, "What the fuck! Philip can't even work! What are you doing?" But I wasn't going to say anything because I wasn't getting along with my husband. Once again, my son was put into the position where he had to say, "Dad, I'm not going to college this spring."

Then I got through teaching that spring and Will came home. Nigel was still away. We hung on. During the summer, I took Will and Philip traveling. First they went to my sister's farm for a few days. They worked in her garden and rode bikes. I guess it was okay. They did all right. They took a lot of pictures from that visit that I still have. Then I took them to Italy. Philip loved the water, and we went swimming in the Adriatic.

They were both really big on Latin. In fact, in sixth grade, Philip got a Latin award in England. I mean, with all the British scholars studying Latin and yet he's the one who got the award! I thought, "Philip likes Latin, I guess!" Ding! A light went on when I got to the ceremony and he won the award! After that, I got them a tutor and they had both studied Latin for seven years by the time they'd graduated from high school, and ancient Greek as well. I'd taken them to Rome before because I thought it was something they'd like, and they could read the little inscriptions. I thought I'd take them again that summer.

We went to Rome. Philip coped. He went around the Forum, but kind of fell apart there. There were too many people. I was beginning to realize: crowds were a problem for Philip, and we needed to protect him from that. The day we went to the Sistine Chapel, he stayed in the hotel room, a dark room. He could lie there all day, which I guess is what he did, and went for a walk. That was the only bad day. I left him for about four hours. But then I rushed back.

After Rome, we went to England and saw various family members. Philip seemed to be hanging in there. I made sure he took his meds. That was kind of a good time. Of course he was around his family and brother. While we were there, the boys saw their father for four days when all three went on a family excursion. Then, in late summer, we came back to the States. Nigel stayed overseas.

When we came back from that trip, it was really bad. Philip wouldn't do anything. He wouldn't do any of his volunteer things. He wouldn't go out. He started to just play games. He bought an Xbox that I helped him get on eBay. He'd buy about twenty videos at a time. Nuts. Nutty things. But I let him. He had money from when he was working. He'd sit in his room day after day. I couldn't get him out.

His father was back in the States by early September. He visited Philip. Philip went on walks with his father, but he didn't do anything else. He played video games and also started listening to pop music a lot. He'd play the same song like twenty, thirty, forty times. I don't know how many other parents have experienced that happy event. But I let him.

Philip and I took Will to college. I have a photo of us all saying goodbye to Will, and Philip looked terrible. Philip was really upset by Will being away. He'd call Will once or twice a day, which he'd always done, even from the mental ward.

I was teaching again. I'd cook Philip dinner and lunch. I made him a cooked breakfast every morning because that is what he got used to in the mental ward. I'd call him during the day if I had to teach. I made sure he took his meds. It wasn't good, though. It was bad. I'd go to my therapist to talk about me, but all I talked about was Philip. I was so worried about him. I didn't know what to do.

Philip was going to a drama therapist whom he'd met on the ward. Nigel had set it up for him to go once a week. Nigel said, "He'll take public transit, no problem." Well, Philip took the train once and he couldn't cope. I realized he couldn't handle that kind of people bombardment. Not possible. Sometimes he could ride his bike there. Usually I drove him to those appointments and sat in the car and worked for an hour. But this became a pattern: Nigel would set him up to do something that he couldn't do. I could drive him, but I couldn't *always* do it. Nigel would want Philip to take the train to visit him. That wasn't going to happen. Fortunately, between Nigel and Philip, they'd eventually work out that Nigel would come and get him.

Increasingly, Philip was less and less able to do anything out there in the world. I took care of him. Sometimes I would take him food shopping just because I didn't want him to be alone. I got kittens so there would be loving things in the house and he wouldn't be alone. He could play with them. I rushed home for lunch. He didn't want to go out, and he certainly wasn't able to work. He didn't even want to volunteer at the church anymore.

Meanwhile, all through the fall, Nigel was planning to take Philip to England for two weeks to have fun and see family. They would go from December fifth to the twenty-first. I sat down with Philip and said, "Gee, Philip, December seventh is my birthday. In fact, it's my sixtieth birthday. Do you think you could delay your trip until the day after so I could have my birthday with you?" Once again, for the second year, he had to go to his dad and say, "Dad, it's my mom's birthday and I'd like to spend it with her." Philip had to choose. He'd been put in that position again.

I came home from teaching on a Wednesday in October. He'd left early that day to ride his bike to drama therapy. He had said he was going to leave at eight-thirty. I had said, "Philip, you're a little late. Shouldn't I drive you? I'm happy to drive you and then go to work."

He said, "No, no, no. I'm fine. I'll do it." He was very agitated. I wasn't going to fight.

I called him at noon at home. "How was drama therapy?"

"Fine," he said.

I reminded him to get lunch and that I'd be home after five when my class was out. I got home and knew there was something up. Newspapers weren't picked up, which is normally what he would do. His bike wasn't in the garage. I went into the house and called, "Philip! Philip!" I thought maybe he'd gone on a bike ride. But that was unusual because he wasn't doing his rides anymore. I went upstairs and found him in his bed. He'd often take naps if he was agitated.

I went to him. "What's up, darling? Are you okay?"

He put his hand up and it was covered in blood, and there was more on his face. I thought, "Oh, shit, maybe he got into a bike accident." I looked closer and all around the room, and saw the bloody knife. I saw then that he'd sliced his left wrist and it had dried. He must have paced around the chair because there was a circle of blood droplets. Blood all over I still haven't been able to get out. Blood in the chair like he'd sat there a long time. On the table was a carton opened up and an empty pill bottle. He'd gotten a bottle of his antipsychotic meds—thirty days' worth—and taken them all. I went into the bathroom later and found all kinds of much worse meds he'd gotten out. He later admitted he'd gotten those out but had only taken his own.

I called 911, and the cops arrived. I was terrified. I didn't know how close he was to death. He was moaning. He was responding to questions, but badly. They rushed him to the hospital. Ten officers were all around the place taking photos. I was numb. I followed them to the hospital, bringing his things, and stayed all night. They sewed him up. He hadn't cut his nerves. The poison group they called decided it was best not to pump his stomach. They let the drugs work through his system. Eventually, I guess eleven o'clock at night, he was taken back to the place he'd been before—the adult ward this time, because now he was a month away from being nineteen. He was there for about a week.

I went to pick him up. He'd been really weird and cagey to me. I arrived with my bag to carry his stuff. He wanted to go straight to family therapy. Throughout this whole struggle with Philip, beginning when Nigel left, I'd found a family therapist to deal with the family breaking up and the father and husband going away. We met in various combinations. Even Nigel went with Philip a few times. I had said to Nigel the very first summer after he'd left, "Obviously this is traumatic. Why don't we all go to a therapist? This is really bad." At that time, Nigel had responded, "You guys go to therapy! I'm fine! I don't need anything!" But later, Nigel did go with Philip and William a few times. I don't know what they talked about.

I picked Philip up and drove him to the therapist. Unbeknownst to me, the plan was that Philip would announce to me, and he did, that he was going to live with his father. He wasn't going to live with me. Not only that, but his father was hiding around the corner. So when we left the therapist, Philip got in his father's car and drove back home to get his belongings. Nigel had done this before when the boys were eight, and I had to spend Christmas with his whole family without him while he was with his girlfriend.

I was distraught. Everyone had known the plan but me. The doctors knew. I kept saying to the doctors when he was leaving the mental ward, "Is he going to be in this program? What's next?"

They kept saying, "Philip will tell you."

"But what's happening next?" I asked.

"Philip will tell you." But they *all* knew. This was exactly how it had happened when my husband left me and everyone seemed to know but me. I started crying, and his therapist kept saying, "Philip has been brave! He wanted to tell you himself." But the whole scene was weird.

Philip came back to the house and I helped him pack his

stuff, and he left. It turns out he stayed with his father only three nights. *Three.* His father got him into a group home. Some free setup. It was called Franklin House because it was on Franklin. It had four bedrooms, and there were three or four other people living there and in the program who were all different ages and genders. But that program had nobody there at night. *Nobody watching them at night.* Someone came once a week to shop for food, and they had to cook for themselves. Philip said, "I'm going to come home on the weekends."

I saw him on the weekends, or various bits and pieces. Will came home from school for my father's ninetieth birthday party. Philip came to stay as well, and we all hung out together. We went to the party and back and forth. It was kind of erratic, but he was in this program that he liked, which is good because at least he was in a steady program again. Then I got this phone call from Nigel in November, before Thanksgiving.

"We just had a meeting. I was invited into a meeting with a therapist this morning, and he's been admitted into the emergency room again because it turns out he hasn't been taking his meds for the last month."

In this house . . . because there wasn't anybody watching him. *I* could see him not taking any meds. If anyone had asked me, which they didn't—they didn't even correspond with me and I had to seek them out—I could have helped him. But they didn't get the signatures and wouldn't talk to me, the woman who'd been taking care of her sick son for the last year and a half.

I know Philip was really upset, and he clearly wasn't taking the medicine seriously. I don't know if Nigel gave him support on that or not because Nigel, all along, had been telling his family and other people that I was making up the fact that Philip was ill for my own reasons. Nigel didn't believe he was ill. "Philip is just agitated and depressed. Philip is not ill." Nigel kept saying, "If we just get him on the right track, get him his own apartment, get him into college, he'll be fine!"

When I visited Nigel's family the previous summer, they had said, "Nigel has been saying Philip's not ill. Why are you saying he's ill? What is it with you, Cate? Why are you spreading this?" I realized that this group of people decided *I* was sick and was using my son for my own devices, which was very hurtful. Philip was a mess, and my husband was writing and saying, "He's not ill; he's not ill! Why are you making this up, saying he's delusional?" I was in an awful place. I was losing it.

I've acknowledged that at first I didn't get it. I didn't get that he was delusional. I didn't get this stuff. Then finally the doctor sat me down when he was in the mental ward for a month and said, "NAMI, books, you have *got* to get caught up on this. You have crossed over to a new realm. You are now in the club of having a mentally ill son. In fact, a *very* mentally ill son. Serious." I'd go see my therapist and they'd say, "Very mentally ill. Serious."

But now Philip was under Nigel's wing. I was out of it. Nobody was watching him and he didn't take his meds for a month, not since he had gone to live near his father. He ended up in the emergency room. I called the emergency room. "Where is he going? I'm coming down."

I got down at seven because I had an afternoon class. He was in the emergency room for *hours*. They couldn't find a place for him. I said, "Why doesn't he go where he went the first time? He knows those doctors and staff; they know him. At least it's familiar . . ."

Right away that hospital said yes. It turns out these mental wards don't take just anyone. They like to take people they know or something. I drove all the way back alone in my car because they don't let you take an ill person. They have to paramedic them. Philip came all the way back.

Because he was off his meds, he had said, "I don't know what I'm going to do to myself." They thought he was a threat to himself. But this therapist who would write to me—she was very good about writing me emails once I'd sought her out—

made it very clear to me that she never thought he was going to try to kill himself again. But she kept telling Nigel that his situation was serious. She'd say, "I tell Nigel constantly that this is not a joke. We don't sweep attempted suicide under the rug." Again, it was pretty clear from that comment that Nigel was acting like, "Oh, that was just being with his mom. That's nothing. He's not really sick."

Philip was back in the ward around Thanksgiving. I finally wrote Nigel and asked, "What's up with that trip? He's in the mental ward. I'm not so sure he can fly on December eighth." I'd thought the trip was crazy but also thought maybe it'd be okay since he'd be with family and friends. But the plan was for Philip to fly with Nigel there, but fly back *by himself.* I kept saying, "Oh, shit! This is not good!" By this point, I knew my son was very ill. This was the padded-cell-protective stuff. You don't just let him go around on his own. I was terrified for Philip. Then Nigel bought him a plane ticket to Ghana in January because Will had done that. Nigel assumed Philip could volunteer in a school and go to Ghana! Because he's normal, isn't he? It's just me . . . his mother . . . saying he's *not* normal!

It was escalating.

Philip was getting all this pressure to be "normal." Nigel was also starting to teach Philip to drive. Will had gotten his driving license during his gap year, and Philip had stopped driving. Nigel was pushing him to practice driving and get his learner's permit. Nigel also bought him tickets to go to a professional soccer game in December with his brother. You know, big crowds. Roar! I was like, "Oh God! I don't think my son can do *any* of this at this point." But I said nothing because it would look like I was fomenting stuff. I kind of kept quiet.

It was December first and Philip was still in the ward, and I confronted Nigel that maybe Philip couldn't go on that trip to England and fly back alone. Nigel finally wrote back and said, "Yes, I've cancelled the tickets to England. It turns out the therapist didn't want me to do that anyway." The therapist wrote and said, "We've been saying ever since Philip got here that he shouldn't go to England."

Poor Philip had to deal with these issues. Ever since Nigel had gotten back, he'd been fomenting this conflict for Philip: "You're good, you're okay! Let's get you into junior college! Let's get an apartment for you! Let's get that driver's license!" He got Philip driving lessons for Christmas. It didn't stop. Philip had to keep saying, "Dad, I can't do that, can't live in an apartment. I can't go to college. Dad, I can't drive. I can't go to England." I don't think that helped Philip's mental state at all, personally. That was incredibly sad for me to watch, and it must have been difficult for Philip. That was all going on throughout this whole time. The day Philip died by suicide, he told his father, "Thanks, Dad. I can't use these driving lessons. I cannot take these driving lessons."

Philip came out of the mental ward on my birthday. I brought him home and he had dinner with me. I took him the next day to the group house and he checked back in. I had a long talk with the therapist and we got caught up. I said, "You have to be watching him at night. You have to be there to make sure he takes the drugs." But she said he was not going to be checked. They were *not* going to check him at night.

Nigel wrote, "I'll check on him at night."

So Philip was living near Nigel. I called him every day. Then Nigel left on the twentieth for England. The boys were with me. We went to my parents' house for Christmas.

Also going on at this time was that whenever Philip was upset or trying to be normal, he would vomit. He'd eat dinner, and if he was in a place where he was trying to be normal and he couldn't cope, he'd go vomit. He did that a lot. His brother came to visit him in December and he vomited the whole time. If someone were here for dinner, he would vomit. I had to be very careful about the vomiting. All this is to say that around Christmas I didn't have anyone over. He made it through Christmas without vomiting. I thought that was good. He spent some time with my parents. My dad had just turned ninety. That was nice.

144

We came back home.

But he was so angry. He'd always called Will two or three times a day—texted and called. He didn't want to be away from Will. He said he needed him. Around that time, instead of waking up and screaming about Allison—although he did that once—he woke up and talked about all that he'd given to Will. He threw Will against the fireplace, and once he threw cookies at us. He was so angry. He would physically attack Will and say, "I gave you everything! I've been protecting you! I've given up my life so you could be good. You're perfect. I left the womb first so you could be alone in the womb. I gave you everything!" That was heartbreaking. How do you think Will felt about that?

On New Year's Eve, Philip and Will were downstairs with friends who were home from school. They were all laughing and playing soccer in the street. All of a sudden, Will came up. It was after midnight. I was watching television all night—my fun time. I didn't want to interrupt their fun. Will said, "Philip's not here. He was playing soccer with Sunil, but I think he's gone for a walk."

"Give it a few minutes and I'll start driving," I said, because we'd found him before by driving around, and once we had to get him off the street. Then the doorbell rang and there was Philip with a cop. He'd been found sleeping on the sidewalk. In the rain. Down on a busy street.

Will left for college. I took him to the airport on Sunday, January third. Philip didn't want to get up and go. Later, Philip wanted to go back to his group home in the projects. I took him back Sunday afternoon. I called him every day. I learned from Will on Tuesday or Wednesday that Philip was the only one in the house that week. No one else had come back. *He was all alone in that house.* He'd had dinner with his dad that Monday and Tuesday. On Wednesday night, some of his friends were over messing around on the computer and then left. Philip wrote a text to his brother that night that said, "I'm a prick." And, at 1:20 a.m., he stood in front of the train across the street from his house.

*Because no one was there in the house.*

I didn't even know until that day. Nigel wasn't checking. He didn't do that. He didn't choose to do that. No one would listen to me when I said, "This isn't adequate." I said that over break. "I don't think this is adequate." Everyone else thought it was a great program.

That was pretty sad to lose my son that way—all by himself.

Nigel said at the funeral parlor, "We did the best we could."

I don't know if we did the best we could. I don't think we did. It's not that Philip didn't want to do all those things Nigel was telling him, or suggesting he should do. Of course he wanted to do those things. Any mentally ill person wants to drive and go to movies and go to college. They want that. *They just can't do it.* I could see that he couldn't do it anymore. He couldn't go out to dinner. He couldn't. We used to go for walks every night after dinner. He couldn't even do that with me anymore. We used to play games. He wouldn't do that. He couldn't watch movies anymore. He just . . . shut down. Maybe it was me. Maybe it was *my* fault. Maybe I was bad. But I let him be. I didn't press him. I asked him if he wanted to go for a walk, not if he wanted to go to *college*, you know? Did he want to eat this or that for dinner? In fact, his last meal was stuff I'd given him to take down there. Fucking frozen pizza. Sad.

While Philip was with me, I'd heard about a research program at the university. I got Philip an interview, and they agreed he was schizoaffective and could join. The research was about rewiring the brain. He worked on these games or questions or whatever, and they did MRIs and would check again and again. It was non-medication. He was helping other people and himself. We were going to learn. I was proud of him. I told him this was something to be proud about because he was helping others. His grandparents and parents are professors. He lived his life around research. This was something he understood. I'd drive him there and work in the library while he was doing it. It was fine by me.

Then, that was it. I was not involved.

I had him doing acupressure, which he loved. He learned to control his leg jitters. He loved cognitive research, too. I thought those were really good things. Even though he wasn't volunteering, I had him *doing* things. Drum therapy and acupressure twice a week . . . therapists. He always had something to do every day. But he stopped everything when he moved near his dad. That was it. After that . . . he was gone.

I think if you asked Nigel now, he would say Philip had a mental illness. I guess I'm a little bitter because of what he told the family. When Philip died, my sister-in-law called up and said, "How did this happen? This is so tragic! Nigel told us Philip was getting better!"

Again, this autumn: Philip getting better? No! I saw him getting worse and worse. Doing less and less. Capable of less and less. He couldn't read anymore. The week of the funeral, Nigel and I went to the therapy group Philip was in. We sat there and Nigel said, "I don't understand it. Philip was engaged. He seemed fine. He could even tell jokes and he had his friends here . . ."

Then there was a pause and I said, "You know, that's really funny because I saw him falling apart. He would come home and go to bed or be really agitated and stay up all night laughing at these videos. He was in this compulsive place, drowning out his brain." Then the head of the group said, "As we often say, the mom is the safest one, and that's where the kid can be himself and doesn't have to act anymore."

The week Philip killed himself, everybody had gone back to college and they'd all been talking about classes they were going to take. He wasn't going back to college. I guess that was too much. We will never know.

Philip wrote a poem that day. I called him on Wednesday. "Whadja do today?"

"I wrote a poem," he said.

"Great! Can you read it to me?"

"I'll read it to you on Friday when you come get me." We had made an appointment, and I was going to get him at three on Friday for the weekend. Then Nigel called me at five in the morning on Thursday and said the police had just been at his house telling him they'd found identification on a body that was in many pieces on the railroad tracks—probably Philip's. I have a card that has blood all over it that was his. The following week he had a dentist appointment. I'd given the card to him to show the people at the center so I could take him to the dentist.

We never got to see the body because it was in so many pieces. I asked the police to show me where the body was. I said, "Could you put this wreath there?"

They said, "On what part of the body would you like the wreath? His head maybe? His leg?"

I mean, his body was smashed. We were told he would be embalmed if we took him to the funeral home and we said, "Yes, we'd like that." Then they said, "The good news is we didn't embalm him. The bad news is that he was in so many pieces that we couldn't." In fact, mixed in with his ashes are rocks from the railroad. They scooped up rocks with his body.

That was pretty sad to lose my son that way—all by himself.

My son.

It would have been better if the therapist on the ward had been able to talk to me more. I would have liked that. I would have liked to talk to his psychiatrist more. I tried. I was a squeaky wheel. My therapist told me to collect all the paperwork. I collected all the medical reports from the hospital and kept track of all the meds he'd been on. I was doing my job. I was told I had to keep the whole record, which I did.

You realize who your friends are. There are some I haven't heard from since this happened. I haven't had the energy to call people, and they haven't called me. I have friends in England and in other states, but not a lot around here. I arrived here from England with two young kids and a full-time job at the university. I didn't have time to make friends. Karen is a friend from grade school and high school.

When making decisions for Philip, I talked to my psychologist and psychiatrist and to Karen, who is a therapist and was really helpful. That was my network for making decisions for what Philip needed. I went to NAMI. I sort of muddled through by myself—a lot of time alone. I went to two therapists that first year after Nigel left because I was so upset. I talked to them a lot about Philip. I was actually getting feedback. I wasn't only talking to his therapist, though I did talk to his therapist until he went into the ward. She was incredibly helpful. But she didn't say he was having a psychotic break. That would have probably been extremely helpful if the psychiatrist had told me that.

I asked Philip what he needed. He said he liked me being in the house but not the same room. I'd be in the house. Once I got home, I'd stay at home. I'd never go out. I like my home, so it was all right. It was a lonely year.

So sad.

He was a beautiful boy.

There's this other picture. It was taken the day before Will left, four days before Philip killed himself. Will and Philip went to see their best friends. Philip is standing beside Sunil, four days before he died. Sunil told me Philip had said that night, "You're my best friend in the world." Sunil said, "You're my best friend." They hugged each other. Philip had connection. He *was* connected to people.

Sunil's mom took the picture. These guys knew he was unwell. They must be sensitive because they knew he'd been in the mental ward. Sunil's mom had even been to the mental ward a few times with me. They knew and they still loved him. They had seen it creeping up through high school. I'm sure they saw him be weird. Will is a sensitive guy also and he wants to be a doctor. He wants to be a psych major. He's pretty sensitive.

Philip lost his mind.

That's my story.

Philip was born in Cambridge, England, the twin of William and the child of Nigel and Catherine on . . . 1991. He has two additional brothers, C— and G—. He attended schools in Cambridge but mainly lived in and attended schools in the US. He performed exceedingly well in all these schools and managed to adapt as he moved between them, despite being amongst the youngest in his class in the USA system. In addition to academic achievements, Philip always played a range of sports, especially soccer, which he played continuously at regional level from 3rd to 12th grade. He was in teams that won regional trophies. He was an avid and loyal supporter of Liverpool FC in England. In music he played the violin through 9th grade and more recently he played guitar. For several years he took ice-skating and tap dancing classes. He enjoyed skiing very much.

Being both British and American and as the son of parents who worked in England, Turkey, Peru, Bolivia, and Italy, he had enormous opportunities to travel and experience other cultures in some depth. He traveled widely throughout Europe and recently visited England, Hungary, Italy, and Holland with his twin brother and a friend. He also visited an elder brother working for aid agencies in Botswana. Partly as a result of these travels, he was proactively involved in a series of initiatives to assist disadvantaged people across the globe. Inspired by the work of *Médecins Sans Frontières* (Doctors Without Borders), in 2008 he raised substantial funds for this organization. His fund-raising included house to house solicitation and an organized group bike ride, leading to a profile being written about Philip in MSF advertising and public relations as well as in local newspapers. He also worked for OXFAM in Cambridge, England.

Through 2010 Philip has been cared for in the hospital, and was in for Mental Health. He died on the train tracks on 6 January 2011. Philip will be remembered by all who knew him as a gentle, kind, and deeply thoughtful person with a sweet, shining smile directed by a sense of humor and fun. He cared very much for those around him and gave much to them. He led by example in his tireless questioning of what so many take for granted and by his commitment to help others. He was a gentle and loving soul, increasingly tortured through his life by the illness that afflicted him. He will be greatly missed by his family, friends, and all those whom he touched. Philip's memorial service will be held on Wednesday the 12th of January 2011 at All Souls Episcopal Church at 11 AM.

———∞∞∞———

*Catherine was alone in her effort to understand and manage Philip's illness. As Catherine readily admits, she was not emotionally stable because of the sudden blow of her husband's infidelity and divorce. Nigel's apparent misunderstanding of Philip's illness and the lack of support or coordination with Catherine for his son's treatment and medication compliance were not beneficial to Philip's mental health. Supporting a caregiver, in this case Catherine, isn't just helpful; it is critical. Pressuring Philip to act "normal" caused stress for Philip, and may have been partly responsible for his medication noncompliance. There is tremendous chaos and confusion when a child's serious mental illness is not stabilized, made only worse when another parent or loved one does not accept the illness, nor support treatment. Parents must find a way to work together to agree on basic care for a child despite differences, hurt, and animosity. A family therapist can be key to establishing communication, but it appears for this family, the therapy went awry. The way in which Philip announced he was going to live with his father and that Nigel was hiding around a corner is illustrative of poor facilitating on the part of the therapist. A family therapist must consider the well-being of all family members.*

*Philip's illness led to Catherine's isolation that continued after his death. She later informed us that even finding a helpful grief group had been challenging because the other mothers were not dealing with the loss of a child who died by suicide. Despite the deep pain Catherine has endured, she bravely came forward to tell her story with hope she could help another family. What can we learn from Catherine's story? With education, awareness, and the same kind of compassion Catherine herself exemplifies, her experience doesn't have to be repeated. Talking about mental illness and accepting that it is a lifelong illness, treatable with medication and other therapies, can make a significant difference for a family. Recognizing the necessity of a consistent treatment plan that is communicated and respected by the primary caregiver, their family, and medical professionals can reduce the isolation and burden on any individual caregiver and improve chances for the ill person's recovery. Open dialogue among family members is necessary. The journey of mental illness can have the best outcome only with the coordinated, nonjudgmental support of many.*

# CHAPTER SEVEN:
## NATHALIE, DELIA, AND GIANNA

*Treatment, hope, and gratitude.*

*It's like living with a time bomb all the time.*

*Parenting a child who lives with persistent mental illness is emotionally exhausting for anyone, even compassionate parents gifted or trained in counseling others to overcome challenges; even for a pastor like Nathalie or a nurse like Delia, especially before a diagnosis and treatment plan come into focus. Finding appropriate treatment and sticking with it, as a family, is monumentally important and epically demanding of time, energy, and emotional generosity. Early diagnosis is beneficial, emotional stamina a requirement.*

*Parenting any child who lives with extreme challenges requires deep personal and spiritual reserves. Some find support groups such as those offered at NAMI. Many lean on their faith or spirituality. The more fortunate may have their child's other parent for support. Family and friends can be supportive. In the end, through all the tribulations, these parents become quiet champions.*

*We first met with Nathalie and Delia in the modest book-lined office of the church where Nathalie is pastor. Her office had a few boxes stacked in a corner, but Nathalie was compelled to apologize for the mess, and as we arranged ourselves, Delia made sure we were comfortable. They sat across from us, a coffee table separating us physically, but soon we all became linked by another power altogether. Both Nathalie and Delia, each in her own way, listen and speak with a directness and purpose honed to a fine art. They epitomize the idea of being present; all else outside our conversation and their storytelling fell away.*

*Their connection to others and relationship between one another is built on intention. Even subtle interaction between them reveals evidence of their deep and arduous history, one of shared and private trauma. Their history doesn't allow for falling into injurious behavior ruts, and there is a deep respect between them. Their philosophy of intent is reflected in the acceptance of all traits and quirks, small and significant, that they embrace in one another. Where they don't budge is in their bond toward one another and their family. The work they have done, and the work they vow to do, is all in keeping with their commitment to loved ones and the value they place in family.*

*To keep a family unit vital and healthy, its members must accept change and growth. The family as a unit, and its individual members' inclusion in community can be a wellspring of support. While Nathalie and Delia have found community in their new congregation, they still struggle over the loss of the one they recently left, a tight-knit geographically and church-based community where they and their daughter, Gianna, felt safe and accepted.*

*Inclusion in some form of community can offer light along the rocky path of mental health wellness. Fortunately, through DBT[22] treatment and their church, Nathalie, Delia, and their daughter Gianna, who was born in 1996, have found the light of hope where there once was only darkness.*

*This is Nathalie and Delia's story.*

**NATHALIE:** Gianna will soon be seventeen. We also have an older daughter, Tanya, a foster child we adopted just before she turned eighteen. She lived with us for about seven years.

**DELIA:** Gianna was a term baby. Of course we had to use donor insemination to get pregnant. Nathalie was in labor for forty-six hours because Gianna kept coming down the birth canal, but then she'd put her head back, which would stop the progression. It ended up in a C-section.

**NATHALIE:** She didn't want to come out.

**DELIA:** That was an interesting foretelling. She's always hesitant to try new stuff. When she was three, four, five, six, we would try to get her involved in group activities like dance class or swimming lessons at the Y. The one that stands out for me is dance class at the YMCA near where we lived. There were four weeks in a dance class session. The first four weeks I took her, she would sit in my lap while we watched the class. For the next four weeks, we had talked and I said, "I'll sit outside." She sat in the corner the whole class time. It was the third set of four weeks when she said, "I don't want to do this." I realized I was wasting my time. She wasn't going to do it. It was the same thing with swimming. The same thing with soccer . . .

**NATHALIE:** gymnastics . . .

**DELIA:** . . . piano as she got a little older . . .

**NATHALIE:** . . . skiing lessons, ice skating lessons, roller skating . . .

**DELIA:** She was always timid and unwilling to try something she wouldn't be able to succeed in immediately.

**NATHALIE:** When she was five, she wanted to be able to do this jump on the school's monkey bars before she started first grade. We lived two blocks from the school, so we went there and she said, "Let's practice. Practice makes perfect, Mom." Then she said, "I don't want it to be perfect." I said, "Okay. Then let's take perfect and put it away." She took perfect, like an imaginary thing, and mimed the act of balling it up in her hands and tossed it as if she were throwing it into a trash can. She said, "Practice makes *possible*, Mom."

We went to the school playground for weeks so she

could practice and launch into first grade with this successful maneuver. It was a pretty big accomplishment, but she was very worried because she didn't want anybody to see her not be perfect at something. She didn't like soccer because she wasn't already good at it, though she's actually quite athletic and well coordinated. She's close to a brown belt in karate. But anything involving a group, like the school play, or doing anything in front of the class was cause for great anxiety. Some teachers helped us adapt; some didn't. It was always like pulling teeth.

But she was a normal baby in most ways except she was always really sensitive and got over stimulated easily. When she would get excited, she would hold her fists in the air and roll her wrists, and when I was pregnant, I would feel these movements that felt like someone doing that inside me. Still, to this day, when she gets anxious, she sort of waves her hands in the air in a similar way. From hours old she did that.

**DELIA:** Before she was able to walk, she would be complacent on the floor on a blanket with toys and mirrors until the dogs went by, and then she'd do that hand movement.

**NATHALIE:** She had sensitivity to big noises like dogs barking, and we couldn't start the vacuum. She still cringes when the dog barks. She needed a quiet home. When Gianna was small, Delia had her own business and I worked evenings, so she was rarely put in child care or aftercare. In second and third grade, I'd bring her home from school and she'd spend twenty minutes just decompressing. She'd get a snack and lie on the bed and stare at the wall. We limited TV and did all those things you do as a good parent. She got over stimulated and overwhelmed easily. And the clothes thing: she stopped letting us coordinate her outfits at about twenty months. She looked like a bag lady a whole lot of the time! She had things she would wear forever because of how it felt. She liked fabrics and having pieces of fabric that felt different and she'd go around touching them.

**DELIA:** She was always a pretty serious kid. It was difficult to get her to laugh or smile. Period.

**NATHALIE:** Gianna likes alone time and always had trouble making friends. She got picked on by kids who figured out she was sensitive. She was not able to understand how to be a friend, really. She felt, "If you're my friend, you're my new best friend, and you can't have any other friends." She wouldn't join groups. We thought about Girl Scouts. She had friends at church. She's been raised in church, and those are her friends in a way. She went to Sunday school and church gatherings. In the pageant, she was always in the back.

**DELIA:** Church has been continuity for her. It was always the same church, the one which Gianna was born into and where Nathalie was pastor for her first fourteen years. There were five other kids at the church who grew up with her. Those were continuous relationships, none of which were ever close or did anything outside of church. Kids from church or school never spent the night but maybe once or twice a year, and it would happen only once or twice. In her almost seventeen years, she's had maybe eight sleepovers in her whole life at other people's homes.

**NATHALIE:** Well, she wet the bed off and on until she was ten. Even now, when she has a friend over, they stay on the sofa bed and she sleeps in her room. Her room is her sanctuary. It's always been that way.

Then at age ten, eleven, twelve, she took the social messages really seriously. I come from a long line of chubby people, but she was appropriately middle-school-age chubby and was getting tall, so we knew she wasn't going to be heavy. We didn't notice at the time, but she tells us now that she really restricted her food. She did lose some weight at one time during middle school, but I never thought she was super thin. She loves to tell the story as if she were one step out of the grave almost.

**DELIA:** I had eating disorder issues in middle school, so I was pretty sensitive to the fact that she was losing weight, wearing baggy clothes, and I was scared to death to broach it with her until it became really apparent.

There's never been any coast time with this child. There's never been a happy-go-lucky, jubilant, jovial, let's go have fun. There's no lightness in this child. There has *never* been any lightness to this child. When you saw something coming, like possibly an eating disorder, even at that time—and that was five or six years ago—I was thinking, "Oh, we get to deal with this, too."

As early as third or fourth grade she had a counselor based on a recommendation from her teacher because of her social ineptness. She also had a counselor all through middle school, primarily for social stuff. But they were all interns and there wasn't much communication with us around specific content or outcomes or assessment.

But, by middle school, it was getting pretty apparent that something was wrong. I kept thinking, "Yes, she has some difficulty with social stuff and, yes, she has some sensitivity, yes, she's a perfectionist, yes, she doesn't like to expend energy for reading or learning new things." But it all came together when the bishop moved us away from the church and community she'd known for fourteen years—her whole life—and what we knew well, to a different county just as she was starting high school.

**NATHALIE:** Gianna was fourteen. And it happened fast. We learned on May first that we would be moving in July. I'm a pastor in a system where, when the bishop says you're going to move, you go. Or I'd have no job or home because we lived in a parsonage.

**DELIA:** We were well established and had a fantastic community both physically in our neighborhood and in that church and it had been a great match for us. Usually, Methodist pastors are moved every five or six years. We were probably left there too long, because we got so weaved in. Then we got ripped up.

**NATHALIE:** Things were starting to come together for her in eighth grade, and then we were notified of the move. She was beginning to have a few more friends, feel more confident, and had begun to break through some of the eating stuff.

**DELIA:** I didn't know that.

**NATHALIE:** Well, it's relative. As you said, there's been no easy time with this kid. We had the baby who slept through the night at seven weeks, and boy, we were like, "We have a baby who sleeps through the night! Ha!" Then she started having nightmares at fifteen months and didn't sleep through the night for ten years.

**DELIA:** Literally.

**NATHALIE:** I remember trying to get her to calm down one night when she was still a baby. We would switch nights and Delia had taken that night. But I came down to help. Maybe biology does have something to do with being close. I said to her, "Did you see something bad?" She was articulate and had started talking at nine months. She talked about, "Black, bad, wind, scary, bad, black." She was describing a nightmare. Then she immediately went back to sleep.

She was always intense. It hasn't been light. We knew that telling her about the move was going to be devastating. I didn't want to move either. But we had to go, and it *was* devastating for her. It was really, really hard.

She started high school after the move at a very white, rich, and privileged community. Before the move, she had attended public schools that were big, interracial, and with students of all socioeconomic levels. Even though she is also white and happens to be cute, she didn't have the Betsey Johnson dress for Friday and the right clothes for Tuesday, and most of the kids here had gone to the same middle school and knew each other. She came home the second week and said, "Mom, I keep trying to talk to people, but no one walks by themselves. They all walk in clumps."

But she did make friends who were also new, and who were ostracized. She got bullied. Now, she looks different. She's got an orange Mohawk and dresses punk. Before, she *looked* like everybody else, she just didn't have the wardrobe. I wasn't savvy enough to know about the wardrobe thing. I didn't have the wardrobe either, and I still don't! But it was horrible for her.

**DELIA:** When Gianna first started high school that fall, the counselor at school had assessed the need for her to see a therapist at school, an intern, who she was still seeing.

**NATHALIE:** We got her into counseling and thought we were doing everything right. Four months later, in January, when she was fourteen and a half, she started cutting. She showed us the cuts and we panicked. We also knew she was beginning to restrict and binge and purge again.

**DELIA:** When she started cutting, she was referred to a community therapist. But the cutting continued. It was all superficial, primarily on legs and arms. Not much torso.

**NATHALIE:** Yeah, it wasn't endangering. But then she carved the word "hate" into her leg.

**DELIA:** That was in July—about a year after we had moved here.

**NATHALIE:** We didn't see it earlier because she always wore pants.

**DELIA:** She carved it, took a picture of it, and put it on Facebook. Somebody saw it, I don't know who it was, and told someone at the high school, who then figured out where this kid lived and contacted the police, who then called us.

**NATHALIE:** It had taken several days for them to locate us.

**DELIA:** Nathalie and I met with Gianna that evening and said, "We know what's going on . . . let's move forward on this."

**NATHALIE:** She was so angry.

**DELIA:** Later, after Nathalie had gone to work that evening, the police came to our house to make sure the child was safe. Gianna was very angry because it was none of the police's business. When they first arrived, I was fearful, thinking that taking her away might be the outcome. They took me outside and asked me if I thought she was going to hurt herself again. I said, "No, she hasn't cut in two or three weeks and I don't expect her to again." The police went back in the house and said to Gianna, "Have you cut since you put that on your leg?" Gianna said, "Yes. I cut yesterday."

The police officer took me outside again and said, "I can't trust that she's not going to cut again. I need to take her." Hearing that, part of me thought, "Maybe she'll realize how serious this is and maybe she'll stop behaving this way." And also, "I wonder if she'll be hospitalized? I wonder if we've lost control of this situation and she'll be taken by CPS?" I saw how angry she was, and because he was being so gentle and kind I trusted his concern that she may hurt herself again. I thought,

"I guess this is the right thing to do because I can't control her. Maybe this is the right path."

I went back in the house again and explained to her very well, very objectively, calmly, and lovingly. Not that she heard any of that. They put handcuffs on her and took her away.

**NATHALIE:** She was taken to the hospital . . .

**DELIA:** I followed to the hospital where they did an assessment for about four or five hours and deemed her safe with us.

**NATHALIE:** Because we're both mandated reporters.[23]

**DELIA:** Gianna came home. Within about two months of that time—September, October—we didn't know what to do. She was still seeing the local therapist.

**NATHALIE:** It didn't seem like she was getting any better. She was looking for an identity. We joked that it was "identity of the month." For a while in the spring she claimed she had Tourette's syndrome; then she was transgender. She had lots of panic attacks. She had OCD. It seemed like she was shopping for a sickness identity. She knew something was wrong.

**DELIA:** Absolutely.

**NATHALIE:** We look back and think, "Why didn't the therapist pick up on the borderline personality disorder?" I understand, with teenagers, especially since she was only fifteen, it's very hard, but we now realize the therapist wasn't as good as we thought. On the other hand, the therapist did deal with her on her OCD behavior a great deal.

**DELIA:** Her OCD was to the degree that when she washed her clothes, *she* had to take them from the washer to the dryer, and straight from the dryer to her bedroom. No one else could touch them. She also could not go into her room until she'd showered each night, and then she'd go to her room and couldn't come out again. It's better now.

The timeline was that we moved in July, and by January, February, March she was seeing a therapist and was cutting . . .

**NATHALIE:** . . . and engaging in anorexic and bulimic behaviors.

**DELIA:** From March through July she was OCD and had a panic disorder. She'd say, "You can't have the guy come in and clean the fleas . . ." Fleas on the dog were enough for her to become insane. She continued searching online to see what was wrong with her. Then in August they took her away for cutting.

**NATHALIE:** Interestingly, one of the hallmarks of this kid is that in the midst of all the craziness through all these years, she had very good gut instincts for herself. Like choosing karate and being able to stick with it. Something we've also heard from people consistently from day one is that she's the most willful child they've ever met. We heard that from her therapist, all of her teachers, everyone we know. More recently, her therapist said, "I've never met someone more willful than Gianna." When she has her mind on something and wants it, she's focused and capable.

During spring of her freshmen year, she had said, "I'm not going back to high school. There's this independent study school called Independent High School, and I want to go there." We did not want her to go there. But she knew Independent was right for her.

**DELIA:** She got the application, figured out all the admissions requirements, and told us, "We need to meet at the school on this particular night." She paved the whole way for herself.

**NATHALIE:** We met with the principal, which all parents are required to do, and were convinced she had a shot. In August she started at Independent High School, which is like a junior college. Independent was one of the things that saved her because it's sort of an island of misfit toys! It's for semi-professional athletes, kids like Gianna, and also kids who get bullied for being gay, lesbian, or are in some way different. Gianna came out through all of this. That was great.

During all of this, she was continuing with her therapist, though we were realizing it wasn't helping her. By October, she got into a good rhythm, but her shopping for an identity continued. She was fifteen then, and what's an adolescent's normal response to moving away from everything she knows?

In the fall, we had started seeing her pediatrician because she was getting dangerously thin. It was pretty bad. She went to her same pediatrician, who is wonderful, and who held her when she was twenty-four hours old and loves her very much.

**DELIA:** Absolutely loves her very much.

**NATHALIE:** Sees her even though she's a part-time doctor.

**DELIA:** Dr. H— referred us to this nutritionist who's an hour away.

**NATHALIE:** Gianna was getting really thin. On two separate occasions she needed an EKG and was almost sent to the emergency room for her heart, which had gotten so weak from not eating. Her organs were so damaged that when she did begin to eat, she was eating 4–5,000 calories a day, and it was six weeks before she gained weight.

We were at the end of our rope. We were doing the best we could and therapy wasn't working, and a year and a half had gone by.

**DELIA:** We wanted to stop in and see Barb, her therapist. We saw her periodically, not frequently enough. There was one visit where Gianna met with Barb for a few minutes and then we met alone with Barb. There wasn't anything substantive in our meeting, but when we got home, Barb called and said, "I need to tell you that after you saw me, Gianna came in and told me she had just swallowed several razor blades and vomited them back up."

**NATHALIE:** Which is a lie. You can't do that and live.

**DELIA:** Barb said, "I need to tell you the truth. This is what she said to me. I'm not sure what to do about it. If it's true, she needs to go to the hospital. If it's not, we need to figure this out." The next morning she called and said, "I was reading last night, and I'm realizing that when I think of Gianna's impulsive behavior, difficulty with social relationships, fears of abandonment, feeling outside the reality of the situation, unregulated emotions . . . that her behaviors fit the criteria of borderline personality disorder, and I'm not sure what to do for you right now. I understand DBT could be helpful. I know there's a program nearby. Good luck."

That was late fall of 2011. She was fifteen and a half.

**NATHALIE:** She was young to be diagnosed, and yet the symptoms were all so clear that we wondered, "Would a sharper therapist have caught it earlier?" But hindsight is twenty-twenty, so you go forward. We knew we had to shake something up. But then it's Christmas and all that. By January 2012, we knew we had to do something different. What we were doing wasn't working.

**DELIA:** The little side of the insurance situation: I researched DBT, and there's a six-thousand-dollar-a-month program nearby, which was not a financially viable option for us. I called our insurance and they said, "There are enough therapists in your community, and we cannot bring in someone else to do DBT because there are enough." I have vivid memories of trying to figure out how to get the DBT through our medical coverage. Dr. H—, the pediatrician, referred us to a medical doctor at the university hospital who assessed Gianna medically and, because of the eating disorder, referred her to DBT at that same hospital. So we got into DBT and then there was the assessment in March.

**NATHALIE:** Four assessment visits.

**DELIA:** Long assessment visits.

**NATHALIE:** Six hours total.

**DELIA:** We also sent her to a neuropsychologist and therapist to get an objective measure around testing.

**NATHALIE:** Which we paid for out of pocket because we didn't want to report through our insurance. Those doctors came to the exact same conclusion: borderline personality disorder. But her IQ test couldn't be scored even though she scored off the charts on the three academic areas. On the part that evaluates *how* you test, her score was low because of her extreme anxiety, which skewed results of the whole test. She's a genius, but her testing anxiety affects her grades in school.

This was not surprising to us. We had sent her to a biofeedback therapist to try to help her learn to be calm. We were using whatever resources we could. We do okay financially, but we're a nurse and a pastor. We don't make the kind of bucks that people who pay for these things make, but we were pretty desperate. A member of our church, God bless her, offered to pay for any private care. She said, "My husband and I used to not have a lot of money and we make money now." She has a bipolar son and said, "I can't imagine not being able to afford his care when my son was diagnosed." We felt blessed.

Then we found DBT. We started with a family skills class a year ago. It was about fifteen hours of therapy a week for each of us.

**DELIA:** Yes. DBT consisted of two hours of family skills class—Gianna had individual, and we had family therapy. In addition, Gianna was seeing her pediatrician about once a week and also her nutritionist. Around this time, Gianna started on an antidepressant and still sees the psychiatrist at the university on a monthly basis.

**NATHALIE:** It was rare, especially at first, for Gianna to reject treatment because she was aware that she was very ill. In fact, Gianna used mass transit to get to appointments. I would take her to the bus station that's fifteen minutes away. She'd take the bus to the city and then a commuter train to appointments, and one doctor was a long commute. Again, when she's motivated . . .

**DELIA:** We started with the same therapist for family that Gianna had for individual. But she left after three months, which was an absolute gift because the therapist that replaced her in July is beyond . . .

**NATHALIE:** She saved our lives.

**DELIA:** Absolutely.

**NATHALIE:** Her name is Irene.

**DELIA:** Yes. A little statement about that team: for probably six or eight months, by the time Gianna would get from her furthest appointment to the university hospital, information would come from the dietician to the therapist and pediatrician two or three times a week. They were all working together. All three are doctors in different systems. It's absolutely amazing. We are very fortunate.

Phase I DBT lasted forty weeks. Now we are in Phase II. Now Gianna goes to a group with her peers led by Irene, the therapist. Gianna's weight is restored, and now she sees both her pediatrician and dietician about every month. We have family therapy on Fridays, and Nathalie and I are back in couples therapy. We got out of couples during the first forty weeks because it was too much, but we're back in it.

**NATHALIE:** The transition from Phase I to Phase II has been horrible and huge, and Gianna has gone back to restricting and she did some binging and purging.

**DELIA:** But yet she's going through the steps.

**NATHALIE:** Transitions have always been hard and horrible.

**DELIA:** Transitions have always been hard for her *and me.* Now that we've moved to Phase II, there is some regression, though Irene said this was normal. She said, "Remember it took you guys ten weeks to get on board during the first forty?" It's been four weeks.

And, she tried alcohol for the first time in the last month, twice. She and Nathalie went out of state to do some college stuff.

**NATHALIE:** The few times she tried marijuana were at home, in her bed. She never drank before, we don't think. We were staying at a friend's house, and she found vodka and drank half a bottle and blacked out. I almost sent her to the hospital. Then she did it again a few weeks ago while at this big, all-ages punk place where she goes to hear live music. She passed out drinking.

**DELIA:** She started doing the punk thing about a year and a half ago. She calls herself a nihilist. What punk offers for her is that it is against the norm, a community in which she feels supported and apart from the norm. She feels, "I'm different, so I'll associate with this group." She loves the music because it's aggressive and out there. Jello Biafra[24] is her god. For her, it's the music, the support, and, "I'm accepted as I am. I can go to the club and into the mosh pit and dance crazy and no one judges me. People love me; they watch out for me." That was her safe place. She was really vehement around, "This is my safe place that keeps me going . . . the club and punk." She has felt like those folks supported her. It was a mistake to allow her to go in the first place; however, it's been a community she's felt supported by, and she has stayed clean, straight edge until . . .

**NATHALIE:** . . . the drinking incident . . .

**DELIA:** Right. She drove herself to the club that night in her car, the one she came home from the hospital in as a newborn, a 1994 beater station wagon that she loves. She and a friend, who is straight-edged, went outside to talk, and another girl, who Gianna doesn't know well but has seen around the club, said, "Do you wanna go drink?" Gianna's friend said, "No, I'm going back inside." But Gianna went and drank. An hour or so later, two friends, who are obviously very caring, called and said, "Gianna can't drive home. She can come to our house." I said, "No, I'll come get her."

When I arrived to get her out of the friend's car, I left the keys on the front seat and got out to help her. She got in my car, shut the door, and locked the door inadvertently. She couldn't figure out how to unlock the door for about fifteen minutes. She was that drunk. She finally unlocked the door, but she was incomprehensible and not really able to walk. She doesn't remember a thing after going out for a drink with a friend.

She's very afraid of that now. She has realized, "Someone

could have hurt me or taken me away if I hadn't had those two friends." She was able to say, too, which is really hard, that, "The club is *not* really the safe place it was for me." That's huge that she could come to that on her own. She had thought the club was safe, the same way it is when she's with us. Her statement to Irene and to us in family therapy about that incident in which she drank to pass out during that college visit with Nathalie was, "I was in a safe place with Mom in this house with just the two of us. Nothing was going to happen. But when I did it at the club, I realized someone could have hurt me."

Now we've created a clear chart. If she wants to go to a show in the future, there are boxes she has to check to be sure it's safe.

We probably haven't been as forceful or as unified as we should have. That's a mistake I believe we've made. Gianna has always pushed back. As fucking hard as she can! From the very beginning, she's pushed to the point where we're worn down. It's been helpful toward validating why we are so worn that others have observed this child's willfulness from the age of seven.

**NATHALIE:** Yes. The living with it is just . . . it's what we do. She got a seventy-eight on a test this week, which was the highest in her class. We're celebrating a seventy-eight, but we don't get positive stuff about this kid from her life. The book that's helped us is entitled *Stop Walking on Eggshells.*[25] That's an accurate description. As Delia said, there's no joy, no excitement. It's not like our kid's on a soccer team and we can say, "Wow, you played well today." There's almost nothing positive. But people love her. She's sociable, beautiful, opinionated, and has a great sense of humor. She loves little kids and older people. For the past couple years, she's been volunteering to read to a ninety-five-year-old blind woman from our church. She's wonderfully engaging. We get positives that way but not like the normal things other parents get.

**DELIA:** And we don't do much together as a family. It's always a struggle to get Gianna to do things, period. Much less something all three of us would be willing to do. For example, Nathalie wants to go bike riding more, so I brought the bikes on the back of the car today. Biking on the bike path together for half an hour would be big for us. I texted Gianna and said, "If you want, put your bike on the back of the car and meet us. We'd love to ride on the bike path with you." She probably won't. I keep inviting her. Even going for a walk around the neighborhood is a challenge for Gianna.

**NATHALIE:** But there are things we do together.

**DELIA:** Such as . . . ?

**NATHALIE:** We have dinner and watch movies.

**DELIA:** We do that. You're right.

**NATHALIE:** We try to eat dinner together as much as possible. When Gianna was at the height of her anorexia, binging and purging, she wouldn't eat with us. But she's been doing it more and more. She's been cooking for us.

**DELIA:** Not in the last couple of weeks.

**NATHALIE:** Well no, but in general. Not now because of her regression. We travel on vacations really well together as a unit. We went to Vancouver for three weeks last year. Alaska the year before. We went to Seattle looking at colleges. We're doing Minnesota this year. That's something we do together.

**DELIA:** Nathalie is great at planning something and marketing it well to the family so that we do it. And yet, I look back at those trips over the years and . . .

**NATHALIE:** They've not necessarily been fun, but . . . Going to see my family around Christmastime has been a big thing we do because Gianna was close to my folks, and is with my siblings. She has cousins her age there. But our daughter really doesn't want to do things, so it's tough sometimes. We're all going to a Green Day concert. When we pay for concert tickets she'll go with us! The problem is that Delia hasn't given up on having Gianna do things that Delia likes, and Delia's trying to learn what Gianna likes.

Gianna has a major impact on the two of *us* getting out. We've been wanting to attend a cocktail hour held Sunday nights in our community, or we say, "Let's go to a play." But then we say, "Can we leave Gianna? Is it safe to leave her?" Or, "Geez, Gianna is having another meltdown." We've not given up 100 percent on our social life here. Maybe 99 percent! We had a few good months recently when she was doing well in the program and we were beginning to do stuff. We went to a party. We met some couples. We said, "We'll have a dinner party." Well, we can have a dinner party, but having the energy to put it together after coming home . . . Both of us have jobs helping people and talking all day to people, and for me to come home and have to process more . . .

We're working hard to get away for our anniversary, and hopefully Gianna can stay with our friend. I mean she *can* stay with her, whether she's able to or not . . . those are things we deal with.

It's hard to do normal things. It's a soap opera drama in our house every day, all the time. She got her first moving violation. She ran a red light in the city and was caught by the camera. She doesn't know it yet, and we have to plot when to tell her. We have to be very careful. I'm really tired of it at this point. We tend to take turns being done with *it*, so to speak.

I don't know how single parents do it.

**DELIA:** We wouldn't have gotten through it with just one of us . . .

**NATHALIE:** We have been pretty close through this. We've done couples counseling and we're trying to stay tight . . . but there are times . . . Sometimes I joke about military school in North Korea. "Ship her away! I just want my life to be simpler!" Of course I don't want my child in military school in North Korea! But it's hard to be exhausted all the time.

**DELIA:** My experience is that feeling too exhausted to deal with the drama tends not to happen at the same time for both of us. When one of us is exhausted, it's not usually verbalized, though it might be helpful for it to *be* verbalized, for us to be clearer for each other. I'm thinking about that Wednesday night when she had difficulty with the dinner and went up to her room and you were very much in "emotional mind."

**NATHALIE:** Yeah.

**DELIA:** For some amazing reason, I was not at the time. We've played it out again and I said, "Would it have helped if I'd said, disconnect the train?" You know, helped us all to disengage from the moment, the drama?

**NATHALIE:** The thing is, there's not *anything* that's easy. We have to have our guard up about everything. Gianna had been really good about food for the previous six to eight months. Food hadn't been an issue. But for some reason, that Wednesday morning she searched for and found the one scale in our house, which is hidden deep within our closet. She weighed herself and decided to restrict that day. That same morning I had said, "What do you want for dinner?" because it had been a pleasure to cook for her. She said, "I want breakfast for dinner." I spent a lot of time making potatoes and all this other stuff, and she came in and said, "The eggs aren't right" and had a tantrum and said, "I'm not going to eat!" She went to her room and I was thinking, "Oh, now it's back to food!" We were off the hook on food! But anything can trigger her and make it all go south really fast, so we're vigilant about everything.

It's like living with a time bomb all the time.

**DELIA:** It's funny to teach people about the impact of chronic stress on one's system . . .

**NATHALIE:** Uh-huh.

**DELIA:** . . . and to know too much about how it affects the system. We have to keep our vigilance up all the time. I've learned recently how to have those things come in that bring balance.

**NATHALIE:** Yes, which is part of the DBT program. It really has saved our lives. It gave all of us skills to at least attempt to live it differently.

**DELIA:** Oh, skill of the day!

**NATHALIE:** Skill of the day . . .

**DELIA:** It's all in the notebook.

**NATHALIE:** ABC: Accumulate Pleasurable Activities, Build Mastery, and Cope Ahead Plan. The first thing means making sure you're doing something pleasurable every day. A lot of the skills are communication skills. For example, skills to help us all learn to ask for something we really want or to communicate in a way that says "no" effectively and kindly. We are learning specific ways of communicating that help us. In the basic concepts of DBT: emotion mind, reason mind, and wise mind . . . there's a lot of mindfulness training. "Let's be mindful for a minute."

Something that has been harder on Delia than me is that

we are now letting the therapist do the heavy lifting on some challenging stuff with Gianna. If there's something we need to convey that's going to trigger Gianna, it's going to wait until our appointment with Irene because she has a way of dealing with Gianna and helping in a way we cannot. That's been helpful.

**DELIA:** There's another skill. We have things up on the bulletin board.

**NATHALIE:** Posters that Delia has made.

**DELIA:** For example, "Can you label the feeling? Anxiety and fear: is it justified or unjustified?" Anxiety and fear is justified when the life, health, or well-being of you or someone you care about is threatened. If not, it's not justified. An example is standing and speaking in front of a group: if you're anxious, that is not justified anxiety because there is no threat to your life, health, or well-being. When fear or anxiety is not justified, you must plough through, work through it. It's similar for sadness, anger, envy, jealousy, or shame. Is it justified or not justified? I try to bring it up frequently, "Can you label the feeling?" Sometimes it's received well by my family and sometimes it's not because, you know, "Mom, stop being the therapist."

What I try to do on my own is validate the most justified feeling that I have now, which is sadness. It's justified, so I give myself the opportunity to be sad at times and I'm not doing anything to buffer it, which I was for the first few years. I express my sadness pretty loud now, so I kind of plan for it. If I feel it coming, I might get in my car and go somewhere and cry for a while. I always feel better. The burden seems to be lifted and I feel great because it takes a lot of courage to experience feelings.

Another tool is "radical acceptance." I move on the continuum toward radical acceptance of mental illness. On the way home from family therapy Gianna said to me, "Mom, what's it like to have a kid with mental illness?"

I said, "It's not unlike having a kid with diabetes. It's just that the disease is thought of differently. Diabetes is not something you can cure. You'll always have it. *You* get to decide how you will control it, how you will treat it. My kid gets to choose to take her insulin or not. I can't take it for her. Sometimes I'm really sad that my kid has diabetes."

Now, I wish I believed all that as readily as I'd said it to her. And that's where I move toward a radical acceptance. It's what it is. I can radically accept it *and* I can be sad.

I try to assimilate the DBT skills as much as I can because there's not one that is not useful.

**NATHALIE:** Yes. It's created a language with our child that she owns and we own and then we can speak together because in the midst of this is what we jokingly call "NAB," normal adolescent behavior. We almost rejoice when we get the stuff that most parents probably scream about because, for us, something normal is pretty exciting. It's learning to tell the difference and when to use the parenting skills DBT teaches us. We now have a language to talk about Gianna.

There's also accountability, and I give Gianna a lot of credit for it. She chose to stay in this program, to do the hard work. We didn't let her off the hook about attending. She's tried to avoid things at times, but if she didn't participate and learn and make the shifts, they wouldn't have moved her into Phase II. I give her a whole lot of credit.

DBT saved our lives and our family because it's given us some hope. She is just sixteen and, even though she's always going to have BPD, hopefully, by the time she's eighteen or nineteen, she can learn all these skills and other things to live within her own personality and body and self. Then we'll be able to let go the way most parents imagine they will when their kid comes of age. She'll have to live her own life rather than living with us. It's the most hopeful thing. I mean, without it, I'm not sure where we'd be.

We're spokeswomen for DBT at this point. From everything I've been reading, it's probably the most effective for young adults and adolescents. I'm not sure whether this is an accurate statement, but I sometimes feel like we lost a year by not knowing about it sooner. But, you know, whatever, best laid plans of mice, men, and women, right?

**DELIA:** Though we've also said that we don't know if Gianna would have been ready if Barb diagnosed it sooner.

**NATHALIE:** That's true. For BPD, it's about finding a DBT program.

For other parents, and of course this is my work so I've done a lot of this for years, one really must find support. For a lot of people it's NAMI, or their church, or something in the community, but that's where we were floundering right before the DBT. We felt like we were isolated and on our own and I was beginning to look at resources when the DBT came to us.

**DELIA:** I get support from friends. Three friends. I don't go to support groups or NAMI. The friends I've chosen have never judged me or our situation. There are three people who know everything—and have for twenty-five years. I've known all of them since before Gianna was born. They've been along on this journey of this child who's not quite like their children. Now that there's a diagnosis, it's even liberating for them.

We probably could access the three other families that were in our family skills group. But I can't imagine relating to one of the families in any way outside of the group. Regarding the other family, I think we don't have much time or energy.

**NATHALIE:** My family has been very supportive to me. I have two sisters and a brother. My mom recently died at eighty-nine, and my dad died a year and a half ago. They were both incredibly supportive. They visited a lot. They watched Gianna every summer for five years—came out and lived with us. My sibs are not judgmental. They don't understand it and they don't really get it, but they've all had challenges with their kids and are all very loving. But we're not geographically close.

We haven't made a lot of friends here yet. Delia commutes still. The church has been extraordinary, though very few know our whole story. They wanted a pastor with a family. The head of the Personnel Committee forgot to check the box that says, "We want the perfect family!" There's a group of moms who drove Gianna places, mostly to school things when Delia or I couldn't. They've been radically and fiercely loving toward me and us because, though they don't say it, they feel, "It's our fault because you've had to move." They believe my work is responsible for some of my daughter's issues, and I say to them, "It's not." But still, they are very compassionate.

We do have a lot of support. That's another thing that is part of our story. Our employers have been incredibly understanding; Delia leaves at four o'clock every Tuesday and one o'clock every Friday for family therapy. This church always had Tuesday night events. Well, no more because I had family class. I had to say to people, "I gotta go." Before Gianna was driving, I was at every one of those appointments. Delia would drive to the pediatrician appointment because it is near her work. Without this community support here, it would have really been difficult. If we had employers who were grouchy about it, it would have been really tough.

**DELIA:** Such a large part of my ability to keep on keeping on is my walking in faith, and that I, and we, have always come out of each struggle on our feet, or knees, and it continues to sustain me. I'm not all clear on how I am held and guided and comforted . . . and yet I always am, and *this* is a large part of how I have made it through the past few years.

Using the twelve-step program of accepting what I am powerless over and trusting that there is something larger than me that can restore me, and then letting go, works. What I've learned does not help: worrying, obsessing, and trying to control. But turning it all over to the care of God has proven to work.

What is funny is Nathalie, the pastor, and I seem to look differently at our being held.

I just know that during those times when it has been so very debilitating and I find myself crying on the floor, I have never not trusted that we WILL be cared for. It just has come to look very, very different than what I had imagined.

This faith keeps me going.

**NATHALIE:** The past several years have been very trying for my faith: moving churches when we did not want to move and, with that, unsure how to serve the new congregation, the death of two parents in eighteen months, the life-threatening illnesses of both a close friend and my sister, Delia and I going through our own depressions, and then, Gianna! I struggled with what it all meant, what God was saying through it all. I tend to keep my faith more in my head than Delia, who is a heart-gal, 100 percent. I make it much more difficult! And yet, I never felt abandoned, even when I doubted. I never felt alone, even if I wasn't sure that God even existed for me anymore. Hope was elusive, but somehow, I never doubted that a firm foundation was there, somewhere.

I'm still not sure about it all. Now that there is more manifest hope in Gianna's recovery and I am moving through mourning my parents, I can see the trail of God's presence with me more clearly. I do not believe that we go through suffering to learn some lesson or because it is God's plan or any of that. What I do believe is that God is always present and our spiritual lives are about being aware of, and living in, that presence. Even if it was just a tiny bit, I always had that through these years. I now have more.

DELIA: Yes.

NATHALIE: We are coming up on our twentieth anniversary. For us, not being married to one another is not an option. We each come from a long line of folk who stay committed, and we love each other very much. I know a lot of families split over hard kids. As a pastor, I know that . . . *I* know that! I don't want to be one of those families, not because it's a statistic, but because my life is so much better with Delia.

DELIA: We now understand that Nathalie and I process life very, very differently.

NATHALIE: We're Myers-Briggs opposites![26]

DELIA: Absolutely!

NATHALIE: It's made life fun for twenty-three years!

DELIA: I'm slowly learning that I cannot expect to process with Nathalie what raising Gianna, especially the acuity of the last few years, is like for me, so I've begun to not broach it—whereas before I pushed with, "Let me talk about this!" As we've been worn down, and Nathalie has stated what doesn't work for her, I've learned: don't even go there. Use my other resources. Nathalie processes it in her head. I don't know how she does it; however, it's not how *I* do it. I can't get silk shirts at Albertson's Grocery, so I'm not going to try to get silk shirts at Albertson's. That's one way I care for her: by not asking her for what she's not capable or able to give.

NATHALIE: And Delia could process forever, needs to talk about very small things till it's what I call "chewing soup." I'm grateful Delia processes with friends, and I think I've grown toward more and better listening so she can do some of that with me, just not all of it. Would you say that's true, Delia?

**DELIA:** Yes.

**NATHALIE:** Because I don't come from a place where continuing to talk about stuff is very helpful. Kind of the opposite. It makes me want to run away.

**DELIA:** She's from the Midwest.

**NATHALIE:** Yes. I'm from the Midwest. Delia and I are radically different about a lot of other things. Delia likes to be outdoors and do outside activities more than I do, so for her birthday last year I gave her surfing lessons, a wetsuit, a surfboard, and said, "Go surfing!" You know, "Go bicycling with friends who want to do fifteen miles. Go do stuff!" I like to take trips and travel by myself, and Delia supports that. Those are the kinds of things we do to care for each other.

We've always been very kind to each other in general. Very loving. You know, "Let me bring you coffee in the morning because I'm getting up earlier than you." The parenting handoff to whoever can handle the situation better at the moment isn't necessarily formal. Once in a while I'll say, "I can't do it tonight. You have to be on." We've been increasing those gestures of kindness and awareness of each other in hard times. Seeing a marriage counselor helps us to be sure we're staying on the same page.

**DELIA:** Here's another example how we are different: Nathalie likes the house picked up. She likes the kitchen clean when we go to bed at night. When the house is in order, Nathalie feels more in control, and I've come finally to realize that. It took awhile.

**NATHALIE:** And Delia leaves stuff around and, to me, it's messy, but you know, her desk, her part of the office and bedroom, I say nothing about. You can tell exactly which side of the bedroom is whose, and that is a radical acceptance for both of us.

**DELIA:** What also helps is not blaming each other for something that happened in the past and what may be perceived to have contributed to the current situation with our kid. I've been there and it doesn't help. What does that help? It doesn't matter. It is what it is today. And that's all we have: it is what it is today.

There has been self-blame. There has also been great judgment from my family. I have a brother and a sister. The lens through which they look is that of my mother. When Gianna was little, my mother was visiting, and her solution was, "Sit her down and *make* her put her shoes and socks on. How can you let her hold up the family?" Which is exactly what I was told growing up. I was whipped into a shape that worked within that family system. There are times I wonder, if I'd whipped her into shape at that time, would it be different now?

My brother, who is a practicing alcoholic, deferred to his wife to raise his kids because he had such a shitty upbringing. My sister, who is in recovery, never had kids. I don't have a good parenting model. I've often acquiesced in situations with my kid because I didn't want to repeat the rigid model I had. I don't talk much with my siblings about Gianna except when she's doing well.

It took until the DBT process that I began to learn this was not our fault. I didn't have any other information or skills to think otherwise. There was nothing specific to read about because it was all so amorphous. I mean, she'd just gone through all these diagnoses and searching and I didn't know what was wrong. I didn't know what to read. What did we do wrong? What didn't we catch?

I did feel shame, and even after we'd lived here a year, I was still really, really angry that we had had to move.

**NATHALIE:** Delia also has had "adoption kid" issues because, legally, Delia had to adopt Gianna. Delia wanted to carry our child but it wasn't to be. I was the second-string uterus! I come from a long line of incredibly fertile women and got pregnant on the third try, though the average is about eleven. When Gianna is eighteen, she has the right to meet the donor who, until then, is anonymous. We had Gianna in the day and age when you had to go through the second parent adoption in our state. Now it's not so embarrassing or hard. I had to give up partial custody. We had special papers to sign and had to pay about $4,000 for a home visit where a social worker came to our home for our own baby. It was weird.

**DELIA:** But I never had issues in terms of the parent role, only in that there were times they connected in ways . . .

**NATHALIE:** Yeah, we're kind of tight.

**DELIA:** They're *way tight*. They think the same way. Gianna actually walks like Nathalie's mom.

**NATHALIE:** She's like my mom reincarnated!

**DELIA:** It was only that I didn't understand some of the ways Gianna thinks. But not being as much of a parent? *Never.*

**NATHALIE:** Never, no. That's why the diagnosis is liberating. I know the illness is somewhat environmental, but since I'm the biological mother, I sometimes wonder, "Hmm. What did *my* side contribute?" But the diagnosis has been liberating. She was "born this way," to quote Lady Gaga. She really was.

**DELIA:** With any mental illness, if there's a recent diagnosis I'd say to another parent, "It's not your fault." But that doesn't mean that's not where their mind is going to go. But that's the advice

I'd offer first, to remember, *it's not your fault*. And also know that if you're not taking care of yourself, you're not going to be there for your kid, which also goes in about as deep as, "It's not your fault." One only can assimilate those two concepts as time goes by. They don't come in and go deep.

There has been so much denial that even I sometimes wondered if maybe it's not as bad as it looks. Especially when it changes faces so often, presents so differently from week to week, month to month, I thought that maybe it's not mental illness. I guess I've come to accept that it is mental illness only in the last six or eight months.

I came to accept Gianna's mental illness piece by piece until the concept of radical acceptance came up in DBT. And yet, it was never associated with the diagnosis or accepting mental illness; it was more radically accepting a specific situation that you are doing in this moment, however it applies.

**NATHALIE:** When Gianna was diagnosed with BPD, I read about it right away.

**DELIA:** Right away. That night.

**NATHALIE:** It is a lot to take in. It's both relief and, "Oh my God. My kid is sick." All the social stigma about mental illness is so internalized no matter how liberal or liberated you want to think you are. I felt, "No, she's only fifteen. She is a baby." But also, "Yay! Now we know." There's not a shot for it, but there's something we can *do* about it. When you have something to do about it, you feel empowered.

One of the hardest things for me as a parent of this kid is that there's only so much power I have, and there's a sense of being out of control and hopeless because, while I can raise her, help her, and give her this program, when she turns eighteen and moves from home—if she decides to move—she may choose not to be treated or medicated. That is scary because you think when you launch someone at eighteen or twenty-one they're going to be okay. That feeling upon learning the diagnosis was, "She's *never* going to be okay." And I'll still never have any control over her.

**DELIA:** That term "letting go with love . . ." At her age it's more difficult, because she's sixteen. We are still the parents; it's our house and our rules.

**NATHALIE:** We're still legally responsible.

**DELIA:** Right. I do vacillate back and forth on "this is my kid's journey, not mine." I can let go of her and her journey and try to focus on my own because I still want to live my life and not lose my life to her. I have vacillated moment to moment, depending on the situation. "Let go, get out of here. It's yours. I'm over it. I'm done. Fine." That's not with love. Sometimes I have to detach to survive. Sometimes it's with an ax. I've learned that in the twelve-step program with Al-Anon: to detach from the alcoholics with love and sometimes not. Sometimes I move toward love. It's a kinetic process.

**NATHALIE:** It's also letting go with love for yourself. It's letting go of expectations for your child. My favorite quote is from Anne Lamott, "Expectations are resentments under construction." It's also letting go of my dreams for her: going to college with good grades and that kind of thing. There is also letting go of expectations around my parenting. Not that I've been a failure, but you can't help but wonder. So it's letting go of all of that and loving myself because, though I didn't do it perfectly, that's the way it is. I did the best I could. That's letting go with love. We really have, for all the imperfection, done the best we could, and more. *And more.*

**DELIA:** Yeah, I do accept that we are amazing parents, and when I don't look at the outcome of our parenting but look at the effort put into it, I know we are super parents and do a whole lot better parenting than anything I would have received if I had Gianna's situation growing up. I'm thrilled for our individual and combined courage.

---

*No parent ever wants to accept his child has any serious illness, much less a highly stigmatized (and often very complicated to treat) mental illness. Most parents want to scream, and many do. And that's where the beauty of "radical acceptance" is realized. Merriam-Webster in part defines "accept" as ". . . to endure without protest or reaction . . . to regard as proper, normal or inevitable . . . to recognize as true . . ." Certainly, mental illness can't be the normal course of things. Most want to deny it or look for signs that the diagnosis is faulty, or wonder if maybe their child is just having a bad day. Yet accepting the diagnosis is the crucial first step toward recovery.*

*The concept of radical acceptance gives us an out. It allows us to have a stance that we accept the diagnosis but not without some internal protest or reaction. We don't regard it as proper, normal, or inevitable. But we can radically accept that it exists and must be addressed. We accept that we love our child, but we don't like it—it being the illness. Not one bit. Radical acceptance allows us to rise to the occasion while acknowledging it's not exactly what we'd wanted for our child.*

*Radical acceptance is a powerful and liberating concept that one cannot arrive at in one step; one moves into it gradually. Parents of adult children who live with serious mental illness learn that one has little control over the lives of their loved ones; each of us has purview only over our actions and reactions, and our commitment to unconditional love and support for our child. Commitment to one's child means being a good advocate and encouraging the ill person to move toward recovery on his own volition.*

*Embracing radical acceptance is recognizing where one can effect positive change. Finding good treatment for one's child and engaging in family therapy is a good use of one's resources. Feeling guilty about the illness, or passing blame for it, is not. It was only after Nathalie, Delia, and Gianna began DBT therapy that Delia began to accept she did not cause her daughter's illness. Delia came to recognize that Gianna's illness is, ultimately, not her own. She says, "This is my kid's journey, not mine." Relinquishing control in this way allows Delia and Nathalie to focus on their own life journey where they are more likely to find fulfillment and therefore be best equipped to support each other and Gianna in tangible ways.*

# CHAPTER EIGHT:
## DAN, REBECCA, AND STELLA

*What recovery can mean, and meeting your child*
*"where they are."*

*Many American teenagers worry about taking*
*their SAT. Our daughter had voices talking to*
*her while she was taking the SAT.*

*Truly knowing one's child provides terra firma in a landscape of*
*many variables that emerge when raising any child, but especially*
*one who is atypical. A parent usually knows when their child is*
*unwell, doing better, or is at his best. Knowing one's child and*
*trusting one's observations and gut instincts are valuable when*
*sifting through advice from medical professionals, a difficult*
*process where important, sometimes life-altering decisions require*
*balancing medical facts with parental intuition. When it comes to*
*treatment for mental illness, one size does not fit all. Those who*
*know the patient best often have the most useful information for*
*guiding another through treatment and toward recovery.*

*Dan and Rebecca's youngest daughter, Stella, was born in*
*1992, and at the time of our first interview, she was nineteen.*
*Dan and Rebecca speak with deep experience. Rebecca, a teacher,*
*is comfortable in sharing her story, though she's selective about*
*the details offered and to whom. But it is clear by the manner*
*in which Dan needed to get up and move during the interview*
*that talking about parenting a child with a serious mental illness*
*was not easy for him. He is not the type to share but did so to*
*represent others like him. Dan's private nature, and Rebecca's*
*comparative openness, is evidence that there are many ways to*

189

*cope, and finding what works is a personal process. Though Dan is less comfortable sharing and talking, both Dan and Rebecca are connected through many years of marriage and childrearing and often finish each other's sentences and thoughts. They both seem quite clear about what each needs.*

*This is Dan, Rebecca, and Stella's story.*

**REBECCA:** Our daughter, Stella, is nineteen.

**DAN:** She was, and still is, very bright. That was apparent from when she was quite young. I remember sitting on the floor with her when she was two or three years old playing a game, and she was basically doing subtraction. No one had taught her this. She figured it out on her own.

**REBECCA:** Stella is a very kind girl.

**DAN:** She's got a good heart. She has a great sense of humor, and as long as I can remember she has been a keen observer of behavior and what people are doing. I remember driving in the car with her and looking in the back seat, watching her, and she was watching everybody else.

**REBECCA:** She thinks a lot about how other people will feel. Too much sometimes. She doesn't want anyone arguing. She doesn't understand that you can argue and it's okay. I don't know how much of that has to do with her older sister, Kristin, who has a very strong personality and could argue with the best of them. Her sister is a strong person.

**DAN:** Forceful!

**REBECCA:** I think Stella decided at one point it was easier and worked better for her if she let her be that way.

**DAN:** Stella cast herself in the role of peacekeeper between her older sister and us, which is a lot for a kid to take on and, really, it isn't her place. But it's how she is. She is that keen observer and she's thinking, "My parents are spinning up what they usually spin up, and I can predict how my sister is going to respond, so I'm going to step in and say something to settle the matter." A lot of times she is very insightful.

**REBECCA:** It works.

**DAN:** But even though she can be insightful, her involvement is not what is needed right then. What's needed is dialogue between the parties in conflict who have a direct stake. She needs to understand that it's better for her to move on. She dislikes conflict but inserts herself less lately, but there's also less conflict going on in the family.

**REBECCA:** She does it less but still tries. For example, if I ask Kristin a question and it's clear that I'm annoyed, Stella will try to explain to me before it becomes a big issue.

**DAN:** Even so, "sensitive" is not the word that comes to my mind for Stella. I think of her as insightful and observant.

**REBECCA:** She's like that about herself, also.

**DAN:** She's analytical and has some intuition. Even though she's very analytical, she understands there is this emotional component to people's interactions and she is able to weigh that into the picture, too . . .

**REBECCA:** . . . and can do that rather quickly. She can cut to the chase in her mind.

**DAN:** It's in keeping with the fact that she's really friggin' smart!

Is she lucky? Well, maybe. Because sometimes when you have the kinds of problems she has, the smarter you are, the worse it can be. That intellect becomes a weapon against oneself.

**REBECCA:** Yes.

**DAN:** She is also extremely competitive. *Extremely.* She enjoyed athletics quite a bit and played soccer for years and also basketball on the boys' team.

**REBECCA:** She didn't know it was the boys' team when I signed her up!

**DAN:** She was on that team and hung in there. She played basketball on a girls' team. She was a very strong rebounder.

**REBECCA:** Very determined.

**DAN:** And stubborn. But socially, she was uncomfortable and awkward. Wasn't quite sure how to fit in or how to make that one really good friend and that bond. Socially, it was always a question mark with her.

**REBECCA:** People have always liked her, but she hasn't always been able to go from "having someone like me" to "what do I do with that?" Even though she wanted to make that leap. It was hard for her partly because she was not a girlie-girl. She liked to build with Legos and play soccer with the boys. She didn't want to play things like, "We're going to pretend we're wolves or little pink ponies" and such.

Even then she was, like you said, very intuitive. In second or third grade she'd come home and say, "I don't want to play these games. They're stupid. But I'm going to do it because I want to be in this group." The unfortunate thing is Stella would pretend she liked it, and the girls would still be mean to her.

Probably because it's hard for Stella to hide her scorn. She doesn't suffer those who she feels are fools.

**DAN:** Yes. The social thing has always been kind of questionable for her.

**REBECCA:** That was a difficulty for her. Always. Kristin is four school grades ahead of her. But luckily, when they were little, they played a lot together. They were good friends, but when Kristin got into fifth grade, middle school, Kristin had her own friends.

**DAN:** Kristin had her own problems as well.

**REBECCA:** Whereas Stella was socially uncomfortable, Kristin always had lots of friends. People were always inviting her over until her high school years when she suffered from major depression.

Stella was the opposite. I could say to Stella, "I'll give you five dollars if you call so-and-so and ask her to do something with you." No. She wouldn't do it. It made her anxious. What if they said, "No"? During middle school, she liked some kids who were in the same honors program she was in. She would get invitations to birthday parties or something like that. In general, she didn't do things with people outside of school. She would say things to me like, "I'm the kind of person that people think, 'yeah, she's really nice,' but I'm not someone they're going to be really good friends with." She was aware that it wasn't that people disliked her.

Then, in middle school, she started playing an instrument in band and decided she was going to do that in high school. That was great for her, because that became her group.

**DAN:** It created a social group.

REBECCA: There was a girl in the group, Abby, who she met freshman year. Before I got to know Abby I thought, "Abby's just a girl Stella likes." But Abby really liked Stella, and they became good friends. She made Stella feel good. When Stella was sixteen, Abby had a surprise birthday party for her and it made Stella feel good. But she still had a lot of social anxiety. When she was going to Abby's birthday party, I had to pull over to the side of the road because she was having an anxiety attack before she could even go in to the party.

DAN: There was a group of girls she associated with. She didn't necessarily feel a deep connection with them, but they were her circle of friends.

REBECCA: She wouldn't initiate things, but with the wonders of Facebook she would know what was going on. She had that group of girls in high school until things got kind of difficult. When Stella went into the hospital the first time, Abby knew, and I think Stella told other friends. Unfortunately, she didn't stay in band with that group of friends.

DAN: In high school, there was one boy.

REBECCA: Yes. She did have a boyfriend. Very sweet boy.

DAN: Who really thought she was it! I probably liked him better than she did!

REBECCA: They were friends from band. He was a year older than Stella.

DAN: He was a nice, sensible kid.

REBECCA: He was smart but kind of goofy. I think Stella thought, "I'm in high school. I'm supposed to have a boyfriend.

He really likes me. Therefore, yes, he'll be my boyfriend." They did a lot of things together.

They were planning to go to prom. She had an anxiety attack about it and didn't want to go because it was after she had been sick and didn't want people to ask where she had been. She told him she didn't want to go, and he said, "Okay, that's fine. We'll do something else." They went to an amusement park the day of the prom. That was kind of him.

**DAN:** There were things where Stella was comfortable, though. She enjoyed team sports and even playing soccer during recess. In elementary school she'd play soccer with the boys, and I remember one kid said, "Stella plays better in flip-flops than everyone else plays in shoes." It wasn't that she was more physically gifted. That's not to say she was weak or slow. But she wasn't especially strong or fast. She had this determination that put a lot of balls in the goal . . . or stopped them, because she played goalie a lot! She was very good as a forward in basketball and goalie in soccer. There were a lot of things she just willed to happen. Not because she had a better shot or more speed or whatever. She had a level of will and determination, competitiveness, and drive that was unusual in a kid her age.

She was this way with school, too, but was pragmatic. She wanted to be the best. She wanted to be among those who were on the accelerated track and wanted to get good grades. But she also understood the balance between getting the highest A in the class and what would be required for that, versus getting by with an A that is not the highest, but maybe you got to watch some TV and do other things. She had a sense of balance about that.

**REBECCA:** But she also would like to be the number one person.

**DAN:** Oh, absolutely. She is competitive. But if she had to make the choice, she would say, "I'm going to watch TV for a while."

**REBECCA:** In high school she could do that. We kept thinking and saying, "It's going to get harder . . ." but for her it never did. Then I thought it was going to get harder when she was in that program with a group of kids similar to her, and even *that* wasn't particularly hard for her. It wasn't easy; it just wasn't hard for her. Kids would say, "Oh, the homework!" But Stella was motivated. We never had to ask, "Stella, have you done your homework?" We didn't with either of our kids. That's just how they were. What was difficult was when her illness made schoolwork more challenging.

**DAN:** Because it had always been easy.

**REBECCA:** The first indications of her illness came in late elementary school or middle school when she started the OCD stuff.

**DAN:** There would be things she'd insist upon. I now feel bad about this, but I'd think, "You can't be serious about this. I mean, *really*? Both armrests of the van seat have to be down? You can't be serious?"

**REBECCA:** On a day-to-day basis I was with Stella more, so I had more opportunities to hear her say, "You're going to roll your window down? Then I'm going to roll my window down." I learned strategies. Then Stella, being the kind of person she is, wanted to see someone who could help her. She was intuitive about herself and what she needed. Stella's concern was OCD and anxiety. During those years, she also was beginning to show signs of anxiety. The psychosis part began between tenth and eleventh grade.

The therapist she saw first, for OCD and anxiety, was very good, but she wasn't used to working with a child who was as intuitive as Stella. I don't think she always listened to what Stella was saying. It wasn't a particularly good fit. She started Stella on some medication. I don't know that it helped. We went to different people trying to find someone. It's very hard to find a *child* psychiatrist who doesn't say, "I'm not taking new patients" or, "I can see you in six months." I guess she was in tenth grade when somebody recommended a doctor. I was present for part of those meetings. Stella was beginning to experience some psychosis by then, and in those sessions she started to act kind of "funny," for lack of a better word. She would look at me and not say anything. The psychiatrist was quite concerned that it was more than OCD or anxiety because of Stella's psychosis symptoms. Stella would smell things that others couldn't. The psychiatrist said it was sensory hallucination. Stella would say, "Don't you smell that? It's orange," or whatever the scent. I could tell it bothered her that I didn't smell it. She knew this was something different and it was starting to get to her.

The psychiatrist said, "I think this is something more." She introduced the word "psychosis" and said, "There's another doctor I want you to see." The doctor she mentioned was at a psychiatric hospital. I went home and, of course, researched that hospital and learned it's a place that treats patients with severe mental illness, including psychosis. This was when I was starting to think, "No, this can't be happening."

**DAN:** To put it in context, a few years earlier our older daughter had experienced deep depression. We learned from a school counselor that she had a blog about suicide that was very dark. She ended up in the hospital for two months and then went to a group home.

We had been down this road before.

**REBECCA:** Yes.

**DAN:** And I can't say our prior experience made me a great proponent of mental health care, to be honest. I have skepticism about mental health practices and believe a lot of decisions made and actions taken are more about legal liability and less about what is best for the patient or what constitutes sound diagnosis. This previous experience was in the mix, too, affecting how we felt. We had experiences with Kristin's illness where some decisions made by professionals were not, I don't think, the right ones. I'm a skeptic by nature anyway. Adding experiences that support the skepticism was compounding.

**REBECCA:** I thought, "I can't believe this is happening again." Also, my brother has schizophrenia, so I knew what that had been like for my brother and my parents. And though my brother has a good life and he's smart and was able to go to college, that's not what you picture for *your* child. I'm sure my parents didn't either. It's probably easier because I can look at my brother's life and say, "He's not out walking the streets and he takes his medication."

But I was trying to reconcile my Stella with *that* illness.

**DAN:** For me, it wasn't so much that she was going to a particular facility that treats serious mental illness that triggered my concern about her mental health.

By that point, I was noticing that discussions with her had become increasingly disturbing. She was talking about a chip implanted in her head for mind control. The first time I heard that, I thought, "Right, yeah, okay." Then I heard it again. I started saying, "What about this or that fact?" I tried to point out the absurdities in her logic. She understood the absurdity of what she was saying but simultaneously had an almost doctrinal belief that it was true. This was where being smart works against her because she was capable of posing a common sense thesis about how having an implanted chip simply cannot be possible, and then she'd provide an equally cogent thesis and rebuttal that it *did* make sense.

For me, it wasn't that we crossed a threshold because we were checking her into this particular mental health facility; it was realizing she was really serious about this flaky stuff. It was like, "You really do believe this." And she'd say, "Yeah, I really do. I don't. But I do." She was torn. Part of her knew it was implausible. She couldn't reach that point where she could say, "I know what I'm thinking is crazy."

REBECCA: Because of my experience with my brother, I had read about schizophrenia. I felt some disbelief. Not so much that "I can't believe this is schizophrenia" as "I can't believe this is happening." But there wasn't disbelief in the diagnosis.

DAN: We didn't question it.

REBECCA: We couldn't question it because our child was telling us that she didn't think we were her real parents and there was a chip in her brain.

DAN: There was one day we caught her going out the front door and she had a toboggan and a backpack . . .

REBECCA: Oh, I forgot about that.

DAN: I said, "Where are you going?" She said, "I'm escaping to warn the others." I tell a story like that and it's funny. You go through enough of these experiences and there's a point where you go, "This is *unreal*." But there are enough sad things and you realize, "She really does believe this. This is real." We accepted the idea that there was a problem. Obviously we'd have preferred *not* to find it was true, but we never had any resistance to the diagnosis.

REBECCA: No, because it was quite obvious.
   Stella's first hospitalization was planned. Stella and I were thinking, "This is like going to camp." We were focused on practicalities. "Stella, which pants do you want me to take

the string out of?" I wasn't as dumbstruck with those logistical things because we knew what it was going to be like in the hospital. We knew the procedures. We'd been through so much with our other daughter that we made jokes about it. Even to Stella.

DAN: The factual aspects and logistics of a hospitalization were not *as* wrenching as the first time Kristin was committed. We'd been through it before and our daughter was there for two months. It was also different with Stella in some ways.

REBECCA: Stella *wanted* to go into the hospital. This was not like she was going, "No, don't take me." Stella didn't feel safe. She felt she was not in control and she didn't know what was going on.

DAN: There was more going on than we realized because she had been hearing voices. We found that out later. Many American teenagers worry about taking their SAT. Our daughter had voices talking to her while she was taking the SAT.

REBECCA: I was driving her to the high school to take her SAT, and I remember her telling me, "I'm not feeling so great." I said, "What do you mean?" She didn't want to talk about it.

DAN: She told me later that voices were talking during the testing, and early into it they said, "We're going to *let* you do this, but we'll be back when you're done."

REBECCA: The voices were also telling her that we weren't her real parents.

DAN: And that people have a chip implanted and when they have a mental illness it's because their chip is not working. The voices said we were part of this plot, and the voices would take over, and at some point she was going to kill us. That's a lot for a kid to have to deal with.

**REBECCA:** That first time, she was relieved to go to the hospital. She was sixteen. I don't remember that much about it. I don't remember how long she was there.

**DAN:** It's kind of a blur.

**REBECCA:** That hospital is good about being aggressive with treatment so the illness doesn't spiral. I didn't know at the time how important that is. The more incidents of psychosis one experiences, the harder it is on the brain and the more damage is caused.

But she did really well on the SATs! When she received the test results, I said to Stella, "You made this score and you were psychotic!" She laughs at that.

**DAN:** When Stella was thinking about conspiracies, the business with the chip in her head and those things, I remember discussing this with Kristin, who in her own right is quite smart and logical. Kristin was in a discussion with Stella and saying, "What you're saying doesn't make sense." It was interesting to hear them talk back and forth, and it was then that Kristin grasped that, yes, there was a problem, and because she had her own problems with mental health and works in the mental health field now, she has insight and knows, "Yes, she is someone who has mental health issues."

**REBECCA:** Kristin feels sad for Stella. She was surprised when Stella became sick. At the time when Stella was experiencing psychosis and hospitalized, Kristin was working and taking care of herself and doing well.

**DAN:** Kristin visited Stella in the hospital. Fortunately, we didn't have to worry so much about what was going on with

Kristin at that time. The biggest worry then was the deplorable state of her room! Kristin is pursuing her own thing and doesn't think much about what is going on with anybody else. She's in her early twenties, consumed with herself. But I see her make an effort to engage her sister. They've found things they like doing together. They play video games with each other, for example. Their relationship has gotten better over the past few years. They've sort of staked out their ground. The big sister isn't quite so big anymore. In fact, Stella is taller!

**REBECCA:** And Stella will stand up for herself. She probably has fewer occasions in which she needs to stand up for herself now.

Kristin is also very protective of Stella. Once, when Stella was in preschool, there was a boy driving Stella crazy, being mean. He had no idea who Kristin was when she confronted him and said, "Leave my sister alone," then walked away. He didn't know she was talking about Stella! But like Dan said, on a day-to-day basis she's not saying, "How's Stella?" If we needed something from Kristin, we would ask her. If it were something she could do for Stella, she would do it.

**DAN:** True.

**REBECCA:** In eleventh grade, after she'd been hospitalized, Stella signed up to take three AP classes.

**DAN:** We were not driving Stella to be competitive.

**REBECCA:** It was what she wanted to do. I remember being in Dr. P—'s office that fall and the doctors were suggesting she shouldn't take a heavy schedule. I thought, "This is one instance where I'm going to disagree with the doctors because this is what Stella wants." It was the right thing to do. Unfortunately, she ended up having to drop every single one of them.

**DAN:** It's kind of a blur to me, but somewhere in this time frame there was a conflict with the band director, which meant she was not in band and lost her social network and the group she felt a part of. That made things more difficult.

**REBECCA:** She went away to band camp then called, asking me to come get her. She wasn't able to be in band. She dropped out in eleventh grade because of the illness. Then, in senior year, she stood up for herself to the band director. I don't even want to talk about it. I feel about him the way I feel about nobody in this world.

**DAN:** He was an odd duck. But the point is that her social outlet was gone.

**REBECCA:** Went away.

**DAN:** And at the same time she was also having to confront the fact that all the young overachievers with whom she'd gone to middle school were taking all AP courses and pursuing the path she had thought would be hers, too. She had to throttle back her academics, and that was in no small measure because of the medication.

**REBECCA:** We went through a period of time where the medications were not right. You know, "Stella is awake all night, Stella is breaking out in hives, Stella is this and that . . ." It's the standard thing. She went through the antipsychotics they like to start with but ended up on an older generation antipsychotic. I can't remember how long it took to get there.

**DAN:** One time she was on something that completely zonked her out. She's on something now that seems to address the issue and strike a balance, but it's not without a price. She knows how quick she used to be. Her intelligence is such that her slow is faster than most people's quick. But it's hard for her to accept that "my brain is not working as fast as it used to, and I have to work harder to remember things." Throughout most of her school experience she was able to pick things up, learn without really having to work too hard, and she hadn't developed the skills to be able to dig in and go, "Okay, I'm not getting it, but I'm going to work at it until I get it." That junior year, she really had to dig in to learn. And she wasn't in AP classes that year.

**REBECCA:** Junior year she had to drop AP courses. The teachers worked well with her and helped her stay in classes. She actually went to a tutor, a teacher who used to be a math teacher at her school, and she thought Stella was incredible. Unfortunately, I don't remember, maybe it was something to do with the medications, but Stella had to drop that one, too.

**DAN:** How she needed to work was not how it once was, and she had to learn to accept that she was on a new playing field.

**REBECCA:** That was what was hardest. Her whole identity was gone. She didn't see herself as Miss Social, but she was really smart, and other people saw her that way too. Even other smart people. That had been her identity since elementary school.

Once, after she'd been in the hospital at sixteen, Dr. P— said to her, "One day at a time." Because Stella would express things like, "I can't concentrate, my memory..." Dr. P— also told Stella that it would take about a year before she'd be back where she wanted to be. I remember thinking, "I can't believe you said to Stella, who can be very impatient with herself and others, that it's going to be *a year*." I felt bad for her. But on the other hand I thought, "You're being honest with her."

**DAN:** Any teenager looks at a year and thinks, "*A year?*"

**REBECCA:** Dr. P— was being realistic with her. It was helpful because Stella could think, "Okay. I have to find out how to deal with it."

**DAN:** It provided her with a timeline.

**REBECCA:** She was fortunate to get into a program at another high school, the Bridge program. A lot of kids were diagnosed with bipolar. I don't think there were any with schizophrenia. For her, that program was excellent. She was quite different from a lot of the kids there in that she was driven academically, so the teachers there loved Stella.

**DAN:** All the kids in that program are diagnosed with a mental illness, but their illness has led each to different problems. They may have gotten into trouble with the law, or drugs, or may have attempted suicide. Fortunately, her problems hadn't led her to acting out and a lot of behavioral problems.

**REBECCA:** The two people there were very good about collaborating with Stella's teachers at her high school. Stella went there for half the day. She wanted to continue her senior year, and they said she could. She did that program for two years.

Stella is currently in college, a good school, living in a dorm, doing really well. She's taking a full load, made really good grades, studying engineering. She's taking classes that make me shake just thinking about them.

**DAN:** Physics, math, and chemistry.

**REBECCA:** Living in a suite and making friends with the girls, and that's been good for her.

**DAN:** There's always concern in the background. If we don't hear from her, we wonder, "Does that mean something?" If you talk to her and she sounds down, then how *down* is she? If she struggles with a course, is that a harbinger? Is that going to put her over the edge? Is that the first in what's going to be a series of falling dominoes? We're always looking for that thing that might lead to the next crisis. Over the last year, for the most part, there haven't been things. We did have one situation.

**REBECCA:** Stella called me on a Friday and said, "I've been feeling kind of weird." I don't remember if it was her idea or mine, but she went to the office of disabilities and they said, "Go to counseling." I could hardly lift my head. I told Stella to call you, and I told you to call her."

**DAN:** I talked to the psychiatrist who had seen her. They were very concerned with her demeanor and presentation and everything. I was told, "You can either come here and take her to the hospital or we are going to take her. Because she's going the hospital."

**REBECCA:** I was just glad they let us know.

**DAN:** So I went and got her.

**REBECCA:** And you stopped at Taco Bell on the way to the hospital!

**DAN:** Well, you know . . .

**REBECCA:** I know! Right?

**DAN:** We went to the university hospital emergency room. Waited forever.

**REBECCA:** As usual. Like, nine hours though.

**DAN:** Had blood drawn and all that. They put her in the room with the soft furniture and we waited forever. The thing is, I was looking at her thinking, "She's all right." We were both tired, and finally I said, "We're leaving. Sorry, but we're not staying here indefinitely. It's not doing any good, and it's probably doing more harm."

**REBECCA:** By then it was three o'clock Saturday morning and they'd been there since five or five-thirty and she hadn't seen the psychiatrist.

**DAN:** "We're done," I said. "We're leaving." They were resistant. I said, "No. We are leaving." They said, "Sign this." Stella was pissed because we were signing that we had refused treatment. But we didn't refuse treatment! We never *received* treatment. We refused to wait indefinitely for treatment. In the end, it was the right decision to leave because it was a single episode on a single day, and who knows how it might have been drawn out or exacerbated and worsened?

**REBECCA:** It would have been worse had they stayed because *we* know Stella and what she really needed was a break. Because it was a Friday, she came home and stayed that weekend with us. We talked with her and she stayed home Monday too, got caught up on work, and then went back.

**DAN:** When it comes to your child's treatment, you have to believe medical professionals and accept that there *is* something going on. But you *live* with this child day in and day out. Medical professionals make a diagnosis based on a sample of information against a backdrop of research and known facts that they try to map to an individual they see very briefly; they must rely upon what you tell them, what your child tells them, and there will be times that it's better to be skeptical. A parent has a perspective that a medical professional doesn't have. That doesn't mean you are against the medical professional. You have to work *with* them. But if your observations point in a different direction, you sometimes have to allow that.

Strike a balance between buying into what professionals tell you and your own thoughts, experiences, and observations of your child and what seems to be working and what isn't, because you might be told, "I think we've nailed it with this combination of meds," and you're looking at your kid and she's not there, it's not her. You have to say, "No, I don't think what I'm seeing is working." Strike a balance between working with medical professionals and trusting your observations and knowledge of your kid.

REBECCA: They wanted her to stay. I understand from their perspective, because they don't know . . .

DAN: They don't want to take chances.

REBECCA: They can't make the assessment on a person they don't know. Didn't you say the doctor called you later?

DAN: Yes, and I was pleased he did. But I was candid. He had done a residency at that university hospital and was a little surprised by what happened. He said, "You could have said this, you could have done that . . ." But it's like, "No, we were there for what seemed like forever, and at some point you gotta say, 'This isn't right.' Sitting in a room with padded furniture and nothing else is *not* going to help."

REBECCA: If she had stayed there, they would have admitted her, and it was a weekend and she wouldn't have gotten treatment. This way, she got a break and a weekend at home.

DAN: She took a day off. She caught up and she was back in

stride. That was the only thing that happened all year. She was stressed. Stress triggers the illness.

**REBECCA:** I'm sure it was related to feeling overwhelmed by schoolwork.

**DAN:** Shortly after that, she dropped one of her classes. She'd had an interaction with one of her professors. I don't even remember the details.

**REBECCA:** Yeah, the professor suggested that she needed to "get over" some of her issues. He said she didn't need her testing accommodations because, in the real world, she wasn't going to get these kinds of accommodations.

**DAN:** She needed to "just get over it." Which is, in fact, incorrect. She's registered with the disabilities office and receives accommodations with exams and tests. She may take tests in a separate spot in the disabilities office and also gets additional time.

**REBECCA:** Pretty much double the amount of time. I think her school's disability office is very good, and I think Stella would agree.

**DAN:** But of course not everything is entirely in the hands of the disability office. You get somebody like that professor who, with the best of intentions says, "You're going to have to buck up, ol' chum." I understand what he means and there's probably an element of accuracy to it, but it's also *not* accurate and not within the letter of the law.

**REBECCA:** Stella also uses special notebooks and pens that look like regular ones. While taking notes with the special pen, it records the lecture. If for some reason she can't pay attention, she can go back and listen to it. Not only that, but she can upload her notes into her computer and they match up with what the professor is saying on the recording. That has been great.

She's going to summer school at a different university and I'm a little worried. I'm trying to get her to send in the disability information there because the accommodations she's had are around reducing stress during testing.

**DAN:** But she did form friendships at college. They are her style of friendships. That's how she is. But you know, she got through a year.

**REBECCA:** She stepped way outside her comfort zone. She had a roommate.

**DAN:** I was holding my breath for her to get out of high school. Then I held my breath that maybe she would get *into* a college, then that she could *go*, and once she was there I was holding my breath that she'd do it!

**REBECCA:** That she could live on campus!

**DAN:** And she ended up doing pretty well!

**REBECCA:** She's told us a lot of funny stories about her roommate.

**DAN:** In the suite that she's in, the others are all good students and nice girls.

**REBECCA:** She's done things with them and gone to the beach.

**DAN:** They seem to be a good match for her. She's getting a different roommate next year, and she's excited because this other roommate seems a little more like her.

**REBECCA:** She's still going to be in a suite with her old roommate, so it's familiar.

**DAN:** She likes what's familiar. She made it through a year!

**REBECCA:** We're happy for her.

**DAN:** I guess we have tried to make her feel like she doesn't need to push her progress any faster than her progress is. We encourage her to be a little more patient with herself, but that is not her personality. If she were different, maybe we would push her a bit more, but with her it's more like, "Relax. Drop the class. It's not the end of the world if you drop this class . . . that's what summer school is for."

**REBECCA:** We didn't have any ideas about what she was going to be like as she got older. No expectations. We've always wanted her, both of our kids, to be happy. If we'd had expectations it wouldn't have been good. She gets to decide that, and we're supporting her in any way we can and trying not to judge what she does. Stella is such a sweet girl, you just want to support her.

**DAN:** It's easy. There are so many parents who have a situation where—and I'm thinking specifically about some kids in Bridge program—their illness has led to behaviors that you have to corral and deal with in addition to treating them for their illness. It could be so much more difficult. In a way, we had it easier.

**REBECCA:** Because of Stella. The way she is.

**DAN:** Her illness didn't translate into other dangerous behaviors as it sometimes does for other kids.

**REBECCA:** I think about the NAMI class and I understand people have different personalities, but we don't have a timetable for Stella. We had that experience with her older sister, also. When her older sister graduated from high school, she pretty much slept the whole year after high school. That's what she needed.

**DAN:** We were just glad she was under our roof. That she made it through high school.

**REBECCA:** We might have been *thinking* things like, "I wish she'd get up. Why don't you do something? How can you do that all day?" But we didn't say that to her because it wasn't going to help.

**DAN:** It wasn't what she needed. Then she *did* get a job, and that provided structure and a sense of accomplishment and that's made a big difference for her.

**REBECCA:** And that's her personality.

**DAN:** But a parent has to have some level of expectation because if there is no expectation ever expressed or implied, then you *are* treating her like a basket case and you're sending the message that "I don't think you can do anything and there is nothing left in the world for you." I think we say things about not pushing and so on, but at the same time we've always had some expectation and expressed the message that "it is within your grasp to have a normal, satisfying life. Your life right now may not be like others your age. There might be some things that are more difficult. There might be some things that take longer and things that are painful. But the possibility of a satisfying life is still within your grasp. You can expect that. *We* can expect that. We might not push in a micromanaging way, but yeah, we can expect that. There isn't any reason why you can't go to college. There isn't any reason why you can't do well. You can do this. If that means you need to drop a class, so what! You don't have to push yourself any harder than you have to. Do what you have to do. There is always more time."

**REBECCA:** Stella has seen lots of different therapists but never anybody she thought was helpful. When she was in the Bridge program, therapy was a requirement. She would see this guy, Andrew, a doctoral student working with Dr. P—. I think he was practicing with Stella. That was fine with Stella, fine with everybody, and it satisfied the requirement. I liked it because she was talking to someone other than *me*.

**DAN:** We understand now that mental illnesses are physiological. A lot of parents probably feel, "What is it that I've done?" I've made my mistakes as a parent. But I don't think those mistakes caused her illness. This is physiological, and the medications that address it get her most of the way there. After that point, it becomes a question of personality. There are personalities who need a therapist to talk, and maybe vent, and work through strategies.

**REBECCA:** To learn strategies is why I wanted her to go . . .

**DAN:** But there are also personality types where talking isn't the thing they need. Every time I've ever had this discussion with Stella, I come away knowing that "talking it out" is not her personality. Her older sister has been seeing a therapist for years. Loves this therapist. And the therapist has been very helpful. That's been the right thing. That's her particular circumstance and personality. But for someone like Stella, who is intensely analytical, it is just not like her to let it all hang out and share feelings. That's not what she's going to do. Even when she expresses feelings, she does so in an analytical, bullet-point way. I want to make sure she's okay emotionally, but this business of the therapist, I don't know if that is her need. The real need is to get that right mix of meds where you're not giving up too much on one side in order to get some gains on the other. It's that weird alchemy of a little more of this, a little less of this, and a little bit of that stirred in. Right now it's an imperfect mix, but it seems to work.

Her academic success has made a big difference as well. She looks at this past year and says, "Hey, I actually did pretty well." In fact, earlier in the year there was a contest within the engineering department and her team won. Not only did they win, but she had done a lot of the work, and it was work that beforehand she had no idea how to do. But, with her determination, she dug in and did it. I think of that picture you took with her standing by the display . . . did she have a medal or something?

**REBECCA:** Yes! She had a medal!

**DAN:** She looks so satisfied with herself that she won. Having a success early in the school year probably paid dividends throughout the rest of the year because she could say, "Hey, wow! I actually did succeed! I can be in this game." Now she can look back and say, "I got through a year of college." Very few people look at their first year of college and go, "That was a cakewalk!"

**REBECCA:** I told her I felt lucky to get a C that first year!

**DAN:** It's a rude awakening for most people.

It was for her because she realized the bar gets reset in college. It's where talent and intelligence carry the day, and there has to be a certain amount of sweat and effort. She's interested in this really weird, obscure corner of engineering called paper technology and science.

**REBECCA:** It's making paper. You work for big paper-making companies.

**DAN:** She's taking this class and knows the most arcane information. She'll recount, "Do you realize that the hog fuel boiler in a paper plant can produce 12 percent of the . . ."

**REBECCA:** She and Dan have this ability to memorize!

**DAN:** She's telling me all these things about the paper market and trees, this compendium of facts. I said, "How do you know all this stuff?" She says, "We *have* to know it. We are not allowed *not* to know it." That has been a really good thing for her, that she had a class that was tangible and where there was a high expectation in this professional program. The expectation is, "We are bringing you into a profession, and we expect you to know this off the top of your head." It fits her.

**REBECCA:** The relationship Stella has with her grandparents has also helped. Stella's illness doesn't make one bit of difference to them. They are excited about anything Stella does and are proud of her. They are like that with all the grandchildren. They don't treat her any differently.

   We don't treat Stella differently than we ever did, either. To us she's the same Stella. Even when she was telling us we weren't her real parents, Stella was still there. I would go into her room and she'd say things like, "You're not my real mother" and, "There's a plot." But she was looking at me because she wanted me to tell her that it wasn't right. She really believed it, but there was always this little part of her that wasn't quite sure. She'd take a toboggan and go outside like that one time, but if we said, "Stella, you're not going to do this," she would come back inside. It's not like she was going to run away or anything.

**DAN:** We don't want to treat her like a basket case. There might be cases where someone is pretty far gone and they need to be treated more carefully, but treating somebody with respect and a degree of normalcy and expectation—not impatience or too much expectation—probably helps too.

**REBECCA:** We are fortunate also that she was able to get good treatment, and that we live where there are good resources. And she was able to go to the Bridge program nearby.

**DAN:** She and I go snowboarding. That's key!

**REBECCA:** Yeah. She loves that! And she's good at it. It's another thing where she feels good.

**DAN:** Yes. If we were to make a general, broad recommendation to another parent, it's that every kid is probably good at *something*. Parents should try to get them doing that thing so they feel some sense of accomplishment and self-worth. About something. Maybe it's not snowboarding. Maybe it's crochet.

**REBECCA:** Whatever. Something.

**DAN:** And do it *with* them.

Maintaining reliability and stability is also important. If we were melting down over this, it would be a big problem. That's not to cast judgment on someone who melts down with this sort of thing because it would be a very natural thing to do. I would never criticize somebody for doing so, but if you can avoid a meltdown and maintain a harbor of stability, that's useful.

**REBECCA:** I work in a very supportive place. I told coworkers whom I knew well a few details, and some people were more aware than others. If I said to my co-teacher, "I need to go out in the hall because Stella's psychiatrist is on the phone," that was fine. It was very supportive. But there was that period of time after Stella got out of the hospital that we were not comfortable with her being by herself at home. And I'm not saying it was easy, but fortunately while I worked, Dan was able to take Stella to the other high school where the Bridge program was located. That's how we did it.

**DAN:** The circumstances of my employment are unlike being a teacher where you need to be there, in-person, and 100 percent there. I was able to work from home even though it's not ideal. I didn't have to explain. If I had been pressed on it, I would have said, "Here's what's going on . . ." But it wasn't questioned.

**REBECCA:** I was also fortunate to have this group of friends whom I met with regularly and were like a support group and knew about Stella's illness.

**DAN:** It was not something I talked about. I talked to my mother about it. She lives locally, as do Rebecca's parents.

**REBECCA:** I have found that it helps to find somebody to talk to. I don't mean a therapist, though that would probably be good too, but somebody who cares about you and your child who is not necessarily a family member, a person who can be more objective. I was able to talk to people who already knew Stella and love Stella and who I knew truly cared about her and weren't going to judge and think, "Oh, here's this crazy girl." Whereas, talking to my mother, she's thinking, "Poor Stella." She's worried about Stella and me.

**DAN:** Because of her experience with her own son, who has schizophrenia.

**REBECCA:** The NAMI Family-to-Family class is a good resource. And anywhere one can find support without judgment of them or their child. It's especially lucky to find a person or a group of people who have had a similar experience. What surprised me with our older daughter was that when I told people, they were like, "Well, my brother has a mental illness . . ." Then they'd start talking because mental illness is a big secret for many people. I feel lucky that I know a lot of people with whom it doesn't have to be a secret. You can talk about it.

**DAN:** Talking and groups are good for Rebecca. That's not necessarily how everybody is, though. A person who feels the need to talk should seek that out. There are resources, NAMI, for example. It's good if one can do that. There are people who want to listen and can talk and share.

But if that's not how a person deals with things, one shouldn't have to feel like they're being railroaded into it. If that's not a person's thing, don't do it. And I'd say that's me! When one goes through difficult experiences, there seems to be this expectation that one wants and needs to talk, and even that a person is obligated to talk until sometimes it gets to the point where a person feels like, "I don't wanna friggin' talk anymore!"

That might be in part why fathers don't often come forward and talk. I did sense it'd probably be a good idea if somebody like me, who doesn't feel a need to talk, *should* talk because otherwise no one hears a perspective from people who are like me. It's great that Rebecca has friends and people close to her who she can talk to, but I don't have a problem with the fact that I haven't done that myself because we're different people and it's not helpful to me in the way that it is for her.

**REBECCA:** I didn't want to talk about every little thing, but I liked knowing that people knew. I might send an email to people and say, "I don't want to talk about this, but I want you to know that Stella is back in the hospital." I wanted people to know, but I didn't want to talk about it.

**DAN:** You did that fairly regularly. You'd say, "Here's what's going on. We're coming for dinner. I don't want to talk about this, but just so you know what's going on. I'm not seeking input." That's a good piece of advice: sometimes just lay it out there. "Okay, I'm letting you know because it's important for me that you know, but that doesn't mean I want to talk about it."

**REBECCA:** That's what I said to some people at church. I'd say, "It's not that I don't want people to know, it's that I don't want everybody asking me about it." I might tell one person. I didn't want *everybody* coming up to me and saying, "How's Stella?" No matter how well meaning, it's a reminder every time. But I like knowing that people . . .

**DAN:** . . . that people close to you know. And you have more people who are close to you than I do.

**REBECCA:** It helps to feel their love and support when you feel bad. I remember a Mother's Day when Kristin had her problems. I was hoping against hope that Kristin was going to call me. I knew she wasn't. We had done something with Stella, and you had gone with Stella to your mother's and I went home. I was feeling pretty sad and came home and there was something at the door from friends. They had gotten me a gift basket. That kind of support was helpful to me.

**DAN:** About coping: I guess I have always felt that there are enough things in the world that are so much worse for so many parents than what I was going through. I was in a position to provide care for my kids when they went through what they did, and they still get the care they need and we live where they have access to help. Who knows, if there'd been a different set of circumstances, maybe we would have melted down and handled things very differently. But we are lucky.

It helps to get a bigger perspective and remember, "It could be so much worse."

**REBECCA:** As for coping: I know what I'd say for you!

**DAN:** What, Scotch?

**REBECCA:** Well, it's very obvious. It's out in the driveway!

**DAN:** Oh! The motorcycle! I'd say it's a good thing to cope with! Having a life of one's own is good. Don't give up those things. I try to keep the interests from my regular life. Are they going to get affected? Yeah, sometimes. But that doesn't mean abandon one's interests entirely either. Keep them around. Let them get affected when needed, but don't let your child's illness become the core fact of your existence because you have your own existence apart from whatever your child is going through. I think that's better for the child, too. Because if the child starts feeling like everything is about *them* and what *they're* going through and *their* problem, your child will feel guilt and a sense of responsibility, which is not positive. Maintain a life, have activities, whatever those might be—whether it's being with friends or other social activities for Rebecca, or riding a motorcycle. Whatever works. Maintaining normalcy sends a very clear message to your kid that says, "Yes, we know there's a problem here but it's not such a problem that everything else is on hold." I think that's probably a good message.

**REBECCA:** What I have said to somebody whose child had recently been diagnosed is that it *is* about patience and time and all that. But as hard as it is right then, it *can* get better. It's very hard to remember that. When you are in the middle of it and your child is telling you, "I hate you and I can't be in the same room with you," which is what our older daughter said to me, or when Stella would say, "I don't think you are my real mother," it is challenging. When you are in the middle of that, you're thinking, "I don't know how I'm going to get through this." It's incredible, and you don't know how you are going to handle it. Having our situation with Kristin made coping easier with Stella.

**DAN:** And it had been so bad with Kristin.

**REBECCA:** It had been so bad with Kristin. But it can get better. This isn't a life sentence. It's not as if there isn't any hope.

**DAN:** There is hope.

**REBECCA:** It's like diabetes. You can't cure it, but you can treat it. And the person can go on to have a regular life.

We are very happy for her.

---

*Rebecca recalls how challenging their lives were when they learned their oldest was suffering with serious depression and while Stella was saying things such as, "You're not my mother." From their experience, they want to tell other parents that it can get better.*

*What helped Dan and Rebecca and their family was the support they have for each other and the manner in which each respects the way the other copes. He doesn't always want to talk, and she has a solid group of dear friends. Their support extends to their children. They recognized that healing takes time and allowed their oldest daughter, Kristin, to do nothing but rest for about a year. They recognize that Stella pressures herself, and they encourage her to allow time for healing, take fewer classes, whatever it takes to stay healthy. Rebecca and Dan support their children but do not coddle. They allow Stella to make her own decisions about college, dorm living, and summer school.*

*Dan and Rebecca possess a clear perspective. They*

have learned to balance their own instincts with advice from professionals. They know their daughters well and respect their individual needs. Dan and Rebecca also recognize their good fortune to have been able to receive early and effective treatment for their children. They recognize their good fortune in not having to address substance use with Stella's recovery.

Dan and Rebecca believe that there can still be hope for a life with serious mental illness. Their belief is illustrated by the way they express their expectation that their daughters can live satisfying lives. It is also expressed in their lifestyle, that their daughter's illness, while top of mind, is not the core focus of family life. Expressing the expectation that a person who lives with mental illness can have a meaningful life is perhaps the most respectful, empowering, and genuine love a parent can have for their child.

# PART III

*Our new normal.*

*Decades ago, medical professionals erroneously believed that bad mothering caused mental illness. Great strides have been made toward understanding and treating brain disorders. Still, compared to other chronic illnesses, relatively little is known. It is commonly held that mental illness is caused by a confluence of factors among which is genetic loading, with stress or substance use—or a combination—providing a trigger. Environmental factors can explain why symptoms appear or escalate following trauma or a significant life transition such as a move, a loss, or starting college.*

*Despite evidence to the contrary, parents often feel irrationally responsible for causing or not preventing their child's mental illness. Almost all parents wish they had done at least one thing differently. Grieving over what one's child lost to the illness is common. But all admit that parenting an adult child with mental illness comes with a steep learning curve. With time and heartache comes the ability to understand the illness and manifestations common for the illness and unique to each individual. Experienced parents learn that life with mental illness, for patient and caregiver, requires lifestyle adjustments such as reducing stressors and managing expectations.*

*The emotional intensity and day-to-day challenges mean a parent/caregiver's own needs are easily neglected. Many parents begin to recognize that caring for one's own needs and living an active life separate from the illness is vitally important for ensuring they will be best equipped to meet their child's needs, particularly during a crisis.*

*As one parent explains, accepting their child's mental illness diagnosis does not mean it is welcomed, or has any agreement with that fact of her child's life. But acceptance is an acknowledgment of what is, a willingness to embrace the new reality of her child's life, and embrace a new normal. A full embrace of one's own or a loved one's mental illness allows the necessary grieving process that can lead to a solid path toward developing real coping strategies and setting realistic expectations. Grief is not a sign of weakness but rather the beginning of gaining the strength to move forward.*

*In the following chapters, author Elin Widdifield joins parent/contributors to share experiences of grief, guilt, and the coping strategies that have helped. Elin's son, Joseph, is currently in recovery. There are no final words, or conclusions, for these stories. These are ongoing, and with hope and good treatment, these stories can have good outcomes.*

# CHAPTER NINE:
# OUR OWN ROLLER COASTER

*Grief, guilt, advice, and coping.*

*The guilt over "What did I do?
How did she get this?"
persists every day.*

*It's okay to let yourself grieve. It's going to be a
lifelong process.*

*If I hadn't worried so much about appearances,
maybe I would have intervened sooner and he
wouldn't have been homeless, or thrown in jail.*

## On Grief

*When my son, Joseph, began showing symptoms of his illness, I
was cast, like all parents, into another realm of existence, at first
bewildered by the behaviors and then overwhelmed over how to
help him. While getting a diagnosis gave us a sense that we had
a starting point for finding treatment, the actual words "bipolar
disorder" had an oppressive power over me. I couldn't even say these
words that delivered me into isolation and depression. I grieved
deeply over the lost hopes and dreams that once seemed possible
for Joe, whose identity was tied to his athleticism, musical talent,
and academic success, all of which had begun to erode because of
the illness. I grieved over what our family always imagined "would
be" and "should be" and the loss of a family life we once knew. Our
oldest son pulled away from the chaos, and I can't say that I blame
him. Our lives had no predictability; family trips were planned and
cancelled; it became understood that any plan was a tentative one.*

225

*Grief manifests differently for everyone. The grief my husband and I experienced was, like for many parents, tangled up with fear for Joe's safety, concerns about when the next crisis would hit and what it would look like, and because of Joe's substance use, the realistic possibility of death. My husband immersed himself in work, whereas my life retracted. I retreated from community and friends, declined social invitations, and resigned from work and volunteer positions and activities in which I'd once been active and found fulfillment for many years. My life changed. I left the house to do only necessary tasks: grocery shop, walk the dog, and sometimes to go to the gym. Once, a display of tangerines at the grocery store reduced me to tears before I fled back home.*

*When I did venture out of the house, I made a conscious effort to "act normal," though in hindsight, it's highly unlikely I appeared to be my old self. I had no desire to participate in activities that had before brought pleasure. The idea of reading fiction, seeing friends, or even practicing martial arts in which I'd recently earned a second-degree black belt could not draw me away from my overwhelming grief. There were times I ranted. I cried a lot, watched too much television, ate too much, and didn't sleep. I had little energy for conversation with anyone.*

**BIANCA**: When a person has a brain disorder it's traumatic for the family, like experiencing a death. If Miguel had been in a car accident and had brain damage, everybody would have enfolded him. The loss Arturo felt about Miguel's illness affected him the way I felt the loss and hurt of my divorce: if the man had died, I'd have gotten a card. Flowers at least. You are left with pain and grief that no one acknowledges.

As with the death of a family member, there are multiple manifestations of grief. Arturo's gone through them all. Arturo started out very angry and thought Miguel could control his illness. Arturo was *mad*. Mad that his brother couldn't function. Mad about his behavior. Mad about the craziness. There were times I yelled at him to go with Miguel when he went downtown and said, "You have to watch him . . ." and then Arturo was *mad* he had to watch out for his brother! He wouldn't talk to him at all for a while. With age and maturity . . . he's grown and is no longer mad at Miguel. He sees that Miguel is not a bad person. Miguel can't control his behaviors.

I am grieving. I lost my son. Somewhere he's still there. I saw him that weekend of the wedding. But he can't sustain that.

I'd tell another parent, you didn't cause the illness. Be nice to yourself. There's a certain amount you can't control. There's only so much you're in charge of. If I ruled the world, my kid wouldn't have this! But I have only so much control!

It's okay to let yourself grieve. It's going to be a lifelong process. You spend years with your child before he becomes ill in his twenties. All that happens between parent and child doesn't go away overnight. Believe in yourself to be a good parent. Give yourself time to grieve, learn, and cope. There's a lot of grief. It can get better. It's never going to be the same, but that doesn't mean it's always going to be bad. It will be different than before, but better than the worst part.

The experience will make one stronger whether one wants it to or not.

## On Guilt

*Years of training and professional experience in the field of psychology fortunately provided me the ability to access resources and understand my son's illness. But nothing had prepared me for the experience of living with a person who has a serious mental illness. And even knowing that brain disorders are caused by a confluence of factors, I couldn't help but wonder if there was something I could have done differently. Was it the virus I had while pregnant? Had we been too hard on him? Too easy? Privately, I railed against my grandfather who was a recovering alcoholic, and against other long-deceased relatives who had the gall to pass this hideous curse of mental illness on to my beautiful boy. I often fantasized about taking on my son's illness so he wouldn't have to suffer.*

*As Joe's illness progressed, home life became chaotic. My husband and I never knew and couldn't imagine what would happen next. We constantly worried, "Will our son start using? Become manic? How will we take care of him, and where will we go for help?" Joe's dual diagnosis seemed overwhelming, insurmountable, and sometimes even hopeless. Making matters worse was that, against every parental instinct, Joe, at one point, insisted on living alone. Though he took his medications, his substance use negated their efficacy. Every phone call, every person at the door might bring unbearable news. I lived with fear, anxiety, sleeplessness, and was constantly on edge. At that time, neither my husband nor I could imagine having hope for the future, much less tomorrow. Tomorrow he could be dead, either intentionally or by accident.*

*With a level of anxiety beyond what I'd ever before experienced, I felt paralyzed and became incapable of doing much of anything useful. I wasn't coping at all. Like all the parents we interviewed, my sense of passing time—days, weeks—was blurred.*

**TESSA:** I feel guilty because when he was sixteen and showed signs of his illness—the rages, the way he talked to me, and behaviors I'd not seen before—I didn't take him somewhere else instead of that psychotherapist who said he was doing what was typical of adolescence. I knew that those rages were not normal, but I also wanted to believe her and that he was going through a phase.

But the main cause of guilt is my denial. If I had accepted and listened to my gut the *first* time, when he was sixteen, I wonder if he would have ended up in a catatonic state in New Orleans. I feel guilty I didn't accept, that I wasn't *ready* to accept that maybe my son's brain wasn't normal. I probably could've done more for him if I'd accepted his diagnosis earlier. If I hadn't worried so much about appearances, maybe I would have intervened sooner and he wouldn't have been homeless or thrown in jail.

There are all these things one thinks one could have done differently. Mother bears kill whatever threatens their cub. I was always that kind of mother, and I think, "Why didn't I do that when he was sixteen? Why didn't I say, "This isn't the end"? Why did I take *one* person's word? Why didn't I go somewhere else? Why didn't I start researching then? Why did I force him *out*? I have a strong personality and can be a little pushy. Why didn't I push it further? It's because I wanted to believe there was nothing wrong.

Having a loved one with a brain disorder wears you down even when everything seems okay. It's a chronic illness. My sister, who has a son with a serious mental illness, apologizes to me for not returning calls. I say, "Are you kidding? Don't ever apologize if you can't get back to me right away. But if you need help, someone to listen, or if you can't talk, just text me: 'Pray.' Because I get how it is." But most people don't understand. Once, my friend said, "I heard that when they're forty it goes away." Sometimes it mellows out, but it doesn't *go away*. Otherwise you wouldn't hear about forty- and fifty-year-old people killing themselves.

After a recent incident where Riley was yelling at me, threatening, pushing that one button that gets to me, "I'm leaving! You'll never see me again!" and screaming at his caseworker, I said, "What if your caseworker put you in jail?" He said, "I didn't treat Dylan the way I treat you." I said, "Of course you didn't." But the way he acted affected me deeply. The following Saturday and Sunday I stayed in pajamas all day until I went to a friend's house.

My personal life has gotten better in the last few years, but it's always hanging in the balance. When Riley came home after being incarcerated, everything was about him for three years.

Not being able to get away and the expense of caring for

Riley are the biggest impacts in my personal life. I can't get away because I have no one else to watch him now that he's out of the judicial program where there was a safety net. I offer to bring him with me on vacation and tell him to bring a friend. My husband and I want to get an RV and take a two-week vacation with the dogs. I really don't want to take my son! I would love to get away from him, and I'm sure he would love to get away from me!

Last year I was able to get away because Riley was still in the criminal justice program that served as a safety net. I went away by myself for two weeks. I didn't even take the dog! I said, "I need to get away from everybody here." The open road! I love nature. Riley called every day I was on the road, sometimes two and three times a day. I sent him pictures and he'd say, "Wow! That's cool!" Of course, the whole time I was gone, I kept close tabs with my husband. Riley got drunk a couple times. He went to jail but got out after only twenty-four hours that time because someone in the department dropped the ball.

Now I go to concerts or to a friend's house for the night. There are other things I'd love to do, including travel the world. But that's not the hand I've been dealt.

What makes me happy is to see Riley happy and getting the respect he needs. He goes to Starbucks for coffee every day. He says, "People must think I'm normal, and they approach me and talk to me. We have conversations about life and this and that. It makes me feel good."

**BIANCA:** I regret I didn't try harder to involve his father because of the closeness he previously had with Miguel. I'm not sure I could have. I wonder, what if I had done things differently and tried harder to get Arturo and Miguel into therapy? His father wouldn't go to therapy, so I don't think I could have gotten the boys to do it. It would have been easier for the boys if Carlo and I had remained friends, but I don't think that was possible. Carlo walked out. He wouldn't go to therapy. He wanted to be done with us.

Once, when Miguel was twenty-four, I almost had him convinced to go to this place for treatment, but he balked and I could demand only so much. I demand he stays on medication, and until she retired, I could demand he went to see Dr. A—. I can negotiate only so much. He shouldn't have gotten out of going into that first facility. It was a great program. The first time I knew that Miguel was reading signs, I should have gotten him help. During his senior year, I told him he needed counseling because his dad had abandoned us and because he was acting out. He went for six weeks, and each session he sat there for one hour and never spoke until the therapist said, "I give up."

I said, "I don't. I don't care if he stays there for six months. Eventually he'll open his mouth."

He said, "No, I can't take your money anymore."

Now I am so tired, exhausted all the time. It's so hard to muster the energy. Finding a therapist and a program takes a lot out of me. I'm just tired. I wish I had more energy to do it. My therapist said, "You should join a support group." I said, "You don't know how much energy *that* takes." I'm getting there. But just to deal with the grief of losing him, to accept where he is, to try and to figure out, *oh my God*, how handicapped he really is, and what can we do about it? Where can we go . . .?

I regret I couldn't jump on his treatment and plow right through it and boom, boom, boom, line ducks all in a row the first time. But I don't think it works like that. Learning how to manage my son's illness is a lifelong process. It takes time and energy. I need to gather the energy again and try to find the therapy he needs.

I try really hard. Some days are better. Some days aren't. You take what you can. Because if I go down, I don't know what will happen to either of my sons. So you do as much as you can. I recognize that I'm my own worst critic.

**ESME:** The guilt over "What did I do? How did she get this?" persists every day. What could I have done differently? What did I do during my pregnancy? These are things I also hear from other parents all the time, and it's none of that. It's hereditary. I know traumatic events can bring on this condition. I know there are also environmental factors that cause children to develop this illness. But a parent can change the outcome. It's not too late to help a loved one. It doesn't matter if your kid is forty or fifty. A parent can still make their child's life better.

When you live with a person who has mental illness, you're always waiting for the other shoe to drop. I was somewhat familiar with that because of my upbringing; I never felt this feeling of *everything's good*. If it *was* good, I wondered why, and what's going to happen next? That was how it was. As a result, I became deliberate about my parenting and family life, making sure the environment for the kids and my husband was not chaotic, not volatile, more planned, loving, and communicative than how I grew up.

I have had to take days and time off from work because of Jennifer for appointments and other unplanned days, which I'm happy to do for her. But it doesn't impact my pay. I am fortunate to have the flexibility to make up hours. I can't imagine what it's like for parents who need their job, who have to be on site to get that hourly rate. I have so much empathy for those parents. It's a call to employers. Businesses allow for medical absences quite easily, but there's still the stigma of mental illness. I often think, what if cancer had the same stigma? Totally different story.

### Advice

*Parenting an adult child with persistent mental illness comes with much internal conflict. While I was sad about Joseph's diagnosis, his struggles and pain, I was also furious he was putting himself in danger by using substances that made prescribed medications less effective. Even understanding that his illness affects cognition, I was angry he wasn't moving forward to help himself. We had provided a loving home, encouraged and supported musical, athletic, and educational pursuits, yet he chose a pathetic, quasi-*

*homeless lifestyle in order to continue to use. But I also felt guilt and conflict for being angry with a person whose behavior was borne out of his illness.*

*When Joe was first diagnosed and lived at home, his illness created constant chaos. To rein in Joe's behaviors, my husband and I were advised to set boundaries and impose stiff consequences. Though we knew it was important to provide structure and lead our son to recovery, our strict treatment seemed far too harsh for a boy who was suffering so deeply. I wanted to hold my son close and assure him we would make everything better just as we had always done. But I understood he would not be able to learn about real life if we didn't "let go," which is another concept for parents of children with serious mental illness so burdened with conflict. My grief left me feeling weak, incapable, and ill equipped to set the firm boundaries my son and our family needed. My husband and I are fortunate to have each other's back. Where I felt conflicted, my husband marched ahead and set rules and boundaries while I hung in the background. We were also fortunate to have support from an Assertive Community Treatment (ACT)[27] team of competent and caring professionals. In addition to stabilizing participants, they educate parents about medication, substance use (if applicable), and mental illness. Parenting mental illness requires tremendous stamina and support. It has always been helpful that either my husband or I can step back, out of the scene, when internal resources are low for one of us. Advocating for a person with mental illness is most effective when a team works together toward the same goal.*

**TESSA:** I've learned from mistakes. It's partly my fault he went off his meds, which led to that horrible break that subsequently landed him in jail. It's also the fault of a prescribing nurse who didn't recognize Riley was beginning to have side effects from the seven different medications he was on. He didn't know whether he was coming or going. He was in unsupervised housing and I wasn't checking because I thought supervisors were watching, but they weren't and he stopped taking medication. During the meeting we had with the whole mental health team to get him back on meds, I made the mistake of questioning the medication in front of Riley, which I never should have done.

I know now that you can't reason with any angry person or a drunk. It's hard *not* to argue or get frustrated, but it's counterproductive. When Riley was fighting with me to get control of his money, I conceded and waited until he was calm. I made it look like it was *his* choice to give control of the money back to me. But I'm still on pins and needles.

I used to try to save him! Rescue him! We all know that doesn't work.

I do it one day at a time, almost one hour at a time! When he's doing well, I relish it! A family member has to stay on top of it 24/7. I am vigilant every single day. My husband, who is not Riley's biological father, doesn't notice things. But I see even slight changes: a little anger, withdrawing, not talking, his moods. I can tell. Then I tread lightly. I don't argue with him. I wait until he is calm or when I can say, "Look, everybody's got bad days. I understand."

I'm still connected to him. You can never, ever give up. I love texting because even when he can't or won't talk, he reads it, and somehow something seeps in during a moment of clarity. If you can't find your kid or if they are not responding: text. They will read it. They will. They may look at it and go, "Eh." But there will come a time, even if just once, where something a parent says connects. Whatever you do, don't put anger in the text because that will give them an excuse to think, "Well, screw you!" And they will shut you out. A parent has to keep saying, "I love you and promise it will get better. Ultimately I can't help you. Nobody can fix it for you because *you* have to make the decision and choice to come home and allow us to help you."

If there is anything a family member must do, it is to never give up.

I have to be real with him. When Riley talks about ridiculous things like joining the army, I'll say, "Are you out of your mind?" It's a phrase I use all the time. People have told me I shouldn't say that to a person with a mental illness, but I believe he should be treated like everyone else. But now when I say that, Riley says, "Yeah, in case you forgot . . ."

I also understand now that it's really crucial at the time of the first break or during early onset, especially during teen years, to get a diagnosis. I'm not saying there won't be years of pain, but I don't think it has to be like what it was for my son if a parent accepts the diagnosis fully and, of course, if the child also accepts it. When a child is underage, a parent has some control to get him into treatment.

My sister is going through with her son what I went through with Riley. Her son needed treatment, and though he was still a minor at the time, she was having difficulty getting him committed. When someone is psychotic, they have physical strength . . . it's not them. It's the illness. And you cannot reason with psychosis. I advised her that when she calls the police, be sure to tell the dispatcher that you don't want just *any* officer. You want a *CIT officer*. I explained that police forces throughout the country are training officers to deal with the mentally ill because it makes for a safer community.[28]

One day, I got this text from her. She said, "We're on our way to the hospital." She said the police came and they were kind and gentle. Her son decided to get in the car and they took him to the hospital. She said, "Thank you for that!"

Here's something practical parents should know: a former mental health director told me that because of HIPAA, doctors couldn't discuss Riley's treatment with me. He said, "The 'Signature of Medical Release of Information' that your son signed is only good for six months." But he was wrong. Riley's nurse recently told me that a legal advisor confirmed that the signature is good forever, as long he's with the same medication nurse. If I'd been able to talk with his doctors, maybe I could have prevented him from being homeless for so long, going to jail, and being arrested.

Another piece of advice for a parent is to definitely get into a support group.

**BIANCA:** I have to remind myself to take care of myself and to find those normal moments. Like, "Miguel, let's cook dinner together." And, "What can we do together?" It can get better, but it can also get worse. So I enjoy the good moments. It's annoying when he doesn't talk. There are times when his behavior is a little or a lot off, like when he sleeps all day. I try not to feel guilty about being irritated by these behaviors. Sometimes he's out walking at night. Then I worry.

Humor helps. Miguel still retains a sense of humor. I don't think we'd survive without it. One time when he was in the hospital, he said, "I met my wife. She said God told her she's going to be my wife."

I said, "What?"

He said, "I don't know, Mom. I really hoped my wife was going to be better looking!"

This woman came up to me and said, "I'm so glad to meet you! You're going to be my mother-in-law." She really believed she was going to marry Miguel.

Later, I said to Miguel, "I was hoping she'd be younger! No! I don't think that's my new daughter-in-law, Miguel! You still have the ability to choose!"

Yes. Humor helps!

**ESME:** A parent must take one's ego out of the situation when a child is being abusive to the parent. I remember at a group meeting I could see the pain in this woman's face at the horrible way her daughter yelled at her and treated her. I've never taken it personally when my kid yells at me. It's not about *me*. Because when I did that to my parents, it was my age and what I was going through. But Doug takes it personally. He feels it much deeper than me. Maybe I'm guarded. Anyway, it's not about me.

Here's something else I'd tell another parent: keep being an advocate. Never stop. Don't trust the doctor if your gut tells you otherwise. Go for second, third, fourth opinions. Seek out experts. Nothing should preclude you, not even lack of insurance, from seeking help, including for yourself. I have to be thankful, which I am every day, and feel blessed to have the means. I know there are people out there who don't. My mother didn't. She had ten kids. How could you possibly have the means to think about yourself and doctors and all that? But denial doesn't work. Secrecy doesn't work. Lived that. Done that in my family. It's horrifying. It only hurts the rest of your family and the kids. Be honest with your other kids. Tell them what's going on. They're not blind to what's going on. If you're *not* honest, they're going to learn to distrust you.

I never had a relationship with my parents because they never talked about anything, and my mother was in denial about her mental illness even though she was institutionalized when she was sixteen. I mean, she would talk about it and the trauma of that still burns for her, and I feel very bad for her. But I know being in an environment where you don't acknowledge or talk about anything doesn't help. Doesn't work. A family needs to have open communication and work together to be healthy.

When Jennifer was still eighteen, a doctor at a prominent psychiatric hospital recommended a conference that Doug agreed to attend with me. The guest speaker, who was very knowledgeable, was an originator of the Family Connections Program, a course I'd attended that had helped me. First there was a talk and patient panel, which I knew would be insightful, and then breakout sessions. This hospital got it right; they involve parents in treatment. Parents have to commit and be involved in their child's treatment.

It was a great conference. Doug learned a lot and I'm

grateful. He said it was helpful and said, "I feel better, but I can't go back and talk about the same thing every week." I said, "Maybe you're thinking about it narrowly because I'd like to learn what to anticipate from parents whose children are older, who've been through similar experiences." At that time, Jennifer was almost nineteen. "Their children are in their twenties but they're still struggling. I want to try to understand and be ready. That's what I'm trying to learn from those groups." He hadn't thought about it that way. The conference piqued his interest. I said, "I'm not trying to say 'I told you so,' but there are things that would have benefitted you, which is why I was trying so hard to encourage you."

I wasn't getting it right for years. Now I'm sometimes getting it right; I'd like to think *most* times right, but certainly not all the time. It's a difficult path. At this point, all I can do is continue to introduce things and lead her. Some kids absorb only so much, I get that. But you need to include them in their own treatment.

**KERRI:** To a parent whose child has been recently diagnosed, I would never say, "Oh, it's going to be fine, don't worry." I would be empathetic. I would say, "This is hard. I remember when Thomas . . ." I would draw upon when Thomas was first diagnosed. "I was so devastated. It was hard. Take it one day at a time. Time will tell."

I would give advice on what to do: "Make sure you have a good psychiatrist with whom you can communicate well, somebody you can trust. You need support. These are the things you should be doing . . . I hope you can come back to our support group next month. Do you have good friends there for you?"

I would offer tangible advice on how to take care of himself or herself as a parent, make sure they have the information they need. I would recommend websites, articles, support groups, and lend a good book if appropriate. Now that I know more about the medication piece, I might even say, "Medication is really tricky . . . if you are ever concerned that your child is either overmedicated or on the wrong medication, you should watch for these signs . . ."

I would give only concrete advice. I would never say, "Oh, don't worry. It's all going to be great, wonderful. I'm sure your son or daughter will overcome this." I wouldn't go there. It's not helpful. I'd be in the here and now. I would never, ever say anything negative because I would never want to discourage a parent. I mean, there's always hope, and there are some people who do fine.

## Coping

*After about five months of deep grieving and isolating myself from the outside world and all the activities I had once enjoyed, I realized that my method of coping wasn't working. One may assume that as a trained therapist this realization would have come sooner, but there is no rationality involved when one's family is blindsided by an epic life-changing illness in a loved one. Mental illness is not like other illnesses. It changes a person's thinking, thought processes, and sometimes talents and learned skills; brain disorder diagnoses manifest differently in each individual. There is wild unpredictability, and some patients suffer from anosognosia, which makes them unaware of their own illness. My husband and I had no idea how Joseph's illness would play out, and feeling helpless was perhaps the worst of all.*

*I sought out a therapist who helped me identify that what I was experiencing was grief. I also went with a friend to a NAMI Family-to-Family class. But the first time I went was too soon. I sat in the chair shaking, wracked by fear for my son who'd completed his first hospitalization and was living on his own, working, and still using substances. Every day, I worried for his life, which seemed to leave little room for me to consider my own well-being. I was still trying to swallow the idea of Joe's diagnosis and that we were in this new club for life. We were on a long and difficult journey that would present many obstacles.*

*I didn't make it through the course that first time, but two years later I returned to NAMI with my husband and completed it. By that point, my son was stable, enabling me to focus on myself and learn from the other parents. NAMI proved healing for me. By the end of the course I could say out loud that my son lives with bipolar disorder.*

*At the advice of my therapist, I reluctantly started to practice a walking meditation in the woods near my home. At first, I could do about three minutes of clearing my head of all the jumbled thoughts that made it impossible for me to stay on task. Soon, I could sustain about ten minutes and then twenty minutes of solid meditation. It has helped me to feel centered and takes so little time in relation to the benefits. But still, I lived with so much fear for the future. Along with deepening my meditation, I began to focus on positive affirmations to help me live in the moment. I would write, "I can live in the moment" and, "I have this day and will make the most of it." Focusing on the moment abated fears I have for a future laden with so many unknowns.*

*Because of my training, and because NAMI had been so helpful to me, I was asked to become a co-facilitator of the Family-to-Family course. This furthered my healing and gave me insight about coping strategies. Hearing the stories of others, and helping others with their struggles was healing. I have always loved hearing stories about other people's lives, and I enjoyed and learned how others care for themselves.*

*Many parents take care of themselves with regular exercise regimens that include anything from walking, hiking, or running, to kayaking, horseback riding, or yoga. Others find creative outlets in arts and crafts, painting, photography, gardening; one parent I met makes furniture. Some perform on stage, making music or singing. Many see a personal therapist. Some bury themselves in work. Others become involved in state or local politics and not always to focus on mental health issues. Simple acts of taking hot baths and watching light movies help many.*

*There may be a single thing or many that help parents cope. As many parents know, the journey with a child who lives with persistent mental illness is long; emotional and physical stamina is needed. Those best equipped for the marathon of parenting a child with chronic illness are those who prioritize their own psychological, physical, and practical needs.*

**ESME:** By the end of Jennifer's junior year, I was definitely in a depression and it was affecting my work, affecting everything. Friends would advise me to seek help, but I thought I was okay. I'd say, "No, no, I'm fine." It wasn't as if I was averse to it because I'd been to counseling in the past. My energy had been focused on what was needed for *her* and I wasn't taking care of myself.

I started therapy in the fall, right before Jennifer moved out. I went on antidepressants, which is the first time I'd ever done that. After I started on medication, I realized I had not been okay because it really did make a difference. That's another message I have. Don't underestimate the stress, trauma, and impact of the emotions and the roller coaster because it's not going to help anybody. You have to be healthy.

Support groups are helpful. Face to face, sitting in a room with others, feeling their feelings and knowing you are being heard, goes a long way toward healing, for the other people in the room as well.

I lean heavily on my spiritual beliefs and take one day at a time, pray and ask for guidance over her, and ask for protection because she is not always smart enough to protect herself. She hangs out with people who aren't my type of people. Trust me, I moved with some tough crowds too, but these folks live day to day. They don't have goals or aspirations. Sadly, they also don't have the opportunities she has because they're in a different economic level. Her boyfriend never graduated high school, and his mother has severe addictions and comes from an entirely dysfunctional family, and Jennifer's around that. It's not what she needs. But I accept that, and he's a good kid. I don't care that he doesn't have a high school education. He is kind to her.

I look at all the positive things and all the strides we've made and I keep that at the forefront. That's how I get by day to day. At the same time, this sounds crazy, but I look at this mental illness journey as a blessing. It has made me more empathic. Not that I wasn't before, but it has made me feel more deeply for other people, understand their pain and circumstances. I saw my brother get admitted into an institution, and I was the one who got called when he was having psychotic episodes and delusions. That was sixteen years ago, and I remember thinking, "God forgive me for saying this, but if anything ever happens to me, put me in a wheelchair. I can't take this mental illness stuff."

You can't see mental illness. You can't wrap it in a bandage. You can't cut it out, although they used to try in the past. Wrong! But if I can make it better for someone else . . . I think we owe that, as a society.

**KERRI:** We've tried to set limits with Thomas. When he was in the hospital, we said, "You can only call us once a day." Sometimes he would call six times a day. Even now, where he is, he calls me not just every day, but *several times* a day. I keep telling him "Please, call only once a day." I'm trying to set limits. "Don't call me for every little thing."

When we went away to my mom's for vacation—my husband, daughter, and me—we tried to enjoy ourselves. I love to read and always have two or three books going at the same time. My husband and I go to restaurants. I go to movies and out with friends. I take walks every day. I meet friends for coffee or walks. I try to do things for pleasure. My husband doesn't have a problem with Thomas's demands. Thomas relies on me more so he doesn't feel the brunt of it. My husband is more likely to ignore a phone call than I am. He plays tennis practically every day and is always working out. Once a week, he meets his college buddies for drinks for an hour and a half. He's good about doing what he enjoys.

**BIANCA:** My sister gave me one really good piece of advice. She said, "You don't have to swallow the elephant whole. You can do it one bite at a time. You may have to eat it, but you only have to do it one bite at a time." She was referring to my whole life. You don't have to fix it all in one day.

Good advice for anyone who has a child diagnosed with serious mental illness is to keep it calm if you can. Hard to practice. I've ripped a few pillows. You have to think positively. I get really discouraged sometimes. Then I remember, "Think further back, and then you realize it's not so bad." There are many who'd trade places with me instantly. They'd give anything to have their child alive no matter what. I see that. I try to be realistic and hope for the best. Slow it down. Little baby steps. I say to Miguel, "It's not always going to be a straight line. You're not always going to feel good. You're not always going to be strong. You're not always going to be able to think clearly. It comes and goes. Figure out what helps you the most and we'll go from there."

I haven't read any books that have helped. Maybe it's because of my medical background. I've been in therapy a long time and probably will be for as long as I'm alive. It's someplace to go and talk things out and put things in perspective. Even my therapist would say, "Between those two boys it's been a wild five years." I'd like a little calm. I'm actually getting more of it. At one point I thought, if all the adrenaline left my life, I would probably drop dead! Having a kid with mental illness means you live on the edge.

What's best for me now is to avoid stressful situations and becoming overly tired. That's why I switched jobs. Those twelve-hour days were too hard to come home from and then deal with him. That was hard. And stress is no good for anybody.

Totally avoiding Miguel's father has helped me a great deal. I now take time to care for myself and take breaks from Miguel. I've realized I can leave town and leave him. He's not going to be so bad in two days that I can't deal with it. I ride my motorcycle. I'm about to take a long trip with my friend.

My male friend has been supportive of both Arturo and Miguel. They've become close to him and he's been there for them. He's down to earth and picks up the pieces a lot of the time. It has helped me a lot that Arturo doesn't fight the reality of Miguel's illness anymore and the two of them have formed a tighter bond again. That's been really, really helpful.

You can't cry all the time. You can't grieve all the time, and I promised myself after that one patient I had that I would find one moment of normal, even if it is a nanosecond, every day that I'm with him, so that our lives are not all about being sick. I find one normal thing that we can do together every single day. That has helped a lot.

**TESSA:** What I'd say to someone who came to me and said their son was just diagnosed is, "Get into a support group." You'll find you're not alone with those thoughts. *Even those thoughts.*

I'm scared.

I started with NAMI about ten years ago and then, "Everything's okay. I don't need NAMI." I sorta dropped out. Then that incident happened to my son where he was psychotic, chased a girl, and was put in jail. You never think something like that could possibly happen. After that incident, I became an avid member of NAMI for a time. Some support groups were really tough, though. My sister supports me, and I have a friend from NAMI who I love and adore. When I get frantic, like when Riley disappears, I'll call my friend.

I tried Al-Anon for a year straight when I first was married. I guess it depends on which Al-Anon you go to. Some people talk on and on, forever and a day, and most didn't seem to be dealing with what I was dealing with: a son with dual diagnoses. I know Al-Anon has helped people or it wouldn't exist. I've never been a "big group person" and not big on group therapy either because I don't trust people. In that way, I'm like my son. Riley stopped going to a bipolar group because people who were not high functioning went around talking, saying, "Did you hear about . . ." It's good for a lot of people, but for me it did nothing.

Ultimately it came down to my faith. For me, spirituality is the path, and exercise is huge. Even though I don't exercise to the degree I did when I was a trainer, I get four to six hours of walking every day. Dogs are the best therapy. My dogs . . . *oh my gosh*, my dogs are my support! You can tell them anything and they're not going to tell anybody! They don't judge!

My husband's emotional support helps also, but I can't say too much to him because he's so sensitive; he is affected by what I'm going through. What helps in addition to my faith is accepting that I have no control over Riley. I can only control myself. How I control my own behavior is what's going to help him.

But if a kid is full-blown psychotic, forget that! Get a team of professionals!

I know this sounds silly, but when I need a moment to myself, I'll tell my husband and son that I'm going into my bedroom and need to be alone. I have orchids, a little altar, and candles. I put on calm Zen music, light candles, and play solitaire or do something quiet. When I'm ready, I come out of my room and I feel so much better. Parents have to do that: take a moment.

I can't cry like I used to. And there are times I get angry with Riley, at everything, but I don't show it to him. I'll take in a run or go in another room or put music on. I have gone into the bathroom and turned on the fan and screamed, "Just take him! I hate his guts!" I have punched a pillow or the bed or something just to get it out for that moment. Then I go, "Okay. I'm good!" But oh, yeah, I get angry. This very morning I screamed in my bathroom. Then I walked out the door and I said in a sweet, maternal voice, "Bye, Sweetie! Have a good day!" And I'm out the door!

People tell you, "Live in the moment" because you cannot predict or plan what will happen the next day, or next week. When an incident happens, you can't think about what happened the last time he had a crisis or all the things that *could* happen. You have to think about *the moment you are in*. It's hard to know how to "live in the moment."

The most important advice for families is to never give up and do whatever works for *them*. Just like everybody's illness is different, for the family, not every group or program is going to work for them. Then you find it and you go, "Ah! Good!"

---

### Eight Bits of Advice from *Behind the Wall* Parents

*The parents we were privileged to meet and bring to our readers are inspiring for the stamina and wisdom gained through their journey parenting and advocating. Their advice is insightful, informed, and realistic. We have summarized below some of the most important bits of advice from this and previous chapters for a parent whose child is recently diagnosed with a serious mental illness.*

1. *Be honest with yourself and your child. As many parents tell us, even when signs are apparent, it is difficult to accept a mental illness diagnosis. But delays in accepting a diagnosis can be a missed opportunity to begin treatment at early onset; early treatment greatly improves chances for recovery. Untreated mental illness increases in severity over time and becomes more challenging to manage. Learning to manage mental illness requires a steep learning curve for the advocate and ill person, who will not reach recovery without fully embracing his own diagnosis. As Tessa says in chapter*

five, "Once I accepted it, then his world got better." A parent or trusted advocate must serve as role model, be truthful about a loved one's behaviors, and accept the diagnosis. A person who manages his mental illness can have a fulfilling, meaningful life.

2. **Trust your gut.** In chapter eight, Dan talks about the importance of listening to advice from professionals but that parents usually know their child best. In one incident, when his daughter felt unwell, he knew that sitting in a "padded room" was less beneficial to her health than coming home for the weekend to rest and be with family. Tessa knew her son's anger was more than what a therapist labeled as just teenage angst, and she regrets not pursuing a second opinion. It is true that there are times when it is easier to be in denial. Arguably, denial is sometimes a useful coping tool. Parenting requires developing skills for knowing what cues are important to notice and what are symptoms of a passing phase, and for trusting one's intuition and not being afraid of the truth. It sometimes seems these skills take a lifetime to sharpen.

3. **Don't be ashamed about a mental illness diagnosis.** One may not want to go around talking about a loved one's brain disorder, as is the case with any illness, but as Bianca says to those who ask, "'My son has schizophrenia.' You know, you guys deal with it. I'm not going to hide it. That's what it is." It may be helpful to remember that mental illness is treatable, not communicable, and is diagnosed in one in four people globally. Feeling shame is not useful for reaching recovery. The more we, as individuals, learn and speak openly about all brain disorders, the closer our society comes to destigmatizing mental illness.

4. **Be informed.** Seeking information about a diagnosis from one's doctors as well as through books, trusted web sites,

and support organizations can help parents cope and better manage a child's illness. Staying current on credible research can improve an advocate's understanding and acceptance of what a loved one is experiencing. For a list of suggested reading, please see References and Resources for Further Reading in this book.

5. *Allow time and space for grieving.* In many cases, symptoms of mental illness manifest in behaviors that are strikingly different or exaggerated, while positive qualities loved ones had once associated with the ill person become obfuscated, sometimes never to fully return. Parents are confounded by the decreased cognitive abilities that are temporary or permanent as well as the ill child's remarkable lack of motivation. Parents grieve the loss of a person they once knew and the abilities and potential he once possessed. A person with mental illness feels this loss as well. Relationships between siblings are impacted. Relationships with those outside the family are affected. The whole family and relationship dynamics are altered by one member's mental illness. Moving through such instability requires time and strength to grieve parts of the relationships that are lost in order to build something new. It is important to remember that grief manifests uniquely for each individual.

6. *Find a method for coping that best fits you and your family.* As Tessa points out, just as treatment for mental illness is unique to each individual, so too are coping methods. For parents whose child has been recently diagnosed, group therapy may feel overwhelming. But when ready, many parents find support groups and classes, such as the Family-to-Family course offered by NAMI, to be resources for coping and general information. Many parents lean heavily on their faith. Meditation, pets, and regular exercise have proven helpful to many for coping with the stress and grief. In chapter

*eight, Dan and Rebecca emphasize the importance of doing fun activities with one's child, whether that is snowboarding or crocheting; it means finding an activity both parent and child enjoy together where the illness is not central. Keeping the illness from being the core focus of the family sends a message that there is hope for mental health recovery and limits pressure or guilt on the diagnosed individual who may begin to feel as if they are always a family problem. And finally, as Bianca advises, have a sense of humor and find "those normal moments."*

7. **Don't blame yourself or anyone else.** *It's not about you. Nobody chooses or causes mental illness. At some point the ill person must own his illness and move forward of his own volition. Parents whose adult children live with persistent mental illness understand that they possess only so much control. Individuals must accept their illness and take responsibility for managing it; this includes identifying a trusted advocate in a parent or loved one who can be depended upon during a crisis. A caregiver or advocate, which is often the parent, can find resources and encourage treatment compliance. But a person with mental illness must be willing to trust an advocate, stay compliant, and ask for help when necessary.*

8. **Stay connected.** *Always. Maintaining a trusting, connected relationship with a loved one who lives with a persistent mental illness can make a profound difference toward achieving recovery. But as Rebecca points out, it can be difficult to feel close to one's own child when they are saying terrible things such as, "You are not my real mother" or, "There's a chip in my head." Behind the Wall parents remind us that these behaviors are the illness, not the child. As Esme says, parents should understand that these tirades are not about the parent. Behind the Wall parents express to their*

*child that "we love you even if we dislike your (recent) behavior." Esme emphasizes that being nonjudgmental, honest, and open to dialogue engenders trust. Parents can stay connected by showing support, listening, advocating for treatment, but also by setting boundaries that keep both child and parent safe. Tessa has a proven history of advocating for her son. When he becomes psychotic and wanders homeless, she continues to reach out to him, texting him to tell him that when he is ready to come home, she will help him. She will not judge him.*

# CHAPTER TEN:
## WHAT WE DREAM FOR OUR CHILDREN

*Revised expectations and recovery.*

*It's hard to rebuild a life. But it can be done.
People with brain injuries do it.*

*We can't look at Miguel's progress over the
course of a month or even two. Sometimes one
has to stop and question, "Where were we three
years ago? Two years ago? One year ago?"*

*Well, recovery is daily.*

*On Joseph's graduation from high school, I felt great pride. He was sober, fit, and had been accepted into a good college. But without structure, he became ill again and couldn't continue after his first year. He spent the next few years struggling, and we realized plans he may have had for himself, or that we had imagined for him, were not to be realized, at least not within the time frame we had previously imagined.*

*When Joseph returned home to live, we insisted only that he stay on his medications and remain sober. We encouraged him to exercise, take a part-time job or college classes, and pursue his other passions. But we never pushed. We always gave him the message that we wanted him to maintain a schedule of purposeful activities that was not stressful. We learned to practice the fine art of being supportive without coddling, and being patient for him to find the volition to drive his own recovery.*

*Joseph is moving forward, and I suppose we are too in our understanding of this illness that tries to hijack one's life. We will never rid ourselves of it, but we can certainly live with it, and have hope for our son's future. It's just a different future than we ever could have imagined.*

*Recovery looks different for every individual and varies over time. A first step toward recovery is to identify the ill person's capabilities and understanding "where he is." Reframing expectations that are realistic, and accounting for a person's limitations and current health status, are as essential for recovery as an evidence-based treatment plan. Progress for an adult child with a persistent mental illness does not travel in a straight line, and setbacks are inevitable.*

*Recovery for a person who is dual diagnosed with mental illness and substance use is particularly challenging to manage. While a person living with mental illness may want to take steps toward recovery for more obvious symptoms such as psychosis, depression, or anxiety, many cannot fully embrace abstinence, in part because substances dampen symptoms and provide a sense of temporary "relief" from reality. Unfortunately, nonprescribed substances do not allow a brain to heal. The first goal in the evidence-based integrative treatment for a person who has a mental illness and a co-occurring substance use disorder is to engage the patient and encourage him to agree to help himself. Substance use can interfere with proper diagnosis and effectiveness of prescribed medications; treatment for the reluctant dual diagnosis patients that has proven most effective is "harm reduction."[29] Harm reduction means that a first step toward progress is measured when one reduces from binge drinking to drinking much less, for example, or switches from more dangerous drugs. Often, a person living with mental illness must work against new cognitive challenges. The goal of harm reduction is to engage a patient in one's own treatment without imposing undue and harmful stress.*

*Parents agree that recovery is when their son or daughter has some measure of stability. There is no cure for mental illness, and symptoms often recur, but accepting and learning to manage one's illness is success. Addressing recurring symptoms and moving forward each day, even if by inches, is success. Having routine and purpose, and satisfaction in one's life, defines recovery. Getting to that goal happens day by day, and those who embrace that journey are to be admired.*

**ESME:** Oh the dreams, yeah. It's not as if I was saying, "She's going to be a track star!" or anything like that. I saw that playing sports made Jennifer happy and active, she had friends and was part of a team. But now I understand why she could never be on a team. We never pressured her, but the coaches had expectations without really saying it. We encouraged her to be active and involved. But coaches were definitely looking and thinking, "Wow, this freshman kid is placing with seniors. That's something we can work with." She had stopped doing gymnastics, so I thought sports were good because she was involved in an activity again. But we didn't know the mental illness was affecting her health so severely and she really couldn't compete.

You have to take away those expectations. You have to accept what *is*. I wasn't worrying as much as I was mourning her future. That was probably the most difficult. I couldn't even go to her high school without crying. The day that would have been Jennifer's graduation, her sister, Laura, wanted to attend because Jennifer's friends who were graduating had invited her. I didn't want Laura to go, but I didn't forbid it either. I drove Laura the four miles to the graduation that should have been Jennifer's. The longest drive I've ever made. I sobbed the whole way home. Even at Laura's eighth-grade graduation, it just stung.

I try to be introspective about the source of my sadness for Jennifer. Was it about *me* and *my* own embarrassment over having a daughter who didn't finish high school? Am *I* mourning her future? It was all of those things. But even more, it was disappointment *for* her. Not me. Because I knew part of her pain was feeling she'd let us down. It was hard for her, feeling she'd let us down. And knowing this about her, I never showed my emotions or my disappointment to her at all in that regard. I would express sadness over things that were happening. We had to be careful, though, because she feels guilt deeply. Guilt is her middle name. She started hiding things from us because she knew how difficult it was for my husband and me.

Now, to think about her dreams of going to college, living abroad, and that she used to teach herself languages—is heartbreaking. None of those things are going to happen. At least not for a while. I need to keep reminding myself: it's not the end of the world. There are things more important and more severe.

I'm very lucky. Jennifer's a very self-aware kid. She can't control herself, but she gets it, 100 percent.

She's reading again. She used to be an avid reader. She's again thinking seriously about going to college because she's always loved learning and was a good student. That's all positive, and I have to keep reminding my husband and myself, *one step at a time*. Have a success, then move to the next challenge and build up self-esteem and the confidence she can do it again. She knows college is a big commitment and she's being cautious.

She's trying to find her spiritual center. Probably not in the conventional way that I, as a Christian, would, but that's okay by me. I'm accepting in that way. I pray for her every day that she's able to find peace and happiness in some way. That's really what I pray for her to have. I don't really care if she goes to college. It's a different expectation now. I mourn for my mother who doesn't have an ability to experience happiness or find joy. I'm sad for my mother, and I know that's not what Jennifer chooses.

I think about recovery for Jennifer because I have a brother who lives with mental illness and is functioning. When I think about what it means for a person with mental illness to function, it means that on a daily basis he or she gets out of bed in the morning, has appropriate personal self-care from nutrition to hygiene. Every day. Not just some days. *Every day.*

Recovery means Jennifer can have a level of contentment and peace. That part doesn't have to be every day but must be 95 percent of the time. That would be "recovery" to me, and that's what I'm hoping the meds will do.

She definitely felt a change in herself when she went on medication. "I feel like I'm standing outside myself sometimes," and I said, "Okay, let it adjust." After a couple of weeks, she said, "No, I don't feel that way anymore. I feel fine. I don't even feel it." I said, "What you just told me is that it's *working*. As long as you feel that way, you have to keep letting it work." I'm trying to emphasize continuity. Jennifer's going to feel good and say, "I don't need this medication anymore." I keep testing her. I'll ask how she's feeling. She'll say, "Good, Mom." I ask, "Really good? Do you still feel the medication is making a difference?"

My expectations now are for Jennifer to keep committing to herself and understanding that we're never giving up on her. We've told her that time and time again. We expect that she will not give up on herself either. If that means she just takes the medication every day and that's as good as it's ever going to get, then I'll take that as long as she remains happy and stable. If I think she can move beyond that, then my expectations are going to increase. Knowing when to expect more is the delicate balance, right? And being able to say, "I want you to work." In fact, I told her recently, "I want you to be busy. Not idle, not hanging out with friends. Busy. Volunteer at a library." I don't care if it's for an hour, two hours a day. She must have some purpose so she can find herself.

Then the next level of her recovery would be for her to acquire some ability to start exploring her purpose in life and have a goal she can move toward. That will take a few years. It's optimistic, but I think she's capable.

My expectations are still low. Because my hopes and dreams are irrelevant for her and I can't impose them. I finally learned that one, unfortunately.

**BIANCA:** It sure isn't what I signed up for. All the hopes and dreams, all the talents Miguel had and what he used to be; I catch glimpses of it, but it's not there anymore.

I don't know if Miguel knows what he's lost because his psychosis comes in the form of religion so he feels he's gained God and deep religious insight. He was really into prophesy-based ministries and feels he gained a lot from that.

At twenty-four, Miguel couldn't work. He was always a slow reader, but because of the illness, he cannot read a page. He complains he can't process information, can't hold on to it, can't remember the material. He has always wanted to go back to school. He knows that's a loss. He gets mad because he can't read. He gets mad because he can't think. He tried a class at Tech but couldn't handle it. Much of his short-term memory is damaged. He's gotten better. He can watch movies. For a while, he could only watch a certain cartoon. He used to be brilliant spatially, at jigsaw puzzles and things like that. He can't put a jigsaw puzzle together anymore. Remarkably, despite all of this, Miguel remains positive. He always works hard, plugs along, and does the best he can.

I said, "You have to work with your church group, volunteer, something. You cannot sit in that room all day long." He agreed. I was told when Miguel was committed that it wouldn't be on his record. It is. When you apply for a job and they look at your past criminal history, the enforced commitment comes up. I don't know what job he could hold, but I want him to feel he can be independent. He managed to work four days a week delivering pizzas and take care of himself. One time the car broke down. He managed to call AAA and used his own money to repair it.

I always remind him to stay on his drugs. I'll say, "Tomorrow you're due to renew your drugs. Pour them out of the container. If you've missed more than four doses, you're not doing well and we need to do something." He has admitted he missed four doses but that's over a month, twice a day, after we changed the dose. I thought that was pretty good. I don't know if I could do as well. When things get stressful, Miguel starts backtracking. I ask, "Are you okay? Do you need different drugs? Do you need to see the doctor?" When he says, "No, I'm handling it," I say, "Okay." I trust him because, until our doctor retired, he'd call her on his own and see her if he needed to. But I'm his checkpoint: "What exactly is going on? Are you being consumed? When you become obsessive with all your thoughts, you need to back up." He now does things that help him de-stress and cope. We've tried hard to help him recognize when he's losing it, to notice the physical signs: jaw clenching, not sleeping or eating. I tell him to stop and recognize his symptoms. That's when you need to call the doctor. But I have to monitor him.

He asks me to please refill the pills. That was a big step forward—that he would even take the pills every day. I thought, "I'm not quite sure what that is, but I'll do that." I've asked him to explain why he needs *me* to set up his pills in the containers, but he says, "It works better." If I were to analyze it, I'd say he needs that boost. Or he needs mommy.

Yeah, maybe we're going to have to check on him once a week, once every two weeks. I want him to stay on his meds and slowly move forward. It would be wonderful if he could go back to school. I don't know if that could happen, but it sure would be wonderful. That would boost his ego. A lot.

Miguel tires really fast. He said it's a combination of the drugs and thoughts constantly going through his mind. But he eats better, exercises more. I said, "You've got to *practice* being normal if you want it to come easily. It's like exercising a muscle. I've seen you do it." His socialization skills are brilliant. He still has friends. For a while he was actually dating someone. It didn't last, but he pulled it off for three weeks. I was thinking, "Now I'm faced with the ethical dilemma of: do I say anything about his illness?" And then I thought, "Naw. I'm not going to say anything because eventually it will show."

I sat with Miguel one night and talked with him about the demons, and "being delivered." He started getting agitated and talking fast, and I thought, "You are better, and 'better' may be as good as we get." He still has psychosis. He still feels demons are there. They're not voices but, rather, negative feelings. "Cured" probably isn't a realistic goal. I said, "I think you can do better than you are now. We have to ask, 'Do you feel stronger than you did three months ago?'" He said he did. I said, "What helped? What are the things you did that made you feel this way?" We keep moving forward.

I told his brother, "We can't look at Miguel's progress over the course of a month or even two. Sometimes one has to stop and question, 'Where were we three years ago? Two years ago? One year ago?' From the day you diagnose him, it's got to be better than today."

Still, I do get discouraged. I try not to dwell on how much he's lost but look at how much he's starting to gain back, because he's made great progress. He's an incredible person. I think it takes great strength to endure what he goes through. There are days where I'm feeling, "Leave me alone. I just want to sit in a hole and cry all day." Then I get over that pity party because one has to do the best with what one has. But it's such a broken life.

We are planning a vacation at the beach. That was not possible three years ago. We rented a condominium so Miguel can have his own room; he can sleep and do what he wants. We don't stress him. The four of us, my male friend and both boys, have taken a couple of trips, and we see what works for Miguel and what doesn't. Stress is a terrible thing. We must plan ahead, make sure he's prepared. If Miguel needs to get up in the middle of dinner and go for a walk, we don't miss a beat anymore. We're like, "Okay, he needs to walk around the block and then he'll come back."

He's coping. It's a new normal. That's fine. If he's clenching his jaw or twitching too much, I'll say, "Do you want me to order dinner for you?" We've learned to meet him where he *is* and respect where he is. I don't try to change him anymore. I try to find out what works best for him and let go of what used to be. Which is not easy and doesn't happen all the time!

Miguel's brother Arturo once said about Miguel, "What I really want for him is to get married and have a family, have kids, and be happy." I said, "Arturo, I don't think that's ever going to happen. There's a genetic component to his illness. I don't know that Miguel should ever have kids." Arturo started crying. I said, "It's okay. You'll just have to have twice as many as you planned, which means you need to start dating!"

If you ask me on a Saturday how Miguel is doing, I may say, "Wonderful." But on a recent Saturday night he wasn't doing well, although we have made progress. He really is doing better. Not perfect, but better. It's an absolutely shitty disease, and it robs these brilliant people of a life. It's an illness they didn't choose or do anything to bring it on. It is what it is, and they are still really good people. My kid is a great young man. He just has a terrible handicap now. It's hard to rebuild a life. But it *can* be done. People with brain injuries do it. He has a life to rebuild. That's the positive subtext. That's all you've got to hold onto.

**KERRI:** I want to express how frustrated and scared I sometimes feel concerning Thomas. His future is so uncertain right now, and I feel deep frustration at his wasted potential. Thomas was such a bright little boy. People and teachers had noted his keen intelligence and curiosity. I look at where one of his former best friends is, a senior premed student, and think Thomas could have been on a similar path because they had the same grades all through middle school, and it's only in high school that their paths started to diverge.

If you had talked to me last year, I would have said, "Well, Thomas is good, he's still in school . . . yes, it's rough and I get a lot of phone calls . . ." A year from now, maybe you'd catch me in a different mindset.

I am frustrated that Thomas is obstinate about medication and therapy. I know if he could trust a good psychiatrist and start back on some low dose of a mood stabilizer he would be able to get back on a path. I don't expect miracles, but I know he could be working and eventually go back to school. I could see him getting a certificate or an associate degree from a community college. I know he could be living independently, perhaps with roommates. For the next five years, Thomas will always need some kind of support. He is intellectually capable, but his illness impedes him.

Recovery for Thomas means that he would be willing to at least take an antipsychotic medication, and if he were living in a group home, he'd be able to get himself up every day. It means that he's taking a course at community college or getting services and some kind of training. He needs testing and career advice to figure out what's realistic for someone like him.

I don't know if college will ever be realistic, whether he would ever be able to handle college on a full-time basis, living away, in a dorm or an apartment. Recovery would mean being able to work toward an associate degree or some kind of certification, maybe having some type of career goal and be completely responsible for himself. Maybe that sounds unrealistic.

**TESSA:** It has been seventeen years of chronic mental illness. He claims he lost his life when the first break came. Riley can be doing really well, and all it takes is for someone to say something wrong to him or hurt his feelings and he gets down on himself and starts to self-medicate. I support positive progress. I can tell on his face when things are going on even if he's med-compliant. I can see when he's sad. It's all over him.

For some reason, Riley also relapses in the summertime. Always. But holidays are the worst. I dread the holidays. By Thanksgiving and Christmas time, I think because of the drinking or—I don't know what triggers it—he gets really weird, down, and depressed. A lot of people do at that time of year. But by Thanksgiving, my eyes are wide open because around Christmastime something always happens. His first break, the big one, happened about a week before Christmas. It was also in December when he went off meds. I think a person living with serious mental illness is always grieving. Something in their brain knows the anniversary of the first break and something is amiss at that time. Every year. Like clockwork. I'm trying to keep him in recovery.

Riley's last relapse began in front of me on June second. On August twentieth, he was finally stable enough for me to again register him at the college. I set his alarm for him so he makes it to class. He has been getting his shots. He's been pretty much clean and sober. Well, he's at least not drunk. He dropped one class, economics, and I don't blame him. I opened the book and was like, "What the hell *is* this?" I said, "Focus on one class," because it's a college-level class that transfers into the university. He has papers due, has to be online, and has to engage in peer discussions. I didn't want him stressing out. He's doing well. He said, "Last time I took English, I had the remedial-remedial." I said, "You're med-compliant. Maybe you can function like yourself. You're very smart."

But the illness has damaged his brain, and he doesn't have the cognitive ability to write down how to get his plans accomplished. He knows what he wants to do, but as far as getting there, he thinks he can do it off the cuff, and he can't. There was a time my son was able to save money and accomplish other things. He bought a car at sixteen and we didn't even know he had it! He worked two jobs while going to school. When he was thirteen, he could make pancakes from scratch and clean his room. But now I don't know if he'd ever be able to manage money again. I don't know if he'll ever be sober, either. Even being med-compliant with the other medication, the alcohol gives a sense of numbness to the pain in one's life. I think if he would continue going to AA it would help. He might meet somebody, a girlfriend, or someone who could be supportive. But he never gives it a chance.

Right now Riley is in recovery. Even if he goes out and has a beer today, he's in recovery because he's in a *routine*. I'm convinced he drinks a beer every day. I said, "If you can master having just one, then you're not an alcoholic. But you can't." But he has done that, so I don't know. With the illness, you don't know if he's drinking because maybe the meds are not dealing with certain symptoms and he's self-medicating. You never know. I do believe he is an alcoholic.[30]

Riley still lives at home. I want him to be independent, but I'm not going to shove him out before he's ready because he's been to hell and back. If he's not ready to conquer the world, I'm not going to push him into that cruel, cold world again. Not when he's doing everything he possibly can in his power. I'd love to see him be independent, but if he needs a place to stay, he's got it. He wants a place of his own. I'm scared to death of that. It's my goal to someday have a home with a basement apartment or detached cottage so I could always have eyes on him yet he'd have separate quarters where he could enjoy life and not worry about having a roof over his head or being beat up by cruel people on the street because he has no home. I'd make sure he stays on meds because, when he's drinking, he forgets to take them.

The recovery is great because he's getting up, he's got things to do, and he's in a routine. Every morning, he gets coffee at the coffee shop and smokes his cigarette. To me that's recovery. Routine is recovery. Also he has a purpose. He has to go to school. He comes home to eat dinner. He'll call and ask, "What's for dinner?"

Routine and purpose is recovery. At least for Riley.

I'm noticing changes in Riley and don't know if it's because I've changed my perspective on how to deal with the illness in the last year or if he's really changing. There seems to be some semblance of maturity happening in his thirties that was not there in his twenties. He knows he has to get his shot. He knows he has to stay on the meds whereas before he didn't.

What more can I ask for? That's recovery.

∞∞∞

*Though there is progressive brain research being conducted, there is no cure for mental illness. But more effective treatment and early detection can mean a greater chance for recovery. Recovery looks different for each individual just as brain disorders manifest uniquely and treatments must be tailored. Setbacks do not mean failure. A setback—or the onset of a psychotic, manic, or chaotic episode—may simply indicate that adjustments to medication, lifestyle, and reducing stressful triggers may be required. Recovery for one individual may be defined as being medication compliant and working a part-time job. For another, it means working full time while also recognizing signs of stress and knowing when to seek help from an advocate.*

*Dr. John Looney tells us in the foreword that, "With a combination of parental patience and strictness, plus good treatment, a recovering state can be achieved." Strictness can be defined as setting clear boundaries for behavior and realistic expectations. Perhaps the idea of setting realistic expectations is the most meaningful lesson* Behind the Wall *parents have learned throughout their challenging journeys. It is a concept invaluable for parenting any child, as is learning nonjudgmental acceptance of the whole child and patience for their pace of progress.*

*Parenting well requires the hard work of truly knowing one's child as a separate, unique being and not just listening but hearing, not just watching but seeing. It is also about understanding the boundaries of influence and control a parent can wield over offspring, a difficult concept to fully absorb concerning one's own. Nurturing is accepting one's child for who he is, assisting in identifying his own goals, then supporting him in failure and success. In his important and comprehensive book,* Far From the Tree, *about parenting children with horizontal identities (differences that determine a child's identity that is not shared by parents such as a child with deafness born to parents with hearing), Andrew Solomon says it best, "Ego confusion between parents and children is pervasive in every demographic; it's no mean feat to find the difference between helping your children formulate their dreams and trapping them in your own."[31] Raising successful humans is about presenting opportunities, identifying options, and providing support for the road he chooses.*

*Accepting a child for "who they are" and "where they are" is by no measure a resignation of a child's future. Unrealistically high expectations or misunderstanding a child's interests and aptitudes doom one to failure, while low expectations send a message that loved ones have given up hope. A parent should never do for a child what he can do for himself. This begins by projecting confidence to a toddler for tying his shoes even if it requires an hour, or to a teen for resolving her own problem with her teacher. But expecting a person only recently stabilized following a psychotic crisis to resume a full-time work schedule, for example, is unrealistic at best and likely harmful. A realistic expectation for anyone is to work diligently and consistently toward knowing oneself and strive for the best life possible given one's abilities and current obstacles. Expecting a loved one to continue marching forward is to respect another's capabilities without judgment. Maybe part-time school is not possible within a year of a critical hospitalization, but it may be possible over time and with healing.*

*A mental illness diagnosis is also not an excuse for inconsiderate or dangerous behaviors, though for minor infractions, distinguishing between what is the illness and irresponsibility can be a delicate line. As Bianca says of her son about not cleaning the mess he made while she was away, "He's not broken!" She is expressing the practical ways parents should not be doing for one's child what he can do for himself. When an individual's illness leads to bad behaviors that may include* disrespect toward loved ones, binge drinking, increased substance use, or medication noncompliance that may lead to psychosis, caregivers must continue to express that an individual is expected to learn to manage one's illness effectively and that he will be supported in this effort. The behaviors are not excusable but illustrate better self-care is required. After Jennifer's near-fatal overdose, Esme tells Jennifer that her overdose is a sign that she needs counseling and emphasizes that Jennifer needs to take better care of herself. Repetition of this message is one way a parent can convey respect and confidence that their child is competent and that their life has meaning. But patience is required to allow one's child to embrace the message and move forward on her own volition

When asked what she would say to a person whose child is recently diagnosed with a serious mental illness, Kerri says she would never say, "Oh, it's going to be fine; don't worry." Because the reality of life with serious mental illness is that in order to properly address the illness, manage it, and weather its consequences, the ill person and her loved ones must accept the profound changes it brings. A diagnosis of a brain disorder requires a dramatic shift in outlook and an acceptance of a "new normal." But it doesn't mean life is doomed. As Esme says, "I look at this mental illness journey as a blessing. It has made me more empathic." When confronted with life-changing challenges, our contributors illustrate that shifting one's perspective makes coping and even gratitude possible.

Behind the Wall *parents are brave for coming forward to share their stories. They are role models for speaking out about what happens behind the walls in homes across the globe. Sharing what we all know about the experience of having a loved one living with mental illness is a positive step toward addressing the stigma around mental illness and helping other families who are beginning this journey. By talking openly, without a dark shadow of misplaced shame and mythology, we help another son, daughter, brother, sister, mother, or father.*

*Continuing honest dialogue about how persistent mental illness impacts families, particularly for the caregiver/parent, creates awareness about the need for logistical and emotional support. Supporting a caregiver in any way possible can make a significant difference in their lives. Relaying these stories educates the general public and policy makers to advocate for early detection of mental illness in children, adolescents, and young adults and to also support cutting-edge research that informs evidence-based treatments.*

*We know from anecdotal sources and research that individuals in mental illness recovery are more successful when they feel inclusion in community. When mental illness is understood, those in recovery are more likely to be accepted in society, including into faith-based communities that often offer invaluable nonjudgmental support and recognition not centered on the illness, but on their whole person. We hope these stories are just the beginning of a sea change about the way society thinks about serious mental illness.*

# ACKNOWLEDGMENTS

We grew up knowing that mental illness is not a character flaw, but rather an illness. Laurence M. Collins, MD—Uncle Larry to us—spoke compassionately about those who suffered with serious mental illness. Many thoughtful discussions held in our great-aunt's living room originated from Uncle Larry's vast knowledge, curiosity, and fascination over the workings of the human brain and ideas about what caused thought disorders. A quiet, kind, and steadfast man, Dr. Collins was a surgeon in WWI and, later, a prominent physician and psychiatrist at Greystone Park Psychiatric Hospital during the years that it was considered to provide the gold standard in mental health care—when it was a self-sustaining community with its own water and gas utilities, post office, police and fire stations, laundry facilities, and working farm with labor provided by patients. Like all Greystone staff, Dr. Collins resided in a home on the campus. Our mother fondly remembers his gardener and cook, both patients of the hospital. Living and working on the campus provided patients with a beautiful, stress-free, purposeful life, while also receiving ongoing treatment. But later, overcrowding and underfunding impacted the original beneficial philosophy of this hospital, like many others in our society, and sadly what is remembered of Greystone is not so positive.

In 1935, by then well into his forties, Dr. Collins became one of the founders of what is now known as the New Jersey Psychiatric Association, which took an active role in influencing legislation for mental health treatment. After WWII, studies on alcoholism were made available, and New Jersey became one of the first states to make progressive steps toward providing medical treatment options.

Our Uncle Larry leaned heavily on his faith and often expressed his deep belief that there was light within all of us, that mental illness was treatable, and that it was an imperative for society to support those who live with mental illness. He would be pleased to know treatments such as DBT and CBT and improved second-generation medications, when carefully prescribed, are significantly improving the lives of many. We are grateful still for his compassion and dedication to the many patients he helped throughout his long career. His influence was certainly a significant factor in our lives and how we have viewed mental illness, even before it directly affected us.

The *Behind the Wall* project came together only with great support from our family and community but was clearly driven by our parent contributors' generous spirits and inspiration. During those frustrating encounters along the path to completion, we had only to think of these heroic parents who considered our effort worthwhile, and who also thought that shining light on the struggles going on behind the wall in homes all over the world was of great value. This book is for every person who cares for a person who lives with serious mental illness.

We are grateful for the generosity of many others. Deborah Rich, MSW, LCSW; Maureen Smith, MSW, LCSW; and Deb Love, Adjunct Assistant Professor, Department of Social Medicine at UNC, all saw the merits of the project and connected us to resources. George Abercrombie provided moral support and practical advice borne out of his years of experience. Sam Abercrombie, Mark Abercrombie, Joan Widdifield, Natalie Johnson, Bernadine Widdifield, Jay Widdifield, and our parents, Joseph and Natalie Widdifield, were early supporters and believers in our project. The ever-enduring Casey McCabe held down the fort and threw in his expertise for our benefit. Gary Ragghianti provided valuable initial and important legal advice as well as friendship; Brooke Hansen gave us an identity; Peg Shultz, MA, provided history about Greystone Park Hospital. Thank you, Dr. John Looney, for your contribution as well as your wisdom, guidance, and remarkable wit, and also Susan Looney, an early reader and avid supporter. We benefitted greatly and were honored to receive advice and clear direction from Pete Earley, David Vigliano, and Thomas Flannery.

Elin wishes to thank Twyla Wilson, MSW, LCSW, for shining a light in the tunnel; Emma, Maggie, and Indie for walks in the woods where I found moments of clarity. A special thanks to the late Amanda Touche Bowler for her enthusiastic love of projects. Thanks to Mary Paulsgrove and Charlotte Margolis for being there with coffee, long walks, and talks; for the magic of Sarah Honer who has kept me upright; and the families at NAMI who have modeled humor, wisdom, and perseverance despite their arduous journey. Of course, my greatest source of strength and endurance to live a compassionate and meaningful life comes from George, Sam, and Mark.

Mary is grateful for advice from Nona Caspers, who said to passionately pursue what holds one's interest and go wherever it may lead. Thanks to my supportive Five Points Tribe; the very talented and generous Marko Lavrisha, and Dr. Ruth Noel. I am grateful for meaningful friendships and early direction from Susan Brandabur and Connie Dillon. Thanks to Richard and Patricia Wootton for too many things. I am grateful for being comforted often by Sweetie and Banksy. I am indebted for eternity to the patient indulgence of those I love more than anything in this universe: Casey, Olivia, and Henry.

# NOTES

[1] *Showed signs of OCD.* Brief descriptions of brain disorder diagnoses mentioned in these narratives are listed in the Glossary of Brain Disorder Diagnoses.

[2] *We were able to get a section 504 . . .* A 504 Plan helps a student with special health care needs to fully participate in school. Usually, a 504 Plan is used by a general education student who is not eligible for special education services. A 504 Plan lists accommodations related to the child's disability and is required by the child so that he or she may participate in the general classroom setting and educational programs. For example, a 504 Plan may include plans to make a school wheelchair accessible, providing for assistive technology needs during the school day, permission to type instead of writing assignments by hand, and permission to hand in assignments late due to illness or a hospital stay.

[3] *Was it PMDD?* Premenstrual dysphoric disorder is a condition in which a woman has severe depression symptoms, irritability, and tension before menstruation. Symptoms of PMDD are more severe than those associated with premenstrual syndrome (PMS), and a minimum of five symptoms must be present for a PMDD diagnosis, some of which may include no interest in daily activities and relationships, fatigue or low energy, feeling sadness or hopelessness or possible suicidal thoughts, feelings of tension or anxiety, mood swings with periods of crying, and panic attacks. For a complete list of symptoms, please refer to www.nimh.nih.gov or talk to your doctor.

[4] *. . . he prescribed an atypical antipsychotic.* Atypical antipsychotics are also known as second-generation antipsychotics (SGAs). The term "atypical" refers to improvements on side effects. SGAs generally do not cause the same degree of movement side effects, tremors, or dyskinesia, for example, common to the first generation, or so-called "typical" antipsychotics.

Typical antipsychotics (sometimes referred to as first-generation antipsychotics, conventional antipsychotics, classical tranquilizers, traditional antipsychotics, or major tranquilizers) are a class of antipsychotic drugs first developed in the 1950s and used to treat psychosis and schizophrenia. Typical antipsychotics may also be used for the treatment of acute mania, agitation, and other conditions. For more information, please go to www.NAMI.org.

[5] *"No. We don't diagnose children under eighteen."* The DSM-IV allows for the diagnosis of borderline personality disorder in adolescence if the symptoms are severe enough to persistently interfere with the individual's daily functioning for one year or longer. On their website, National Youth Mental Health Foundation cites a twenty-year longitudinal study that provides strong support for the argument that borderline symptoms in adolescence cannot be considered a developmental stage that passes. For more information, see www.nationalyouthmental-healthfoundation and www.neabpd.org.

[6] *I really can't help you.* For a person who struggles with a serious mental illness and co-occurring substance use, a best practice is an integrated approach to treatment, addressing the two illnesses simultaneously. For more information on treatment for dual diagnosis, see Dr. Robert Drake's articles cited under References and Resources for Further Reading in this book.

[7] *When an adult child refuses to sign a release . . .* Parents must be part of the recovery team. Part of HIPAA law states that a therapist can use their best judgment:

> *The provider may ask the patient's permission to share relevant information with family members or others, may tell the patient he or she plans to discuss the information and give them an opportunity to agree or object, or may infer from the circumstances, using professional judgment, that the patient does not object. A common*

*example of the latter would be situations in which a family member or friend is invited by the patient and present in the treatment room with the patient and the provider when a disclosure is made.*

More information on the HIPAA language may be found on www.hhs.gov.

[8] *"Your daughter exhibits symptoms of _____"* See endnote number 5 regarding diagnosing borderline personality disorder before the age of eighteen.

[9] *. . . parents become frustrated by HIPAA laws . . .* The Health Insurance Portability and Accountability Act of 1996 (HIPAA) addresses the use and disclosure of individuals' health information as well as standards for individuals' privacy rights to understand and control how their health information is used. A major goal of the Privacy Rule is to assure that individuals' health information is properly protected while allowing the flow of health information needed to provide and promote high quality health care and to protect the public's health and well-being. The U.S. Health and Human Services website provides details at: www.hhs.gov/ocr/privacy/hipaa/understanding/summary/index.html.

[10] *. . . where the treatment is dialectical behavioral therapy-based.* Dialectical behavioral therapy (DBT) is a mode of treatment designed for people with borderline personality disorder (BPD), particularly those with suicidal ideation. DBT works toward helping people living with BPD validate their emotions and behaviors, examine those behaviors and emotions that have a negative impact on their lives, and make a conscious effort to bring about positive changes. Though Thomas was not diagnosed with BPD, this therapy benefits most individuals who live with mental illness.

[11] *She was going to prescribe an SSRI antidepressant.* An SSRI, or selective serotonin reuptake inhibitor, is any of several drugs that inhibit the re-absorption of serotonin by nerve cells,

leading to more serotonin activity in the brain. SSRI drugs are used chiefly as an antidepressant.

[12] *Thomas cannot be on any SSRIs. It activates him.* Patients with undiagnosed bipolar disorder or in the early stages of their illness often seek medical help to address depression. Medical professionals who may be inexperienced or uninformed may fail to thoroughly examine the patient and incorrectly prescribe an antidepressant, which for about one-quarter to one-third of bipolar patients may result in inducing an episode of mania. Prior to prescribing antidepressants, physicians must first consider possible physical causes of depression, such as thyroid conditions, and obtain a patient's personal and family medical history. Consulting the patient's loved one, as was the case with Thomas, can be crucial. A patient may not relay information he does not identify as important and may not display all symptoms during an office visit. Bipolar patients with a strong genetic loading and whose initial illness begins in adolescence or young adulthood may be especially at risk for antidepressant-induced mania. For comprehensive information on bipolar disorder and antidepressant-induced mania, refer to scholarly articles in the journal *Bipolar Disorders, An International Journal of Psychiatry and Neurosciences* listed in References and Resources for Further Reading in this book.

[13] *The only thing he's willing to take is an antianxiety medication* . . . It is a concern that this patient would be prescribed antianxiety medication given his history of drinking to black out. Many antianxiety medications have potential for dependence and addiction. A person with a history of substance use is at risk of becoming dependent on these medications, which in turn complicates treatment for mental illness.

[14] *There is a higher incidence of death* . . . Information provided by National Alliance on Mental Illness (NAMI) states that substance use complicates treatment of mental illness:

> *Abuse of drugs and alcohol always results in a worse*

*prognosis for a person with mental illness. People who are actively using are less likely to follow through with the treatment plans they created with their treaters: they are less likely to adhere to their medication regimens and more likely to miss appointments which leads to more psychiatric hospitalizations and other adverse outcomes. Active users are also less likely to receive adequate medical care for similar reasons and are more likely to experience severe medical complications and early death. People with mental illness who abuse substances are also at increased risk of impulsive and potentially violent acts. Perhaps most concerning is that people who abuse drugs and alcohol are more likely to both attempt suicide and to die from their suicide attempts.*

*Individuals with mental illness and active substance or alcohol abuse are less likely to achieve lasting sobriety. They may be more likely to experience severe complications of their substance abuse, to end up in legal trouble from their substance use and to become physically dependent on their substance of choice.*

For more information and resources on mental health, please visit the NAMI website at www.nami.org.

[15] *For years I tried to get him into cognitive behavioral therapy (CBT).* Cognitive behavioral therapy (CBT) is a common type of mental health counseling. Patients work with a mental health counselor in a structured manner, attending a limited number of sessions. Cognitive behavioral therapy helps one become aware of inaccurate or negative thinking so as to address challenging life situations more clearly and respond in an effective manner.

[16] *But at twenty-five, he did finally receive supplemental disability (SSI)...* The U.S. Social Security Administration's Supplemental Security Income (SSI) program pays benefits to disabled adults and children who have limited income and resources. SSI

benefits also are payable to people sixty-five and older without disabilities who meet the financial limits. People who have worked long enough may also be able to receive Social Security disability or retirement benefits as well as SSI. For more information on SSI eligibility and benefits, please see www.ssa.gov.

[17] . . . *what can happen if their child doesn't have a loved one advocating for him.* The Family Education Institute of the Community Residences Foundation in Arlington (VA) helps parents plan future care for their developmentally disabled or mentally ill children. The foundation also provides services ranging from group homes to case management. In some cases it accepts Medicaid or private insurance. NAMI also provides resources for finding lifelong care by state.

[18] *He was a 5150.* California's Welfare and Institutions Code (WIC) describes a 5150, or seventy-two-hour hold, as a means by which someone who is in serious need of mental health treatment can be transported to a designated psychiatric inpatient facility for evaluation and treatment for up to (but not longer than) seventy-two hours against their will. If the facility determines that further treatment is indicated, the person can be held involuntarily for additional lengths of time providing he or she meets the legal criteria, which is defined as being a danger to self or others, and is unwilling or unable to remain voluntarily. For specific and current parameters for obtaining a seventy-two-hour hold for a loved one, please refer to the NAMI chapter in your state.

[19] *I got him on a seventy-two-hour hold and quickly got conservatorship.* Rebecca Woolis, MFT, provides valuable practical advice for the loved ones of individuals living with mental illness. Obtaining conservatorship for a loved one can be an effective way to keep a person from endangering oneself:

> When people have a serious mental illness, and due to the
> illness, are a danger to themselves or others or are unable
> to provide for their own basic needs for food, clothing,

*and shelter, someone else may be given legal authority
to meet the person's needs and to make certain decisions
about the person's life and, sometimes, property. This
legal structure . . . court appointed, is called conservatorship or guardianship . . . Only by means of a guardianship or conservatorship can someone be treated involuntarily for any length of time. To find out the specifics of
how guardianships work in your state, contact your local
NAMI or public guardian's office . . . "When Someone
You Love Has a Mental Illness," (pp. 182-183).*

[20] *He was on seven different medications.* Most parents express concern when their child is prescribed any medication or a combination, commonly referred to as a "medication cocktail." It is important to note that pharmacological treatment of mental illness can be helpful to many, and a particular mix of medications is not a "one-size-fits-all" solution. Side effects and efficacy must be carefully monitored for ongoing changes. Each patient and their advocate must carefully weigh benefits and side effects with their medical doctor.

[21] *. . . nearly twice the rate of homicides.* Statistics and resources about mental illness can be found on the National Institute of Mental Health website at www.nimh.nih.gov. Refer to Note 14 regarding increased rates of self-harm by those who have co-occurring mental illness and substance use disorder.

[22] *Fortunately, through DBT . . .* See Note 10 above regarding DBT.

[23] *Because we're both mandated reporters.* Each state has laws requiring individuals to report suspicion or observations of child abuse and neglect. While some states require all people to report concerns, many states identify specific professionals such as social workers, medical and mental health professionals, teachers, and child care providers, who have regular contact with vulnerable people such as children, disabled persons, and senior citizens. Specific procedures are usually established for mandated reporters to make referrals to child

protective services. More information can be found at: www. childwelfare.gov.

[24] *Jello Biafra is her god.* Jello Biafra was a founder, lead singer, and songwriter for the punk band Dead Kennedys.

[25] *Stop Walking on Eggshells: Taking Your Life Back When Someone You Care About Has Borderline Personality Disorder,* written by Paul T. Mason, MS and Randi Kreger (New Harbinger) is included in References and Resources for Further Reading in this book.

[26] *We're Myers Briggs opposites!* The Myers-Briggs Type Indicator (MBTI) is a widely used personality inventory, or test, employed in vocational, educational, and psychotherapy settings to evaluate personality type in adolescents and adults age fourteen and older. In an educational setting, the MBTI may be performed to assess a student's learning style. Career counselors use the test to help determine what occupational field one might be best suited for, and organizational settings assess management skills and facilitate teamwork and problem solving, including communication skills. Because the MBTI is also a tool for self-discovery, mental health professionals may administer the test in counseling sessions to provide patients with insight into their behaviors.

[27] *We were also fortunate to have support from an Assertive Community Treatment (ACT) team . . .* The treatment that helped Joseph and was supportive to us in our efforts to keep him in treatment was assertive community treatment (ACT), which helps a person reintegrate into the community by living semi-independently, engaging in everyday required tasks, working and/or attending school while also engaging in some type of group or independent therapy. This evidence-based treatment can significantly reduce hospitalizations for the qualified individual. For more information about ACT, see www. dualdiagnosis.org.

[28] . . . *because it makes for a safer community.* Crisis Intervention Team (CIT) programs throughout the United States and in other nations worldwide promote and support collaborative efforts toward effective interactions among law enforcement, mental health care providers, individuals with mental illness, their families, and communities.

[29] . . . *has proven most effective is "harm reduction."* Because patients are usually unmotivated to pursue abstinence, most dual diagnosis programs focus initially on education, harm reduction, and increasing motivation rather than strict abstinence (Drake et al. 1993a; Carey 1996; Mercer-McFadden et al. 1997; Ziedonis and Trudeau 1997). Motivational approaches are designed to help the patient to recognize that substance use interferes with his own goals and to nurture the patient's desire for abstinence. It cannot be emphasized enough that the patient must take responsibility for his own treatment. A second, common approach for substance abuse treatment involves CBT. These two approaches are often combined or offered in stages so that skills for achieving and maintaining abstinence are taught after motivation is developed (Bellack and DiClemente 1999). For more information on treatment of dual diagnosis, please refer to Dr. Robert Drake's articles listed in References and Resources for Further Reading in this book.

[30] *I do believe he is an alcoholic.* It is significant to note here that Riley's recovery is an example of the need to redefine progress for individuals who live with persistent mental illness, particularly when there is co-occurring substance use. Also important to note is that setbacks are common in mental health recovery. One evidence-based approach for treating co-occurring mental illness and substance use is to motivate the individual to employ *harm reduction* as a first step to recovery, with the ultimate goal of embracing a sober lifestyle. Harm reduction is defined as significant decrease in quantity, frequency, or a transition to a less harmful method or substance; the primary objective is for

a patient to willingly choose abstinence. For more information about harm reduction and treating dual diagnoses, see also Note 29, above, and refer to Dr. Robert Drake's articles listed in References and Resources for Further Reading in this book.

[31] . . . *and trapping them in your own."* Andrew Solomon, *Far From the Tree*, page 680.

# Appendix
## Parent Questionnaire

*Questions designed to guide parents toward exploring*
*and understanding their own journey.*

The stories of our contributors led us to similar themes and answered most of our questions without prompting. Almost every contributor expressed relief at the end of our interview sessions after having had the opportunity to talk openly and deeply about their experience. For most, the process of telling their story was a cathartic exploration. We have provided similar questions here for other parents to benefit from careful self-examination of one's journey. Perhaps parents can work through the questions together, or if this is not possible, journaling using these questions as prompts may be beneficial. Not all questions may be relevant to all parents, and some may not be relevant now but may become so at a later stage of one's journey.

I.      Childhood.
- 1. What good memories do I hold from my child's infancy and childhood?
- 2. What qualities of my child are dear to me?
- 3. Can I access these memories during trying times?

II.      The Journey.
- 1. Am I able to fully acknowledge how my child's behaviors affect me and other family members?
- 2. Am I able to separate behaviors associated with the mental illness from the person my child really is?

III. The Diagnosis.
    1. Will others support my efforts to help my child?
    2. Do I fully accept my child's brain disorder diagnosis?
    3. Does my child accept his/her diagnosis?
    4. Does my spouse/partner/significant other accept my child's diagnosis?
    5. Do other family members accept my child's diagnosis?
    6. Do the people close to me accept my child's diagnosis and make an effort to learn and understand it?
    7. Do I blame myself for my child's illness?
    8. Have I made a concerted effort to learn about my child's diagnosis?
    9. Do I have reliable people in my life to help me during crisis?
    10. Do I and/or my child's other parent have a crisis management plan in place that provides directives about which professionals to contact and how to cover emergency care for other dependents?

IV. Family Relationships.
    1. In what ways has my relationship with my spouse/partner/significant other been affected by my child's illness?
    2. How has the relationship between my child who lives with a brain disorder and his or her siblings been altered? How does this affect me?
    3. How has the parenting of my other children been affected by my child's illness?
    4. If the child lives at home: have I established clear and specific house rules? And, if so, are they abided?

V.   Treatment.
1. Do I still question whether my child has a chronic illness?
2. Does my child have medical professionals I trust?
3. In determining treatment options for my child, do I feel included, overly involved, or left out?
4. Have I been given either conflicting medical advice or advice that goes against my own instincts?
5. For a child whose doctor determined hospitalization was the best treatment option: did I feel supported by other family members or loved ones in this decision? For a child committed unwillingly: how do I feel about that decision now?
6. For a child who uses alcohol and/or drugs: how do I define "substance abuse?" Has substance use been addressed by medical professionals, my child, or me?
7. What are my limits and boundaries regarding substance use? How does my stance on substance use affect (or not affect) my child's treatment?
8. Has a medical professional informed me that my child has co-occurring mental illness and substance abuse? Do I understand this diagnosis?
9. Does my child understand his illness and treatment options? And, is there open communication?
10. Am I on the "same page" with my spouse/partner/significant other and in agreement regarding treatment?

VI.    Recovery.
     1. Am I able to define what recovery means for my child at this stage?
     2. Is my vision of recovery congruent with my child's other parent?
     3. Can I find gratitude in aspects of my child's current stage of recovery?
     4. Can I find gratitude in other areas of my life?
     5. Am I able to "live in the moment" and, if so, what does that mean for me?

VII.    Coping and a New Normal.
     1. What do I miss most about who my child was before his or her illness?
     2. Does my child's illness create feelings of grief? And, if so, can I identify how I express grief?
     3. Does my spouse/partner/significant other respect my expressions of grief?
     4. Do I respect and acknowledge expressions of grief by other family members even though it may differ from mine?
     5. Am I able to participate in work, recreational, or social activities that had, prior to my child's illness, given me pleasure or fulfillment?
     6. In what specific ways do I take care of myself?
     7. Is there a person in my life who understands the difficulties associated with parenting a child who lives with a brain disorder, and do they provide support?
     8. Have I made an effort to find support in my community such as through NAMI, my faith community, or extended family?
     9. What is my biggest fear or worry for my child?
     10. Have I limited interactions with old friends and/or extended family members since the onset of my child's illness?

11. Are the interactions I do have with old friends and/or extended family more difficult in any way?

12. Are there times when my anger or frustration negatively affects my relationships? Have I addressed ways to manage anger and frustration?

13. Have I found activities our family can do together? Have I found fun activities to share (one on one) with each of my children and significant other?

14. In what ways, if any, has my perspective on parenting, life, and family, for example, changed as a result of this journey?

15. What is the biggest change in my life since my child's illness?

VIII.   What We Dream for Our Children.

1.   Do I have any expectations for my child's future?

2.   How do I convey expectations to my child?

3.   Based on where my child is now, with his recovery, do I believe my expectations are realistic? Does my child own these expectations as well?

4.   Do I acknowledge expectations my child expresses? And are these expectations realistic?

5.   Are the expectations held by the other parent consistent with mine, and with my child's?

6.   Do I believe that my child's other parent coddles, is too harsh, or holds unrealistic expectations?

# GLOSSARY OF BRAIN
# DISORDER DIAGNOSES

The following are brief definitions of brain disorders mentioned by our contributors. Definitions are excerpted from the National Institute of Mental Health and NAMI websites. For more detailed descriptions of brain disorders, please visit: www.nimh.nih.gov or talk to your doctor.

**Anosognosia** is the inability of one's brain to recognize one has a serious psychiatric illness, which presents a tremendous challenge to family members and caregivers who try to engage a person in treatment. About one-half of people living with schizophrenia, and a smaller percentage who live with bipolar disorder, as well as those with Alzheimer's disease or dementia, have this clinical feature. Anosognosia, also known as "lack of insight" or "lack of awareness," raises the risks of treatment and service noncompliance.

**Anxiety disorders** are defined by excessive reaction to stress. Anxiety is a normal reaction to stress and can be beneficial in some situations. For some people, however, anxiety can become excessive. Even recognizing that one's anxiety levels are too high, one may have difficulty controlling it, and it may negatively affect day-to-day living. There are a wide variety of anxiety disorders, including general anxiety disorder (GAD), post-traumatic stress disorder (PTSD), obsessive-compulsive disorder (OCD), and panic disorder (PD) to name a few. Collectively, they are among the most common mental disorders experienced by Americans.

**Attention-deficit/hyperactivity disorder (ADHD)** is an illness characterized by inattention, hyperactivity, and impulsivity. The most commonly diagnosed behavior disorder in young persons, ADHD affects an estimated 3 to 5 percent of school-age children.

**Bipolar disorder** was formerly known as manic-depressive disorder. Bipolar disorder is a chronic illness with recurring episodes of mania and depression that can last from one day to months. This mental illness causes unusual and dramatic shifts in mood, energy, and the ability to think clearly. Cycles of high (manic) and low (depressive) moods may follow an irregular pattern that differs from the typical ups and downs experienced by most people. The symptoms of bipolar disorder can have a negative impact on a person's life. Damaged relationships or a decline in job or school performance are potential effects, but positive outcomes are possible. In most cases, bipolar disorder can be managed with medications and psychological counseling.

**Borderline personality disorder (BPD)** is a serious mental illness that can be challenging for everyone involved—family members and loved ones, and even the individual with the illness. Loved ones often describe life with a BPD family member as "walking on eggshells." BPD is characterized by impulsivity and instability in mood, self-image, and personal relationships. Treatments and longer-term studies of BPD offer hope for good outcomes for most individuals who live with BPD.

**Dual diagnosis** is a term used to describe people with mental illness who have coexisting problems with drugs and/or alcohol. The relationship between the two is complex, and the treatment for people with co-occurring substance abuse (or substance dependence) and mental illness is more complicated than the treatment of either condition alone. This is unfortunately a common situation—many people with mental illness have ongoing substance abuse problems, and many people who abuse drugs and alcohol also experience mental illness.

**Major depression** is a mood state that goes well beyond temporarily feeling sad or blue. It is a serious medical illness that affects one's thoughts, feelings, behavior, mood, and physical health. Depression is a lifelong condition in which periods of wellness alternate with recurrences of illness. Each year, depression affects 5–8 percent of adults in the United States.

**Psychosis** is not a diagnosis, but a symptom or set of symptoms that can have many different causes. Psychosis may be transient, intermittent, short term, or part of a longer-term psychiatric condition. Psychosis is defined as a loss of contact with reality. It typically involves at least one of two experiences:

*Hallucinations* can be auditory in nature (e.g., hearing voices), less commonly visual experiences and, even more rarely, smelling things that no one else perceives. For the person who experiences hallucinations, they are very real and can be frightening.

*Delusions* are false, fixed beliefs that may involve paranoia (e.g., a man who believes the FBI is chasing him) or mistaken identity (e.g., a woman who believes her mother is an imposter). What makes beliefs delusional is that they do not change when a person is presented with new ideas or facts that demonstrate they are false.

**Schizoaffective disorder** is a serious mental illness that affects about one in one hundred people. Schizoaffective disorder as a diagnostic entity has features that resemble both schizophrenia and also serious mood (affective) symptoms. Many of the strategies used to treat both schizophrenia and affective conditions can be employed for this condition.

**Schizophrenia** is a serious mental illness that affects 2.4 million American adults over the age of eighteen. Although it affects men and women with equal frequency, schizophrenia most often appears in men in their late teens or early twenties, while it appears in women in their late twenties or early thirties. Schizophrenia interferes with a person's ability to think clearly, manage emotions, make decisions, and relate to people. It impairs a person's ability to function to their potential when it is not treated. Unfortunately, no single, simple course of treatment exists.

# REFERENCES AND RESOURCES FOR FURTHER READING

*This list includes sources cited in the foreword by Dr. John Looney, MD, MBA.*

Aguirre, Blaise A. *Borderline Personality Disorder in Adolescents: A Complete Guide to Understanding and Coping When Your Adolescent has BPD.* Minneapolis, MN: Fair Winds Press, 2007.

Amador, Xavier. *I AM NOT SICK—I Don't Need Help! How to Help Someone With Mental Illness Accept Treatment.* New York: Vida Press, 2007.

Amen, Daniel G., MD, and Lisa C. Routh. *Healing Anxiety and Depression.* London: Penguin Books, 2004.

Beers, Clifford F. *A Mind That Found Itself: An Autobiography.* New York: Longmans, Green & Company, 1907.

Carlson, Trudy. *The Life of a Bipolar Child: What Every Parent and Professional Needs to Know.* Duluth: Benline Press, 2000.

Drake, Robert E., Gary R. Bond, and Deborah R. Becker. *Individual Placement and Support: An Evidence-Based Approach to Supported Employment.* New York: Oxford University Press, 2012.

Drake, Robert E. and Deborah R. Becker. *A Working Life for People With Severe Mental Illness.* 1st ed. New York: Oxford University Press, 2001.

Earley, Pete. *Crazy: A Father's Search Through America's Mental Health Madness.* New York: Putnam, 2006.

Fast, Julie A. and John D. Preston, PSY.D. *Loving Someone With Bipolar Disorder: Understanding & Helping Your Partner.* Oakland: New Harbinger, 2004.

Fine, Carla. *No Time to Say Goodbye: Surviving the Suicide of a Loved One.* New York: Broadway Books, 1997.

Ghaemi, S. Nassir. *Mood Disorders: A Practical Guide, Second Edition.* Philadelphia, PA: Lippincott, Williams and Wilkins, 2008.

Hornbacher, Marya. *Sane: Mental Illness, Addiction, and the 12 Steps.* Minneapolis, MN: Hazelden, 2010.

Jamison, Kay Redfield. *An Unquiet Mind: A Memoir of Moods and Madness.* New York: Vintage Books, 1996.

Jamison, Kay Redfield. *Night Falls Fast: Understanding Suicide.* New York: Knopf, 1999.

Kaye, Randye, PhD. *Ben Behind His Voices: One Family's Journey from the Chaos of Schizophrenia to Hope.* Lanham: Rowman and Littlefield, 2011.

Lafond, Virginia. *Grieving Mental Illness: A Guide for Parents & Their Caregivers.* Toronto: University of Toronto Press, 2000.

Leahy, Robert L., Stephen J. Holland, and Lata K. McGinn. *Treatment Plans and Interventions for Depression and Anxiety Disorders.* New York: The Guilford Press, 2012.

Levine, Madeline. *Teach Your Children Well: Parenting for Authentic Success.* New York: Harper, 2012.

Looney, John G. (ed). *Chronic Mental Illness in Children and Adolescents.* Washington, DC: American Psychiatric Association Press, 1988.

Lyden, Jacki. *Daughter of the Queen of Sheba: A Memoir.* New York: Penguin Books, 1997.

Mason, Paul T., MS, and Randi Kreger. *Stop Walking on Eggshells: Taking Your Life Back When Someone You Care About Has Borderline Personality Disorder.* Oakland: New Harbinger, 2010.

McKay, Matthew, Jeffrey C. Wood, and Jeffrey Brantley. *The Dialectical Behavior Therapy Workbook: Practical DBT Exercises for Learning Mindfulness, Interpersonal Effectiveness, Emotion Regulation, & Distress Tolerance.* Oakland: New Harbinger, 2007.

Miklowitz, David Jay. *The Bipolar Disorder Survival Guide: What You and Your Family Need to Know.* New York: The Guilford Press, 2002.

Mueser, Kim T. and Susan Gingerich. *Coping with Schizophrenia: A Guide For Families.* Oakland: New Harbinger Publications, 1994.

Plath, Sylvia. *The Bell Jar.* New York: Harper & Row, 1971.

Prochaska, James O., John Norcross, and Carlo C. DiClemente. *Changing For Good: A Revolutionary Six-Stage Program for Overcoming Bad Habits and Moving Your Life Positively Forward.* New York: Avon Books, 1994.

Reiland, Rachel. *Get Me Out of Here: My Recovery From Borderline Personality Disorder.* Minneapolis, MN: Hazelden, 2009.

Saks, Elyn R. *The Center Cannot Hold: My Journey Through Madness.* New York: Hyperion, 2007.

Sheff, David. *Clean: Overcoming Addiction and Ending America's Greatest Tragedy.* New York: Houghton Mifflin Harcourt, 2013.

Soloman, Andrew. *Far From the Tree: Parents, Children, and The Search for Identity.* New York: Simon & Schuster, 2012.

Soloman, Andrew. *The Noonday Demon: An Atlas of Depression.* New York: Touchstone, 2001.

Steele, Ken, and Claire Berman. *The Day the Voices Stopped: A Memoir of Madness and Hope.* New York: Basic Books, 2001.

Styron, William. *Darkness Visible: A Memoir of Madness.* New York: Vintage Books, 1992.

Swanson, Sarah J. and Deborah R. Becker. *Supported Employment: A Practical Guide for Practitioners and Supervisor.* Minneapolis, MN: Hazelden Publishing and Educational Services, 2008.

Temes, Roberta. *Getting Your Life Back Together When You Have Schizophrenia.* Oakland: New Harbinger Publications, 2002.

Torrey, E. Fuller. *Surviving Schizophrenia, A Manual for Families, Consumers and Providers.* 4th ed. New York: HarperCollins Books, 2001.

Turkington, Douglas, et al. *Back To Life, Back To Normality!: Cognitive Therapy, Recovery and Psychosis.* New York: Cambridge University Press, 2009.

Vine, Phyllis. *Families in Pain: Children, Siblings, Spouses, and Parents of the Mentally Ill Speak Out.* New York: Pantheon Books, 1982.

Wasow, Mona. *The Skipping Stone: Ripple Effects of Mental Illness on the Family.* 2nd ed. Palo Alto, CA: Science & Behavior Books, 2000.

Whitaker, Robert. *Anatomy of an Epidemic: Magic Bullets, Psychiatric Drugs and the Astonishing Rise of Mental Illness in America.* New York: Crown Publishers, 2010.

Woods, Mary and Katherine Armstrong. *When The Door Opened: Stories of Recovery From Co-Occurring Mental Illness and Substance Use Disorders.* Manchester: CreateSpace Independent Publishing Platform, 2013.

Woolis, Rebecca. *When Someone You Love Has a Mental Illness: A Handbook for Family, Friends, and Caregivers.* New York: Penguin Group, 1992.

Young, Joel L. and Christine Adamec. *When Your Adult Child Breaks Your Heart: Coping with Mental Illness, Substance Abuse and the Problems That Tear Families Apart.* Guilford, CT: Lyons Press, 2013.

## ADDITIONAL ARTICLES

Drake, Robert E., Susan M. Essock, Andrew Shaner, Kate B. Carey, Kenneth Minkoff, Lenore Kola, David Lynde, Fred C. Osher, Robin E. Clark, and Lawrence Rickards. "Implementing Dual Diagnosis Services for Clients with Severe Mental Illness." *Psychiatric Services* 52, no. 4 (April 2001): 469–76.

Drake, Robert E. and Kim T. Mueser. "Psychosocial Approaches to Dual Diagnosis." *Schizophrenia Bulletin* 26, no. 1 (2000): 105–18.

Drake, Robert E., Kim T. Mueser, Mary F. Brunette, and Gregory J. McHugo. "A Review of Treatments for People with Severe Mental Illnesses and Co-Occurring Substance Use Disorders." *Psychiatric Rehabilitation Journal* 27, no. 4 (Spring 2004): 360–74.

Ghaemi, S. N., D. J. Hsu, F. Soldani, and F. K. Goodwin, F. K. "Antidepressants in bipolar disorder: the case for caution." *Bipolar Disorders* 5, no. 6 (Dec. 2003): 421–33, doi: 10.1046/j.1399-5618.2003.00074.x.

Goldberg, J. F. and C. J. Truman. "Antidepressant-induced mania: an overview of current controversies." *Bipolar Disorders* 5, no. 6 (Dec. 2003): 407–20, doi: 10.1046/j.1399-5618.2003.00067.x

Regier, D. A., M. E. Farmer, D. S. Rae, B. Z. Locke, S. J. Keith, L. L. Judd, and F. K. Goodwin. "Comorbidity of Mental Disorders with Alcohol and other Drug Abuse. Results from the Epidemiologic Catchment Area (ECA) Study." *Journal of the American Medical Association* 264, no. 19 (Nov. 21, 1990): 2511–18.

# ABOUT THE AUTHORS

**Mary Widdifield** received her MA in English and creative writing from San Francisco State University. Mary is a grant writer for nonprofits. She received San Francisco State University's Wilner Award for short fiction and her work has appeared in *Transfer Magazine, San Francisco Chronicle,* and *Able Muse.* She lives in Northern California with her husband and two children. (Photo credit: Marko Lavrisha.)

**Elin Widdifield** received her MA in counseling psychology from Tufts University and completed an externship in family therapy at The Philadelphia Child Guidance Center. She has worked extensively with adolescents, families, young adults, and sexual assault survivors. Elin has documented oral histories, including life experiences of combat veterans. She resides in North Carolina where she is on the boards of NAMI (the National Alliance on Mental Illness), and the UNC Center For Excellence in Community Mental Health. She is the mother of two sons. (Photo credit: Amy Stern.)